Snakes! Guillotines! Electric Chairs!

Dennis Dunaway

Snakes! Guillotines! Electric Chairs!

My Adventures in the Alice Cooper Group

Dennis Dunaway and Chris Hodenfield

OMNIBUS PRESS

London / New York / Paris / Sydney / Copenhagen / Berlin / Madrid / Tokyo

SNAKES! GUILLOTINES! ELECTRIC CHAIRS! Copyright © 2015 Dennis Dunaway and Chris Hodenfield
This edition published in 2015 by Omnibus Press
(A Division of Music Sales Limited)
This edition published by arrangement with St Martin's Press

Portrait of Glen Buxton, p. v, by Ingo Gierdal
Handwritten note, p. 291: Dennis Dunaway private collection
Lyrics to "Black Juju," p.153: Courtesy of Ezra Music

Designed by Steven Seighman
Cover designed by Rob Grom
ISBN: 978.1.78305.993.5
Order No: OP56485

All rights reserved. No part of this book may be reproduced in any form or by any electronic or mechanical means, including information storage or retrieval systems, without permission in writing from the publisher, except by a reviewer who may quote brief passages.

Exclusive Distributors
Music Sales Limited,
14/15 Berners Street,
London, W1T 3LJ.

Macmillan Distribution Services
56 Parkwest Drive
Derrimut, Vic 3030,
Australia.

Printed in the EU

A catalogue record for this book is available from the British Library.
Visit Omnibus Press on the web at www.omnibuspress.com

Dedicated to my two wonderful daughters, who urged me to write this book, and my beautiful wife. They are my true loves.

In fond memory of Glen Buxton
1947–1997

CONTENTS

Acknowledgments ix

Prologue: The Opening Chords... 1
1. School's In... 7
2. Headliners and Guillotines 31
3. Sunset Stripped 52
4. Threadbare, Broke, and Spacey 70
5. Topanga 81
6. Your Music Is Killing My Wife's Petunias 93
7. *Pretties for You*—The Accidental Album 114
8. So Fine in '69 125
9. Blood, Sweat, and Toledo 140
10. The Freak Farm 157
11. Spidery Eyes 163
12. *Love It to Death* 175
13. Killer on the Loose 193
14. Bowling Them Over in Hollywood 219
15. Hello, Dalí 227

16.	Conceiving *Billion Dollar Babies*	234
17.	*Muscle of Love*	252
18.	Breakup	261
19.	The Cold Room	268
20.	There's No Business Like No Business	275
21.	The Hall of Fame	279

ACKNOWLEDGMENTS

It seems like a previous lifetime, but it was 1964 when the idea to combine conceptual art and music entered my teenage mind and consumed me with a do-or-die passion. My friend Vince was enthusiastic about the idea from the beginning. The concept was fun, which made it easier for us to convince others to join in. The seed was planted and nurtured and it led to the birth of Alice Cooper. Vince Furnier, Glen Buxton, Michael Bruce, Neal Smith, and myself—along with Charlie Carnal, Mike Allen, and Cindy Smith Dunaway—laid the groundwork. And with the brilliant help of Shep Gordon, Joe Greenberg, and Bob Ezrin, we all made that dream come true.

That really would have been my previous lifetime if Crohn's Disease had gotten its way. On Easter of 1997, when the Reaper was looming around my bed during a serious, extended hospital stay, another idea struck me. I would act on my daughter's suggestions and write a book. In my mind, that meant that I had to make it through the surgery. You can't kick the bucket if you're writing a book! And once again, I had a creative dream to pursue. And once again, I would need the help of others to make it happen.

My greatest thanks go to my beautiful and talented wife, Cindy, for keeping our life together while I typed the days away. When my head is in the stars, she keeps me on the ground, and she does it with great style. Our daughters, Renee and Chelsea, also deserve tons of credit for their hard work, talents, and positive support.

Everlasting gratitude to Sharyn Rosenblum and Dereck Walton for believing in this story as much as I do, and for making me feel welcome in the exciting literary world of New York City. I had spent a decade pounding the sidewalks for a publishing deal when Sharyn, with her infectious enthusiasm, introduced me to the rock star of literary agents, Jim Fitzgerald. Jim had heard a thousand pitches before mine, yet he gave me a considerate listen, and in his gritty voice that reminds Cindy of Glen Buxton, he agreed to give it his best shot.

I needed an accomplished writer to polish my manuscript into a smooth-flowing read. It had to be someone with enough insight and firsthand knowledge to maintain the proper tone of the times. Chris Hodenfield was the first writer that came to mind. Man, that turned out to be the perfect call.

I'd like to thank David Cluett and Paul Brenton for their generous help on the photographs. We saw a lot of dead ends, detours, and roadblocks along the way, but we managed to track down some rare treasures.

Most important, I needed the right publisher. That's where Jim Fitzgerald swung into action, and no writer could hope for a more insightful and enthusiastic editor than Rob Kirkpatrick and the stellar team of experts at Thomas Dunne and St. Martin's Press, including Jennifer Letwack, David Lott, and copy editor Jenna Dolan.

The creative energies flowed together as one, and we all made this dream come true.

—D. D.

Snakes! Guillotines! Electric Chairs!

PROLOGUE

THE OPENING CHORDS...

I WAS CURSED with the gift of a vivid memory. It's so funny now to sit with fellow road warriors and hear them recounting some epic, razzle-dazzle story of our rock-'n'-roll years, while I holler, "*No, no, no,* that's not how it happened!" There are, of course, a lot of reasons for my buddies to suffer memory slippage. We were pursuing the amusements, and there were a lot of ear-splitting screams in the fun house.

Early on, Alice gave me the nickname Dr. Dreary. It was for my habit of getting lost in deep thought. This was during our days together as art students. When it came to conceptualizing projects, we were like mad fiends. Art was our true calling, and it seemed to spring from the habit of observing people. An artist just sees things. I began faithfully keeping dream books and diaries. Even during the roller-coaster years, I always wrote letters home. It meant a lot to me to remember things right, especially as my artistic ventures went rocketing into Bizarro Land.

When I was a teenager, I got the idea to apply the weird inventions of my art world to a rock band. My best friend shared my enthusiasm for the notion, and we got together to talk others into joining us. Some people got it right away; some people wanted to punch us in the face. Still, we were driven to share our mission with the whole wide world.

Our collective dream came true. That is the essence of Alice Cooper.

You might be here to read about your hero, Alice, or to learn of some injustice that detoured the original group. I'm here because I'm proud of what my closest friends and I accomplished. Blame is not important. Blame does not override the memories of how goddamned great it was to be a fast-moving rock-'n'-roller in the '60s and '70s.

Hold the tragedy. We had cubic *fun*.

Being stars then and making it through that era was a monumental miracle. The choices we made were done while shooting through deep space and dodging in and out of a massive meteor shower. Were poor choices made? Everyone makes his share, and some choices get heavier amplification than others. Want to hear more? I'm here to tell you about it as I remember it.

And I do remember it. Some of the events in this recounting have been combined, and the order of things may be slightly askew, but it's as close to real as I could get. If you were a fan of the Alice Cooper group, you might have sharp-red recollections of seeing Alice hang from a gallows while we blasted "Killer" at you. Our specialty was the creation of glaring, graphic shows designed to send you out to the sidewalk reeling.

Sometimes our own doom seemed imminent. This is what happens when you come up playing penitentiaries, air force bases, and cowboy bars with a dangerously high hostility content. We liked getting in people's grills, but sometimes the audience was ready to put a razor in *our* faces.

Then there was São Paulo, a concert that really sticks in my brain, and not just because it was our last together. It was huge. You just don't expect to see 158,000 people *inside* a venue. It was, in fact, the largest indoor concert ever, according to *The Guinness Book of World Records*. I just know that when I looked around the curtain at the crowd, it was like staring into the Milky Way.

For the Alice Cooper group, reality was not a given. We always made sure it was going to get stretched, as the saying goes, like a weary snake. And from our earliest days, we had to accept the reality that our fans were going to honor us by getting seriously weird themselves.

For that São Paulo gig, it seemed that every freak in the Southern Hemisphere had come to lay on a big helping of Brazilian crazy. All the trashed-up, sexed-out regalia made us feel right at home, too. Unfortunately there was a kind of heaviness in the air.

The police, for one, had put us right on edge. Brazil was still in the throes of being run by a military dictatorship, and the police were glad to show they were unstoppable. That afternoon, for the sound check, we'd been stuffed into military vehicles that bulldozed through the crowds on the streets. We were sure we saw a kid get run over. Alice pleaded with the driver to slow down, but he only yelled back in Portuguese, laughed, and drove faster.

That night, we looked out onto the crowd and there they were, right up front, clutching automatic weapons and looking as antsy as meth heads, the very same itchy-fingered cops. These were going to be our *protectors*!

On top of all the cops, there was a strange emotional weight hanging over the group. We couldn't talk about it, because that wasn't our style. But it was there. It was like we'd lost control of the dream. We'd constructed this powerful locomotive, and now the brakes were shot, the wheels were coming off, and up ahead the bridge was out . . .

Michael Bruce caught my eye and gave me the disgruntled nod that said, *Can you believe this?* He had his guitar over one shoulder while his other arm was around a captivating Brazilian girl from the opening band. Michael was tireless in his pursuit of the beauties. He always had some sort of scheme going offstage, but onstage he was as reliable as a Mack truck. In his hardened face, though, I could see his sense of disillusion. We had sold-out crowds everywhere, a No. 1 album in the racks, stories in the magazines proclaiming us the highest-grossing band in the world—bigger than the Stones, bigger than Zeppelin—but where were those kinds of checks? No wonder Michael often looked aggravated.

Our other guitarist, Glen Buxton, wore the same expression he'd had for about a year—a distant look. His gaze had a sinister depth. Glen had been the first to see something was wrong in the group. His response, though, was just to party it out. In Brazil, the purest bad substances came to him piled on silver trays. Just two nights before, I'd seen him crawling down the hallway of the Copacabana, loaded into a world beyond recognition.

This book is dedicated to Glen, clearly one of life's sterling originals. He only had to walk into a room and the inflammatory wisecracks would be scorching the earth. We expected this, just as we knew, as musicians, to expect him to deliver a blast of jagged guitar from the planets beyond. But now Glen was just more interested in getting blasted.

Towering over him was Neal Smith, our flamboyant, golden-god drummer. No, wait. Gold wasn't good enough for him—he was the Platinum God, always entertaining us, always carrying us to some higher, more explosive level. Neal and I had formed a tight bond, and not just because I was sleeping with his sister Cindy. My bass and his drums had found some unaccountable connection that went way beyond our being "the rhythm section." My rolling bass lines fed off his primal drumbeat, and we would get totally locked in, creating more thunder than bombers in the sky.

Then there was Alice, our comedian-philosopher, the caring preacher's son who doubled onstage as our embodiment of evil. He was in a good mood tonight, even though he seemed more anxious than usual. Maybe it was the violent tension in the air. He wasn't too drunk, but he sure smelled of beer. His face was blackened by his heavy eye makeup. He had on his leather stage costume and stained athletic cup. He whipped his sword around and seemed ready for anything.

The brotherly harmony I had felt with Alice for so long had hit some interference lately, but the group's tension never followed us out onstage. Once we were out there, everything was all right. We had spent a decade loving the music more than anything else, and it had become our final refuge.

We had not brought our big stage set to São Paulo. It was just us and our music. Like old times, we were a rock band again, happiest when in a primal, teeth-baring state.

We took the stage and gave them the whole infernal onslaught. Although we had no way of knowing it was our final show, we had all the mad fever of a romantic couple going out in style, having a final fling and a good-bye kiss and a quavering bunch of *Don't forget me, nows*.

Hey, I'd known these guys since high school. We'd lived together, cheek by jowl by armpit, in flophouses and mansions, ever since we were gawky teenagers, and we all knew the deepest, darkest. Some years back, when we were sharing a farmhouse in Michigan, I noticed a recurring phenomenon. If one guy ever walked into an empty room and flopped down on the couch, very soon another guy would come in, then another and another, as if we were an organic machine that worked only when all the parts were assembled.

Such closeness can get to be too much, of course. By the time we got to São Paulo, our round-the-clock hilarity was now freighted with responsibilities to a larger machine.

It had all become a nerve-frying hallucination. The pleasures were huge, sure. No sense in denying it. There's no life force quite like what you feel onstage, the mix of cascading love and demanding fury, the firecrackers thrown at your feet along with love trinkets and foaming beer cans.

The tide rushes in, the tide sweeps you out.

Five high school guys who liked fast cars, we'd jumped into the super stock car called rock 'n' roll and peeled out. I'm going to share our dream with you. Like any dream, the logic sometimes falls apart like a blown Marshall amp.

The Alice Cooper group *liked* working hard. We were always writing songs and cranking out albums and devising stage shows. On the road, we'd get to the arena and turn the afternoon sound check into a two-hour rehearsal. We liked being so damned good. We *liked* seeing the audience go absolutely nuts. When the five of us melded together, we were as strong as a longshoreman's fist.

Michael Bruce once noted that the early group seemed like my band. That was kind of him to acknowledge, but it's critical you think of us as a group of five.

Indeed, fans might now think of "Alice Cooper" as one person, but my perspective is different. The man now known as Alice has talents that can be fully appreciated only in the context of the original, full-blown vision: as a member of a *group* known as Alice Cooper. He deserves his present fame as a solo star, but we earned something as a group.

He wasn't always called Alice, of course. When I met him he was Vince, which is what anyone back in Phoenix called Vincent Damon Furnier. As I tell the tale of the band here, I'll be calling him Vince in the first half of the story.

He was Vince, and sometimes still is. When I saw him the other day, for example, I automatically called him by his real name. He had just come offstage, shining and stinkin' with sweat, but within seconds of our sitting down, we were just two kids from Arizona, hunkered down in my Ford Falcon with a bagful of tacos, wishing we could get to first base with some unattainable girl.

When I call him Vince, I'm thinking of the guy who sat at my kitchen table or who walked around the house in only a bath towel.

Sometimes it was just like the authorities used to tell us: When teenagers hang out, they can get into some real trouble. Our whole story begins with that simple fact: Vince and I just liked to hang out together. And when we did, things happened.

1.

SCHOOL'S IN...

"WHEN WEIRD PEOPLE BECOME THE MASSES, WE'LL BE FAMOUS."
—VINCE

VINCE'S CHAIR SCREECHED across the paint-speckled linoleum. All around the art class, heads popped up like a bunch of startled antelope. Everyone was instantly on the brink of illicit laughter. Vince turned to see if Mrs. Sloan had noticed. What he saw were her staring eyes, peering over the top of her reading glasses, locked on him, signaling to all that *she* was in charge.

Vince had a reputation for clowning his way out of trouble. So the class just waited. Mrs. Sloan was attractive and well liked, but she usually maintained a stern attitude. It was just about to meet its match.

Vince's eyes grew big as he mimed the TV character Barney Fife. He mouthed a silent, "Sorry." He was like an actor in the spotlight and could just as easily have turned into Inspector Clouseau or Stan Laurel or any one of a dozen characters in his repertoire. So now he acted out the shaky lawman, nervously picking up his chair and easing it over the floor next to mine.

A snot-snorkeling giggle erupted in the far corner of the room. It was from Maurice Kluff, a kid who always wore bright orange socks. Mrs. Sloan snuffed out his laughter with a deadly stare.

The class settled down, and Vince and I went back to flipping through a heavy book about modern art. It was our pirate's treasure.

We came upon a Salvador Dalí painting of Sigmund Freud, vivid in its Surrealism.

Vince looked at the next one and pointed to each word in the title: *Soft Construction with Boiled Beans (Premonition of Civil War)*. He laughed and muttered, "Boiled beans?"

I propped my chin on my fist and studied the picture. Vince did the same, like we were modeling for that statue *The Thinker*.

Before I could come to a grand conclusion, Vince started nodding his head up and down like one of those wobble-headed dogs in the back window of a Chevy.

"Neat," he said.

"Really neat," I elaborated.

On the next page, another sweeping Dalí painting showed a grotesque structure that looked like a stack of disjointed body parts. It was crowned with a butt-ugly head. But right off, Vince spotted Freud again. It was the same image as the previous portrait, only smaller. The tiny Freud suddenly seemed even more amazing in the context of Dalí's full-blown vision.

What happened in that moment of discovery? I'd like to say we knew something big had happened. Something *did* happen.

I'd entered Cortez High in the fall of 1961. The school, on the northern edge of Phoenix, had just opened and didn't have air-conditioning yet. Every room felt like a furnace. The rules there weren't set in stone yet, so the kids were testing and pushing the limits all the time.

I joined the Cortez track-and-field team. Coach Emmett Smith noticed that I was pretty good at going the distance. Big glory. I soon found out that cross-country was about as popular as the parched dirt we ran on. During our meets, the bleachers were entirely buttless. The janitor and his dog watched us.

I met one of my future musical partners on that team. John Speer had dark curly hair, a big barrel chest, and the stamina of a bull. He had a great sense of humor, too, even if was clouded with pessimism. We developed a friendly rivalry.

Not everyone at Cortez got along as well as the guys on our team. A lot of times guys settled their differences with their fists after school. Any kid who wanted to build a *reputation* had to prove it regularly in the parking lot.

The worst hombre in school, though, was a big hulk named Ruben. He had three older brothers who would come pick him up after school, all jammed into a white Corvair that sagged down low. The brothers would be peering out with their dangerous stares, making the Corvair look like a nest of rattlesnakes.

Ruben's favored shtick went like this: He'd come up to you with an outstretched paw you couldn't refuse, then crush your hand till you dropped to your knees in agony; then he'd drag you to the trash can and drop you in it. Your pain made him happy.

Then a skinny little freshman named Vince Furnier showed up. He was the least likely human for anyone on earth to fear, and this struck Ruben as funny. So he "volunteered" Vince to join his handshaking reign of terror. Side by side, they looked like cartoon characters, Tweety Bird and Spike. Ruben would stand in the shadows while Vince, his scrawny puppet, lured their prey.

Vince would introduce passing kids to Ruben, who'd come out grinning and raising his paw. As long as Ruben was entertained, Vince had immunity from the dreaded handshake from hell. Vince was in his glory, and seemed perfectly happy to lure these victims. After all, it wasn't *his* fault—Ruben was making him do it.

In our school, Journalism class was considered an all-girls thing. Naturally I signed up for the class, which also meant writing for the student newspaper, the *Tip Sheet*. The girls saw me as an interesting novelty and showered me with special treatment and outright pampering. Oh, I was bad. The girls didn't want me to get all stressed out over missing a deadline, so they'd write my stories for me. I even won an award for one.

The guys on campus also gave me special treatment: They called me a pansy. John Speer gave it to me the worst. But after a while, seeing what a cushy life I had in that class full of cuties, Speer and the other slobs recognized my genius. Vince joined the class as soon as he could and became the *Tip Sheet*'s sports editor.

Although he was a year younger, Vince was a character, and I was drawn to him instantly. Making friends seemed so effortless for him. He didn't need to go anywhere to find new friends—not even across a room. He drew people in with his congenial magnetism.

When we met, Vince's family had just moved in from Detroit, and it was only the latest move. A kid whose family picks up and moves all the time learns how to shed friends and make new ones. Sometimes it's just too tough to adapt. Vince's older sister Nickie dealt with all the moving around by just avoiding friendships. That cut down on the number of sad goodbyes she had to endure.

Vince took the opposite approach. No matter where he was, he treated everyone like a friend. He could talk to anybody about any subject. He'd quickly figure out what the person wanted to hear and then he'd say it, even if he had to stretch the truth to do so. You might even say he preferred exaggeration. In his world, the plain old truth was just so dull that he had to dress it up in its Sunday best. Yet he knew exactly how far he could stretch his embellishments.

After all, his father, an aeronautics engineer, was also a part-time minister. (He was a cool guy, though, with an interesting hairdo and a riverboat gambler's pencil-line mustache. Funny—in all the sketches that Vince compulsively drew, the characters often had that suave mustache. Vince and his father shared that duality of being strongly religious and extra hip.) So with religion in the home, Vince believed in being truthful and would never have lied. This was not entirely out of respect for his father; he held the same beliefs. Yet, as I said, he did have a constant need to exaggerate, which he rationalized as a simple matter of making the truth more interesting. There's nothing bad about that!

To make his enhancements believable, he spoke with casual confidence and laughed a lot, as if to say, *Wow, I can hardly believe that myself.* His laughter signaled to everyone, and perhaps to himself, that it was only a fun conversation, nothing serious. It was easy to enjoy Vince's conversation, too, because he never tried to make himself look better than other people.

And we're talking about a teenager named Vince, not our sinister stage character named Alice. We're talking about the skinny underclassman with a relaxed but energetic manner, the witty guy with an unlimited repertoire of tales.

That limitless stream of wonderfully enhanced tales is a big part of why I like Vince so much. It's a big part of how he charms the world.

Vince's universal congeniality didn't cramp our closeness as friends. We were best friends. What created our tight bond was our mutual interest in Surrealism and Pop Art. Vince and I were so inseparable that people rarely talked about either of us as individuals.

Girls liked us, even though Vince and I were pretty shy in that department. I was pathetically shy. For an introvert like me, I had to gain friends by association. Still, I was voted as having the "Best Personality" in the 1965 Cortez High School yearbook, although I never felt that popular. I'm sure the football quarterback was scratching his helmet over that one.

Art class was the place where Vince and I hatched plans for revolution. We'd sit in back and talk quietly of artists and art movements. One day, he showed me the famous Magritte painting of the businessman whose head is obscured by a green apple. I realize now how this influenced Vince's style of odd character portraits. But it was also easy to segue the conversation to the latest hit song, like "Surfin' Safari."

I loved hot rods, and Vince favored sporty cars like Volkswagen's Karmann Ghia. We agreed that whichever the ultimate dream car was, Brigitte Bardot should be riding in the passenger seat wearing pointy harlequin sunglasses and a polka-dot dress with her blond hair blowing in the breeze.

Vince's conversation overflowed with television references. He'd watch anything and everything: *The Steve Allen Show, The Twilight*

Zone, *The Ernie Kovacs Show, Peter Gunn, The Untouchables, Ozzie and Harriet, The Andy Griffith Show, My Three Sons, The Dick Van Dyke Show*. When programming ended at ten o'clock, the screen would show a test pattern of an Indian chief's head before it went to static snow. Vince claimed that he'd even watch the static Indian chief.

That day in art class we snapped back to reality when we noticed Mrs. Sloan standing behind us.

"I hope I'm not interrupting you two," she glowered as she plugged in a portable record player. "You two think you're so hip. I want you to sit quietly, if that's possible, and listen to this."

She handed an album jacket to Vince. On it was a photo of a couple of young bohemians walking down the middle of a snowy city street. The guy appeared to be engaged in a game of pocket pool while the girl clung to his arm. The title was *The Freewheelin' Bob Dylan*.

Mrs. Sloan lowered the needle on the record. Out came a strumming acoustic guitar sound and a froggy voice asking socially pertinent questions.

We'd never heard this kind of seriousness in a song. Vince laughed at the guy's weird voice, but he had to admit it seemed like important stuff.

We also had to admit we'd just been out-cooled by our art teacher.

It hits me now, all these years later, how Vince and I were knocked off balance by this woman and sent down our slightly crooked path.

Mrs. Sloan was so tough-minded. There were no indulgent pats on the head from this woman. She'd tell us right out that we weren't Living Up to Our Fullest Potential.

Maybe she didn't care for our stunts. Once, when Vince returned from the bathroom wrapped from head to toe in toilet paper, staggering like he was a wandering mummy, the class erupted in laughter. But Mrs. Sloan just grabbed a pitcher of ice water from her desk and dumped it over his head. "*Touché!*" she said.

For the rest of the day, slivers of wet toilet paper fell from Vince, blowing his image as a sharp dresser.

Mrs. Sloan had stunts of her own. One day she presented the class with a black bag. "You've been struck blind," she said, and told each of us to reach inside and touch the bag's contents and then draw whatever we think we'd felt. "Let your hands be your eyes."

Vince slinked his hand into the bag and then yanked it out fast. "Whoa, what *is* that?" he said, aghast. He held out his hand as if it were contaminated.

I watched my own hand disappear into the bag. Ugh. Whatever was in there was nasty. It felt like dry leather, a twisted spine with a tail, and a head with needle-sharp teeth.

One by one, the students were grossed out by this thing in the bag, while Mrs. Sloan, perched on a stool, grinned like the Cheshire cat.

It was only the next day, after we'd put our interpretations down on paper, that Mrs. Sloan hauled out the object of our terror. What she pulled out was far more disturbing than the grossest of our drawings. "It's a dried-up devilfish from the Gulf of Mexico," she said, beaming while holding up the petrified thing.

Diane Holloway's arm shot up. "May I go wash my hands?" she pleaded. All the girls rushed over to the sink.

You think this experiment had an influence on me and Vince? You think?

Vince liked to draw. His character sketches were a zany stew of Magritte, *Peter Gunn*, and *MAD* magazine. The characters were heavily stylized and usually looked like him. If he wore a sharkskin suit and a pencil-thin tie to school that day, so did the character on the pad. Or he'd do himself as a beatnik, and you could almost hear the bongo drums pattering in the background.

My own paintings had bold slashes of color and rarely any discernible subject matter. I just liked letting go. My artistic orgasms usually came out looking like an explosion in a scarf factory.

Mrs. Sloan's painting style was also somewhat vivid, so I looked to her for guidance. One day, I found her standing in front of my canvas with her hand to her cheek, staring at my painting in unnerving silence. Finally, she turned and said, "When everything is screaming, nothing is screaming."

Her comment puzzled me for days. But the next time my brush went to work on a canvas, I gave my screams some solitude to shatter.

Little life lessons. Vince and I would later apply this advice to song structure, album order, set lists, and theatrical presentations.

Another of Mrs. Sloan's pieces of wisdom came from her method for getting a fresh viewpoint on a problematic composition. "Just hold it up to the mirror," she said. "Sometimes the reversed image reveals the imbalance." The artwork's problem, she explained, becomes hidden—the brain simply gets accustomed to the imbalance and your objectivity is gone.

This was another life lesson we took with us to the world of music: If you're writing a song and it's problematic, do it on a different instrument, play it through a tiny speaker, perform a reversal on it, and hear it fresh.

The film version of *West Side Story* influenced how Vince and I dressed that year. We bought white sneakers and rubbed dirt on them so we'd fit right in with either the Sharks or the Jets. One night, we hid behind some bushes at the end of my block, and when a car drove by, we'd jump out and fake a rumble. The car sped on, and we cracked our knuckles, confident that our staged scene had left the driver terrified.

Little frauds like that were the highlight of our drab existence. We didn't own cool cars. We weren't California surfers. Our sex lives, if we were lucky, stuck to the pages of *Playboy*. But we knew that something more was out there. Vince had seen the stories.

Our daily conversation was a rummage sale of pop culture effluvia, all spoken in *very authoritative* terms, and music was becoming more and more the focus.

I had already lived through three pretty significant revelations about music. My first big eye-opener—and ear-opener—happened on a scorching 102-degree day in Phoenix, "the Valley of the Sun." I was happy to be in an air-conditioned movie theater balcony, devouring my popcorn and watching a double bill of *Peter Pan* and *Hercules Unchained*. During the intermission, the red velvet curtain swished closed over the screen and some guys began setting up a drum set and amps on the narrow stage. Then the announcer tapped the mike.

"And now," he said, "the Fox Theater is happy to present—[*squeak*]—Phoenix's own Duane Eddy and the Rebels!"

The theater was suddenly filled with the blistering electric guitar of the Twang Meister himself. The word *twang* is always used to describe Duane Eddy's lowdown guitar sound, but it doesn't really describe the barreling thunder he created in hits like "Rebel Rouser" and "Forty Miles of Bad Road." You've got to understand, this was so many years before anything like acid rock or heavy metal. Duane Eddy was one of the early kingpins of heavy guitar raunch. Guys like Duane, Link Wray, and Bo Diddley laid it down early.

Duane Eddy—even his name sounded like a guitar lick—was strutting one way across the stage while his wailing saxophonist slid the other way. "Go git 'em, man!" yelled the drummer. "Go! Go! Go!"

A guy on the far side of the theater balcony belted out a bloodcurdling "Yeeee-*haw*!"

The Rebels rocked through three of their guitar instrumental hits, then waved like heroes and trotted off behind the curtain.

The Hercules movie came on, with all its images of the muscular dude busting out of chains. But, for me, the movie didn't stand a chance against the echoes of the twangy guitar still bounding around in my now-enlightened head. Whatever I'd expected to happen that afternoon in the movie house was gone now. Detour City.

Seeing Duane Eddy wasn't the first time I'd witnessed music as big fun. As a small boy in Creswell, Oregon, I listened to my dad and his friends and family play music well into the wee hours. They loved that ol'-timey country music, with the authentic fiddle-playin', guitar-pickin', everyone-singin' kind of homegrown refrains.

They'd scatter salt over Grandma's wooden floors so their shoes would make a scuffling sound as they danced the two-step. Some of the womenfolk frowned on drinking, but as the evening wore on, it was easy to figure out who'd been sneaking a few nips. The men would be drunk as polecats, arguing about who was making eyes at their women. I was spellbound.

Lust. That's most important, right? Of course it was Elvis who led the charge of rock-'n'-roll lechery. As a kid, I'd watch my teenage babysitter go into *heat* every time she heard Elvis. I'd be watching slack-jawed. Her girlfriends would show up with the latest platter, and the poodle skirts would be flying as they danced the Dirty Bop.

The Dirty Bop involved a lot of suggestive hip movements, and of course it had been banned all over the nation. I'd already heard the inside story on it from a local hoodlum. He was always polishing his black '53 Ford with C. C. RIDER painted on the fender. "Girls," he said confidently, "don't wear panties when they do the Dirty Bop." Goggle-eyed, I had to find out if this was true.

I was watching all this lusty stuff from afar, and then it happened: the eighth grade. Washington Elementary School. The Friday night dance. The lights were low. A teacher announced that it was time for the Spotlight Dance, and to my shock, he announced that I was to lead it off. Even more surprising, he indicated that my partner would be a nice young miss named Sharon. Thanks to her blossoming figure, I was already well aware of her. Sharon galvanized the gonads of guys up and down the school halls.

Sharon cruised up to me under the glowing spotlight, gently pressed her blessings against my chest, and proceeded to glide me around the dance floor inside a circle of onlookers. She danced much slower than the tempo called for.

"In the Still of the Night," by the Five Satins, tugged at my heart as the clean fragrance of her white blouse held me paralyzed in a heavenly trance. Then my slacks began to tighten. Oh no, I thought. Not this. Not here. *Not now.*

In desperation, I tried to think of something else: The car crashes in the automobile safety movies, for instance. While I struggled with the woody from hell, the song came to an end. The glorious female lifted her arm from my shoulder, whispered, "Thank you," and left me standing there all rubber-legged. I slowly became aware of the stares of my drooling friends.

So, the connection was made: music=sexual force.

On the Social Ladder of Cool, long-distance runners ranked far below baseball players and wrestlers. But we learned something, John, Vince, and I, and that was the value of being part of a team. We endured the same miseries, pulled cactus thorns out of our ankles, perspired profusely, stank like hell, and even threw up together. We proudly called ourselves the Pack.

After Vince and John joined me on the *Tip Sheet*, it was only natural that the track team started getting all the publicity it so richly deserved.

We weren't complete phonies, though. The Pack had a season record of nine wins and no losses. We won the Division II Cross-Country Championships. When we tallied up the season, we realized we had run more than 450 miles. And I set a record for the 20-mile run that stood for years after I graduated.

What happened next might seem to be some cheesy high school prank, but it started the wheels rollin' to the big time and infamy.

Thanks to our cross-country heroics, John, Vince, and I became eligible to join the Lettermen's Club. Vince was good enough to letter as a freshman. Entrance into this prestigious organization was by no means automatic. And we were nervous about all the rotten initiation pranks we'd heard about.

You might get dropped off in the desert with a choice of what to wear on your walk back—shoes or a jock strap.

You might have to drink from an unflushed urinal. (Later, we'd learn that the "urine" we were to drink was only water doctored with yellow food coloring.)

You might get a string tied to the end of your wiener, knowing that at the other end of the string was a clipboard that held the message PULL ME. A letterman would toss the clipboard into the girls' locker room while you were at the other end of this long piece of string, outside, behind a bush, waiting for the fateful pull.

As potential victims, John, Vince, and I were shaking like wet Chihuahuas. The lettermen all had a real flair for heavy drama, and they gave us the works. But we got in at last. We were suddenly cool guys in the coolest club on campus.

When it came time for the Lettermen's Club to host an annual fund-raiser, we were tossing out suggestions. I said, "Hey, how about, as a big goof, we put on a talent show?"

The guys grumbled, but grudgingly gave in. To our surprise, the other clubs in the school came forward with so many impressive ideas that we were suddenly at risk of getting upstaged in our show. We called an emergency meeting.

"Tell them your idea, Dunaway," John Speer said.

"Since we don't have much time," I said, "how about a surprise, gag entry? Maybe it could be a phony act of some sort. A phony Beatles act."

I made my pitch as if the inspiration had just hit me, but it was all part of my scheme. I had seen Duane Eddy and the Rebels. I knew what kind of hell you could raise on a stage. John wasn't much help, but Vince backed me up.

The jocks went for it. They relished the idea of poking fun at the longhaired Beatles. It was early 1964, and the Beatles were ripping through America like a gang of joyriders. After the vote, they appointed Vince, John, and me to organize the performance. The upperclassmen glared at us heavily and said we'd better be good.

I'll admit that if we wanted to copy the Beatles, we were lacking a few critical skills. Up until then, our talent was limited to singing Beatles songs during long-distance workouts. Vince, John, and I would break the boredom by substituting our own track lyrics: *I'll beat you / Yeah, yeah, yeah.*

We went to Woolworth and bought some skuzzy-looking Beatles

wigs. I borrowed my dad's guitar, and Vince nabbed his father's ukulele, but neither of us could actually play these instruments.

All through the week, various hulking lettermen pulled us aside in the hallways and explained how our future health *depended* on our success.

We needed someone who could actually play an instrument. So Vince and I approached an offbeat loner we'd seen in photography class. He was the kind of guy who liked to hang out in the darkroom because he knew that if the orange light was on outside the door, no teacher would enter. This allowed him to sneak smokes—and be alone.

His name was Buxton. One day, Vince and I cornered him and introduced ourselves.

"Howdy do," he said, extending his hand. "Glen."

For a desert dweller, Glen had unusually pale skin. But while he was thin, he still looked pretty tough. His waterfall hairdo had an attempted ducktail in the back. His nose supported thick Buddy Holly–style horn-rim glasses, which was like an open invitation to the hard guys to start a fight. The hair, the stance, the look, the 'tude—I think it came from James Dean in *Rebel Without a Cause*. This blatant disregard made Glen seem fearless.

"We heard you have a guitar," I said.

"Yeah," he said, "an Epiphone hollow-body electric."

That sounded better than my dad's guitar. We told him about our talent show and need for a guitarist.

"Sure," he said, "I'll give it a stab."

The very next day we found him in class, sitting at his desk with a brown guitar case at his feet.

"Hey, how ya doin'? I brought my guitar." He knelt down and unsnapped the latches. When he opened the lid, we could see it, nestled in a soft, fuzzy compartment, a beautiful blond sunburst guitar.

We asked if he knew the new Beatles song, "Please Please Me." Glen lifted up the guitar and began strumming the chords.

In low voices, Vince and I sang along: *Last night I ran four laps for myyyyy coach* . . .

Glen was as far from being a letterman as he was from his hometown, Akron, Ohio. Still, he thought the phony Beatles idea was cool as long as he was only a sideman. Besides the wigs, part of our costume was the black Cortez High letterman jackets. While he considered that part lame, he *did* like the idea of wearing something he wasn't supposed to wear.

"I know a guy who plays rhythm guitar," Glen said one day. "And he can get beer."

Vince and I didn't care about the beer, but having some more musical ammunition sounded great.

The second guitarist was John Tatum, a confident, good-looking guy who knew a lot of guitar chords. He sported a blond waterfall hairdo like Glen's. Both of them were so proud of their hair that they refused to muss it up with any Beatle wigs.

But Glen did have one style tip. He handed Vince a pair of sunglasses and said, "We gotta wear shades. With a little attitude, you'll look too cool for school."

Vince and I found that a fellow letterman, Phil Wheeler, owned a drum kit and had even taken lessons. We asked him to help out.

"I'll do it, but no wig!" he said. "I'll keep it simple by using a snare drum and a cymbal."

We didn't care. We had a drummer!

Vince and I taught John the lyrics during track practice. Our list of fake Beatle songs was pretty slim. Our version of "She Loves You" was "I'll Beat You." Then there was "Please Beat Me," sung to the tune of "Please Please Me." (*Last night I ran four laps for myyy coach / He said I didn't even tryyyy much.*)

When I mentioned a song I liked called "Foot Stompin'," a catchy tune by an R&B group called the Flares, Glen just shrugged.

"That's easy. It's just a three-chord progression." He might as well have said $E=mc^2$. But he started strumming, and we commenced singing. Then Vince chimed in with a request for the Contours' raucous hit "Do You Love Me (Now That I Can Dance)." Glen quickly worked that out. We had two more songs.

Rock 'n' roll has a history of bands with bug names: Buddy Holly's Crickets, then the Beetles with an *a*. I suggested the creepiest bug of all: the Earwig. This is a squirmy little bug with a pincer at the end of its tail. Anybody who camped in the desert was afraid of having one of these things crawling inside his ear and clamping onto his brain for eternity.

"And when you step on 'em, dey stink," said Glen, "so you can't do nuttin' wid 'em."

I also liked the idea of the Earwigs wearing wigs. So we became the Earwigs. A good rock 'n' roll name, it seemed to us.

Come the night of the Lettermen's talent show, our performance was supposed to be a surprise. It was, typically, a sweltering hot night in the Cortez "Cafetorium," the school's combination cafeteria and auditorium. Backstage, we watched nervously as the other acts performed under the purple stage lights. The international flavor was big that year. There was a Filipino dance, and music from Spain and France. Also, three teachers did themselves up as a hootenanny act, the Klunkstone Trio, and sang an anti-A-bomb song.

When the curtain finally closed and it was our turn, Phil Wheeler rushed to get his drums set up onstage. As Vince, John, and I donned our wigs and sunglasses, we heard three girls from the Pep Club giggle at us. Vince grabbed his ukulele; John and I posed with our guitars.

"And now, we have a special surprise," came our introduction over the mic. We began stomping our feet in time to our opening song. "Direct from Cesspool, England! The Earwigs!"

The curtain swept open and we were looking at a sea of surprised faces. As John Tatum joined Glen in laying down some electric guitar racket, we stomped our way to the front of the stage and sang our phony lyrics: *Listen to my track shoes / Stomping all over you . . .*

Beyond the footlights, I could make out the faces of friends, faculty, and parents—everyone roaring with laughter. Even the janitor's dog seemed to be laughing.

In the high of the moment, we didn't think we looked goofy. The loud guitar and the drums and our voices booming out over the speakers created a rush inside us, an incredible feeling.

We rocked, stomped, and jumped around as if we knew what we were doing. We could see that the folks out there were equal parts entertained and dumbfounded.

The Beatles had a signature move at the end where they'd all bow deeply from the waist. So we Earwigs did a cartoon curtsy.

The curtain closed on us and we heard the Cafetorium rock with rowdy cheering. We looked at one another in shock. Make that ecstasy. This had gone over *far* better than we'd ever imagined.

Mrs. Axelrod, our chemistry teacher, bustled up to us and said, "You guys should be on *The Ed Sullivan Show*!"

The entertainment bug had not only bitten us; it had clamped down hard on our brains, and like the deadly earwig, it meant to stay there in perpetuity.

Our infamy didn't let up over the next few weeks. Naturally it was pumped up a little by a front-page story in the next issue of the *Tip Sheet*, complete with a spoof about our early days in Cesspool, England.

Our popularity skyrocketed. Football players grudgingly acknowledged that we belonged to the same species as they. Teachers actually nodded at us. And the biggest shockeroo of all: Girls actually *smiled* at us.

Girls smiling. This is the nuclear power plant that fuels every rock musician and gets him off the living room floor. Suddenly we were getting a little leak of this wave of electricity. *That girl back there—she just gave me a warm look . . .*

Overnight, the Earwigs had become more popular than the Edsel. But we weren't a real band—or were we? Vince and I didn't have to think twice. We sure as hell *were* a real band. John Speer was game to continue, too. Handsome Phil Wheeler didn't need to be in a goofy band to get girls, but for the time being, he'd go along with the scam, just for the heck of it.

It would take some real convincing to get the two actual musicians,

Glen and John, "the cool duo," to join up with us rank impostors. After school, I approached Glen and asked if he wanted to get together.

"Sure! Wanna come over to my house tomorrow? We can play some records. Bring your guitar, and I'll show you some chords."

The next day I jumped on my bicycle and followed Glen's scribbled directions to his house. It was in a middle-class neighborhood like mine, dotted with one-story cinderblock homes. His house was painted lime green.

I rang the bell. After a long wait a woman opened the door, and there was no question this was Glen's mom. She was thin but by no means frail. Her expression gave the immediate impression that she would not put up with any foolishness. I put on my Sunday-best voice and asked for Glen.

"Come on in," she said. "He's in his room." She pointed down the hall and went into the kitchen. I felt like the parole officer in some B-movie about youth gone wrong.

I knocked on Glen's door. Mrs. Buxton's voice echoed from the kitchen: "Go on in. He's there."

The door fell open slowly. The windows had been covered with sheets of aluminum foil, and only pinpoints of light broke through. I stumbled over to a lamp on a table. The low-watt orange lightbulb gave off a vague, funereal illumination. It was like we were back in the photo darkroom. As my eyes adjusted, I looked around. What kind of cave dweller was he?

Scattered across the floor were issues of *TV Guide*, a guitar case, the remains of various electronic gadgets. Then I saw Glen's bare foot, sticking out of the bedsheets. I looked up from the sleeping form crumpled up in the sheets to the wall, where pictures of Ozzie and Harriet were pinned crookedly. There was a smaller photo of the *Leave It to Beaver* sidekick Eddie Haskell. The wise guy.

A Chet Atkins songbook was open on top of Glen's guitar case. Other books were scattered around. A W. C. Fields biography. A worn-out *Catcher in the Rye*. Some of the things still had their original price tags attached. I'd learn the reason for this later—when it came to shopping, Glen was something of a Light-Fingered Harry.

"Glen," I said, "it's afternoon. Want to play some records?"

"Mmmm-aahhh-nggg" was his response from under the covers. "Go away."

After a lot of this high-minded debate, he dragged himself from bed and zombie-walked to the kitchen. He poured himself a cup of black coffee and slowly came to life.

After he unlatched his guitar case, he was strikingly more alert. With great love, he laid hands on the Epiphone nestled in a bed of burgundy velvet. As he tuned it up, I thought of an important question. "What note is that?" I asked.

He looked up, smiled, and explained what he was doing. The chalky blear had left his face. Now his expression was suffused with a beautiful warmth. This guy loved music. It was like watching a deep believer at a moment of religious uplift.

He asked where my guitar was. When I said I had ridden my bike over, he shrugged and rifled through his stack of records.

This was my first session with Glen. It stands out in my mind so sharply not just because he was such an unusual character, but I think because I recognized that it was an important moment. Over the years, this little scene would be repeated countless times.

Glen pulled me into a very real world that so far had only been the stuff of my fantasies. This was Glen—seemingly lost in a dreamland of broken-down kitsch, but revived by playing music. When notes tumbled from his fingers, he entered a zone where he actually possessed world-class talent.

He gave me a conspiratorial look. "If Gerry asks," he said, referring to his mother, Geraldine, "pretend we're gonna do some homework."

"Your living room is nice."

He looked at me. "You're not allowed to sit on the furniture. Those plastic covers are to keep our grubby mitts off. Gerry buys everything with cash, and she makes it last forever 'cause nobody's allowed to use it. They bought most of this stuff back in Akron, but it still looks brand spanking new. I mean, flies gotta have a lookout before they'll land on it. Ya know what I mean?"

I knew what he meant, but I had *never* heard anyone talk like this.

Then we got down to business. He showed me the bare-bones basics: the names of the notes on the guitar's neck and how a chord worked. He said he'd keep going until I got it. I had grown up around guitar pickers, but this was different. This guy knew rock.

In class, Glen was the guy who'd do as little as possible save for sitting in the back and firing off low-volume wisecracks. But now that Vince and I had discovered him, we made him part of our inner circle. He became the main photographer at the *Tip Sheet*, so we could all duck into the darkroom under the pretense of working on an important photograph.

Glen was also in my Physical Education class. His bowed legs looked like a couple of albino snakes. After class he'd wrap them back up in his pegged jeans. His arms were equally white, which, as I've mentioned, was rare in Arizona. He always wore long-sleeve shirts.

The next time I went to his house, I brought along my Duane Eddy record. In pretty short order he picked out the notes and played along with it. Then he handed me the guitar. I could see he was worried that I'd dent its perfect finish.

"Relax," he said, pointing to a fret. "That's a G." He adjusted my left hand on the fretboard and taught me how to hold the guitar pick with my right. The action on this electric was so much easier than on my dad's old cowboy clunker. Within a few minutes Glen had me playing the main lick to "Rebel Rouser."

It all began to happen. Vince decided to play harmonica. John Speer chose drums. That left me to play bass. I didn't really know what a bass guitar was. I sure couldn't hear one on my crappy little turntable. It didn't seem a standout instrument. I thought if I was going to play it, I'd make it into a standout instrument.

Urgency fueled our plans. It did, however, seem a tall order to scrape up the money for a bass guitar and an amp. Salvation did not fall from heaven, but it did come from a cool place. My mother handed me a letter one day and said, "Here. Read this. It's from your grandpa."

"You can stay here with your Grandma and me," it read. My grandfather's penmanship was perfect. "We'll feed you and grow some string beans. And if you're a good worker, you'll go home with enough money to buy that guitar."

The lush green farmland of Oregon was a world apart from the sun-bleached Arizona desert. I knew Oregon well, though. My first home had been next to Grandpa's farm. As kids, my little brother, Dean, and I ran through Grandpa's fields with our toy six-guns, pretending to be rootin', tootin' cowboys. So I went there for a three-month stay.

Somebody might easily think that being on a farm for the summer must have qualified as a living hell for a fledgling rock-'n'-roller. But it was a great summer. I learned how to operate a tractor, plow a straight line, and string up young vines. After three months of lifting sacks of string beans, my muscles were toned. Since I had a dark Arizona tan, long hair, and always wore a Levi jacket with an Indian chief embroidered on the back, the workers there figured I was a Native American. I stayed quiet and thought a lot about what the band could become.

One morning I jogged down the long dirt driveway to the mailbox on River Road. Inside was a letter from Vince. I tore it open. He'd bought a sharkskin jacket at a summer sale. He was running three miles a day. And he said he'd like to try "Mr. Moonlight" when I got back.

Back home in Phoenix, I took but one day to drum up some action. Glen accompanied me to the Montgomery Ward department store to look at their Airline-model bass guitars. We stood in the aisle and took turns plucking the strings. Glen gazed down the neck of one with a marksman's eye and checked for trueness. Satisfied, he handed it to me and said, "There ya go, Mr. Bassman."

It was like he'd just handed me the scepter that made me King of the World. We hustled right over to the checkout, and I plunked down my summer's wages.

I had no amp, but Providence stepped up again, this time in the person of my cousin Glynnell, who was married to a guy named Tyke, who played steel guitar in a country band in Oregon. Tyke gave me his old Fender amp. It was covered in that brownish twill called "tweed," and it just seemed to stink of raw music.

I was officially ready to rock.

John Speer answered an ad in the *Phoenix Gazette* and found a decent set of drums. Vince took up tambourine, maracas, and harmonica. Though he never seemed to practice, he had good rhythm and could make the harmonica wail.

You'd never have asked Vince to lug a guitar case or drum set, of course. That kind of yeoman activity was amusingly beyond his capabilities. In fact, he had a hard time keeping track of even his small cache of instruments. Vince went through life leaving a trail of things in his wake, secure in the knowledge that others would double back and find them. That was just the way he lived. He'd grown up with a mother who doted on him like a prince. It may have been a habit left over from caring for him after his many childhood operations. But he carried on in life with the trusted knowledge that any old thing he dropped to the floor would eventually find its way back to his hands.

Vince had a thin, nasally voice, but he could hit the notes and remember the words. His greatest possession, really, was his wonderful, gregarious personality. It made him a natural front man. He's just a likable guy. Did he have charisma? Well, once you looked past the skinny body and the big honker, there was a desire to entertain socially that was as deep and constant as the Colorado River.

Whenever Vince started into one of his fantastic stories, Glen and I only had to share the slightest glance to know: *Get out the shovel, the bullshit's gettin' deep.* But I never found myself *not* wanting to hear Vince reel off one of his tales. Even repeats. He was right, too: It did beat plain old everyday life. It was interesting also to hear his new twists on old yarns. Vince's storytelling didn't have good days and bad days—he was always on.

Glen's conversations were just as entertaining, but he was more a curmudgeonly W. C. Fields character. To Glen, all of life was so absurd it required him to keep up a running commentary. We quickly got used to this babbling river of sulfuric mockery.

The Earwigs had no rehearsal hall, so we moved around to our respective houses. Glen's house became the favorite because it had the semiprivacy of an enclosed garage. In Phoenix, a garage is really just an oven annex. It should come with buttons on the side that read, BAKE, BROIL, ROTISSERIE.

Glen's father worked alongside Vince's dad at a factory called AiResearch, where they made turbochargers and rocketry equipment. Mr. Buxton hoped that Glen, with his interest in gadgets, would work there someday, too. It sure seemed to offer a more promising future than the Earwigs. But anything that involved an alarm clock inspired in Glen a phobia bordering on revulsion. If daylight hours were involved, Glen was wary.

Like many younger siblings, Glen fell under the shadow of an accomplished older brother. He felt he was always being compared to Ken, who was more intellectually savvy and far more practical.

During one sweaty rehearsal, the garage door slid open and Glen's folks announced that they were going away for the weekend. Mrs. Buxton fixed her gaze of steel on Glen. "We're trusting you to watch the house," she said. Glen's house was as neat as a pin. If we misbehaved, Mrs. Buxton's threatening expression stopped us cold. This look of hers became known as the Evil Eye.

Glen slid his hand through the air and said, "Don't worry about a thing."

With more stern looks, his parents got in their car and drove away.

After peering down the street, Glen turned and said, "We're practicing in the living room."

"Are you nuts?" I said.

"How can I watch the house if I'm out here?"

We marched into the forbidden paradise of the air-conditioned living room. John snagged the welcome mat from the front door and put it under his bass drum pedal, so he wouldn't get grease on the powder-blue carpet. Then we plugged in our amplifiers and began tuning up.

I was just making a joke about pulling the wool over the Evil Eye when the room fell silent. I turned around, and there stood Mrs. Buxton wearing the most intense Satanic gaze ever. I felt sheets of skin burn off my guilty face. Apologies flew, and we groveled back out to the Oven.

Had they forgotten something? Or did they just know Glen all too well? It was clear that he was, again, a disappointment.

"I've never been in so much trouble without getting yelled at," Vince said. "If only we could harness that power."

Instruments in hand, we stood there working out various TV commercials for our new product, Evil Eye Drops.

Vince's father, Mr. Furnier, was a cool guy. He proved this when he booked the first, no-foolin' paying gig for the Earwigs. We had pounded out enough lunchtime concerts at Cortez High; it was time to go big.

The Dunes Lounge was a semirespectable dive down the road from school. Although the adobe exterior suggested a desert oasis, it was just a beer joint. The stage could barely accommodate five musicians. It was the first time we played to an audience that could actually walk out.

Oddly enough, they walked out.

The last remaining customer stumbled out of the bathroom door marked SHEIKS. As he wiped his hands on his slacks, he staggered up to the stage, fished five bucks out of his wallet, and slurred heavily, "Melancholy Baby."

We all looked at Glen. He shrugged. The customer dropped the five on the floor and staggered to the exit. The open door let a wave of sunlight flash across the empty room.

Then we saw Mr. Furnier sitting alone at the bar, looking as supportive as he could. He'd been there the whole time. When we finished, he handed us our pay and gave us an encouraging smile. We all told him we thought he was cool.

Vince frowned. "I can't believe people really request 'Melancholy Baby,'" he said. "I thought that only happened in cartoons."

2.

HEADLINERS AND GUILLOTINES

ENTER HERE FOR THE THEATER OF ROCK

A FEW YEARS LATER, when we were headliners pioneering a new kind of stage warfare, a number of rock critics had a lot of fun with our theater of rock stuff and gave us some outlandish write-ups and interpretations.

What did we know about rock theater? As far as we knew, we were the first. We knew the *records* of Screamin' Jay Hawkins, the barrel-voiced soul singer of "I Put a Spell on You," but we didn't know about his act of singing it while sitting in a crypt, surrounded by voodoo hoodoo.

The whole notion of "rock theater" (*Hair*, *Godspell*, and so on) was still a long way off, but we were gradually getting into a groove of making spectacles of ourselves. Three events occurred that taught us about showmanship.

Inspiration Event No. 1: On the night of October 23, 1964, the Earwigs played for the Cortez High "Pit and the Pendulum" Halloween dance. Somebody must have been inspired by the Vincent Price horror movie.

For the occasion, the father of our photographer pal Scott Ward built a working guillotine. The "blade" was made from wood and spray-painted silver. Mr. Ward assured us that it had stops built in to keep it from lopping off any heads.

We got the girls from journalism class to weave giant spiderwebs from white clothesline and hang them from each side of the stage. Vince and I created a coffin out of cardboard and painted it to look like old wood.

Inspiration Event No. 2: Going on TV. People think America was all clean-cut and preppy in the early 1960s, but pop culture even then was filled with all kinds of tasty ridicule. Comedians such as Peter Sellers, Ernie Kovacs, and even Steve Allen worked at the edge of the surreal. And on the local level it was even freakier. Before the television industry got all syndicated and homogenized, there used to be regional programs on stations all around the country. Our big deal in Arizona was a local show full of skits and cartoons called *The Wallace and Ladmo Show*. Boy, they fed us a big bowl full of crazy every day.

Wallace, the straight man, wore a beanie and a propellor. Ladmo was the goofy sidekick with an oversize top hat and polka-dot tie. Wallace and Ladmo's skits were outlandish, and naturally there would be moments of awesome failure—props would malfunction, actors would come apart. But as far as I'm concerned, on this show, *there could be no failure*. They just grabbed hold of catastrophe and rode it out like champs. In fact, the more it fell apart, the funnier it became.

One day Vince got brave and dialed up the show's station, KPHO. Wallace himself answered the phone. Vince told him about the Earwigs and explained how we'd love to be on their show.

"Sure," Wallace said. "I'll have you on."

Over the next weeks, we dove into our preparation for our allotted two songs. Vince painted John's bass drum. We wore black turtlenecks and matching gold corduroy jackets with no collars. We still managed to look scruffy.

The day we walked into the television studio, we were surprised to see Wayne Newton. He was a young singer from the area who specialized in the old standards. He watched us set up.

"Stand very close together," said the future Mr. Las Vegas in his silky, high-pitched voice. "It will have more impact on-screen." We figured he knew what he was talking about; we had seen the Newton Brothers perform on *Lew King Rangers*.

There we were, facing these TV cameras that were as big as dirigibles. As Porky Pig signed off, "Th-th-that's all, folks!" we got a brief, cordial introduction and the nervous Earwigs catapulted into a song. We were so keyed up that the song came out like a sped-up Charlie Chaplin movie. On our second song, we got so confused that we had to stop playing. Vince saved our bacon by waving into the camera and saying, "Yabbada-yabbada, that's all, folks!"

The lights dimmed. Our heart rates slowed to the low hundreds. Wayne walked past us casually and nodded: "Good save."

It was 1964. Our hair was getting longer now. In school this made us marks for the tougher teachers and their stooges, the hallway monitors, who loved to report us. Any guy with long hair must be a dope fiend. Worst of all, Arizona was chockful of dudes whose sole ambition on weekends was to get cross-eyed drunk and go pound somebody. Whaling the tar out of some longhairs seemed to be easy pickins.

The parking lots of the teen clubs turned into battlefields. In our case, though, the confrontational sneer "Are you a boy or are you a girl?" didn't always work out for the cowboys. Quite a few ended up sprawled on their backs with bloody teeth while the athletic John Tatum looked down on them with a devilish grin. Glen's flying fists also did some damage.

We were barely old enough for our parents to allow us to go to these places, but we'd heard all about the most popular teen club in Phoenix, the VIP Lounge. One night, we showed up unannounced and introduced ourselves to the owner, Jack Curtis, who agreed to an audition. Jack had a wholesome Dick Clark kind of style.

He didn't have to hear much at the next day's audition before he agreed to hire us. But the band name, he said—that had to go.

"We couldn't have made it this far without that name," Glen said.

"How about the Spiders?" Jack said. "It has more radio appeal."

"The Spiders!" Vince said. "It's still a bug. I like it!"

Jack said we could have a new stage to go along with the new name. It would be called the Spider Sanctum.

"I haven't the slightest idea what it should look like," Jack said, "but you're going to build it."

Later that week, the band met at the VIP to build our magnificent set. We scrambled like a pack of chimpanzees. Mr. Ward, the dad who'd built our guillotine, showed up with a station wagon full of wood. Even Mr. Furnier and Mr. Buxton came to offer engineering pointers.

Just like at the Cortez "Pit and Pendulum" dance, we used clothesline to create spiderwebs. I painted a giant spider on John's drum head. Glen found a sparkly curtain in a faded brown color he called "shitania" and stapled it up to be our backdrop. I plugged in some indigo and magenta lights. We stood back and admired our pit of doom.

Jack, meanwhile, had radio ads going with an echoey voice announcing the Spider *Sanctum-sanctum-sanctum* . . .

It was then that we made a major musical discovery. Glen showed up at my house with a Yardbirds album, *For Your Love*. The guitar just exploded from the tracks. Searing triplets would reinforce the melody and then echo off somewhere as if they were soaring down a canyon.

Glen and I couldn't wait to tell our guys, but first we decided to learn a couple of the songs. We spent the afternoon figuring out the parts, lifting the needle off the vinyl record and playing it again and again. One number, a Mose Allison song called "I'm Not Talking," required a raft of repetitions.

Later, when we sat Vince down to hear the record, he picked up Keith Relf's harmonica parts quickly. Their nasally teenage voices matched perfectly.

Paychecks on the horizon, we went to the Arizona Music Center and bought new Fender amps. Glen bought his dream guitar, a Gretsch Chet Atkins Tennessean, an ornate, single-cut hollow body. Vince bought harmonicas in every key. He didn't get any fancy chromatic ones, but rather the three-dollar Hohner Marine Bands, the kind Paul Butterfield blew. Vince claimed that blues notes sounded better on cheap harps. He liked saying "harps," too.

I was the proud owner of a spanking-new Fender Bassman amp with two twelve-inch, heavy-duty speakers. It even smelled new. I heard those big fat notes thumping out of that thing and shivered. In my mind, that amp made me a bona fide professional.

Jack's idea was to provide nonstop entertainment at the club. On the main stage he'd have headliners like the Byrds and the Lovin' Spoonful, and when they were done, the audience could turn around and face the shadowy Spider Sanctum at the other end.

When the big Friday night debut arrived, we pictured ourselves arriving by limousine. Instead, we chugged up in a 1956 Mercury. We were four hours early, so we went to the nearby Jack-in-the-Box for a sackful of tacos.

Our debut actually wasn't modest at all. Jack had rented two searchlights, and he had them sweep the night skies. He also hired two go-go girls to dance on the corners of the stage.

We watched the parking lot fill up. A candy apple red hot rod cruised in. Then came a woody with a surfboard strapped to the roof. Then a dusty black pickup rolled in with a whiskey-sodden dude hanging out the window, hollering that he was gonna kick some ass.

A normal Phoenix night.

Several members of the Maricopa County Sheriff's Office stood ready to break up fights and keep an eye out for any steamed-up windows on the cars, the better to protect the virtue of young ladies.

The doors opened at seven. Peanut Butter, a local group with psychedelic intentions, hit the stage, and by the time they finished their set with "Laugh, Laugh" (a cover of the Beau Brummels' hit), the VIP was packed.

The lights faded, and the Spider Sanctum began to glow. I counted off the first song like a trick pony, and John's drums went off at a full gallop. The go-go dancers began to gyrate crazily. The audience immediately turned around to see what all the ruckus was.

We knew some of the faces, and they were startled at our transformation. The silly Earwigs were gone, and in their place stood a fresh, more professional incarnation. We had our cool, snazzy new jackets, and all this nifty lighting that helped us perform with confidence. John and Glen had also worked out perfect blond hairstyles—John was aiming for Brian Jones of the Rolling Stones—and the lights made them look like Nordic gods.

For my own mysterious new image, I'd combed my hair over my eyes. I hope I was mysterious, because I couldn't see jack diddley.

We were used to being hassled by cops for our long hair, but while Glen was putting some fiery guitar work into the Yardbirds song "Shapes of Things," we spotted a police officer grinning hugely and giving Glen a big thumbs-up. I mean, this was no cowboy song. It was the Yardbirds' cosmic anthem to world peace, set off by Jeff Beck's soaring Morocco-by-way-of-Jupiter guitar solos. And there was the cop groovin' and appreciating it.

After the set, Jack congratulated us and said we had a long future as the VIP house band. The club was ours anytime for rehearsals. Best of all, he assured us we'd get steady paychecks.

From then on, every Friday and Saturday night, we were burning down the VIP Lounge, and that cop was always there, pointing his nightstick at Glen and ordering up another round of "Shapes of Things."

The club had a legal capacity of eight hundred but a thousand kids jammed in there on good nights. Now we were rolling in dough. Heck, we all still lived at home. John Speer went out and bought a peppy old Corvette with faded paint. Vince bought a brand-new bright yellow Ford Fairlane convertible. He dubbed it the Chick Pleaser.

Then: the blonde.

It happened at the Back to School Bash at the Arizona State Fair grounds. The Turtles were the headliners, and we were among the local support bands. To eliminate changeover lulls, we had agreed to share the same equipment. It was all going smoothly until a surf band called the Laser Beats took the stage. Everything had to be moved out of the way so an enormous riser could be built for their golden-haired drummer.

I thought it was ridiculous. So, standing out with the crowds, I start ranking on him. "What a jerk!" I said loudly. "What does he need a drum riser for? So he can play 'Wipe Out'?" I used a dorky voice to emphasize my disdain.

A blonde girl in front of me spun around and faced me. She was pretty, but she was *mad*. "He's *not* a jerk," she snapped. "He's my brother and he's the greatest drummer in the whole world."

This was how I found myself face-to-face with Neal Smith's pretty sister. She gave me a dirty look and turned back around.

Feeling like a dope, I remained dead silent for the rest of the long delay. The Laser Beats finally went through their surf songs, and the crowd went crazy for Neal's drums scorching in their rendition of "Wipe Out."

I couldn't stop thinking about the tall, cool blonde, even as we waited for her brother to take down his drum riser.

Then it was our turn. It was the biggest stage we'd ever performed on. The room sounded huge. We tore into our versions of other people's hits, leading off with a revenge-driven version of Bo Diddley's "Road Runner." Vince's harmonica was wailing. In our imaginations, we felt like pop stars.

Maybe that's just what it took to be as strong as we were. After the show, an ecstatic Jack Curtis met us at the side of the stage and said, "Whatever it is, you boys have it."

One hot night, the Yardbirds came to play the VIP Lounge. They might have been *our* heroes, but they were only just then on the verge of national recognition. Jack was still able to get acts like this for a decent price.

As the opening act, the Spiders came up with a real nice way to salute these guys and show them our respect. We did a set that was *all* Yardbirds numbers. It wasn't until the Yardbirds blew everybody away with the same songs that it occurred to us we might have been a trifle inconsiderate.

One of the new things that Glen had been doing was incorporating silverware into his act. He clacked spoons against his thigh and even played slide guitar with a spoon. The Yardbirds' guitar player, Jeff Beck, thought Glen's spoons were hilarious. After we finished our set, Beck sneaked into the Spider Sanctum and swiped Glen's tray of silverware. During their show, Beck was doing one of his blistering solos. He fretted the guitar with his left hand while his right pinged spoons off the neck. One by one, they clanged off his strings and flew into the audience.

After the show, Glen and I were backstage and struck up a conversation with Yardbirds singer Keith Relf.

"I'll bet you didn't expect anyone to know all your songs," I said.

"We've never had to follow that before," he admitted.

"We really like your band," Glen said, "especially the guitar player."

Relf just shook his head. "You should have seen the guy we had *before* him."

Glen and I laughed because we were sure he was putting us on. Better than Jeff Beck? C'mon. Beck was probably the most original, outlandish guitarist on earth. It was only later, when we heard Cream and found out that Eric Clapton had broken in with the Yardbirds, that we understood Relf wasn't joking.

But the biggest assault on my senses that night was seeing their bass player, Paul Samwell-Smith. His experimental style was a revelation. It was Glen Buxton who taught me my first musical notes, and Bill Wyman and his "Famous Framus" bass playing on early Rolling Stones records gave me a foundation in blues patterns and structure, but it was hearing Samwell-Smith's original style that fueled my desire to be as different as possible on bass.

In rehearsals and on the road, Vince was growing more comfortable with his role as the lead singer—and the leader. If we were all about to walk across the parking lot to Taco Bell, Vince would walk in front and say, "Let's go get some tacos." It's like the skinny kid had someone to back him up; it was the Ruben Lukie bullying scene all over. Glen would just cackle.

During live shows at the VIP, Vince's stage confidence drew on whatever singer he was imitating in a cover song—singers like Mick Jagger, the Animals' Eric Burdon, or the Kinks' Ray Davies. He didn't imitate their movements so much as their confidence. Without that imaginary shield, he was only Vince.

We had no taste for happy songs. We had an edge and delivered it times five. Vince drew strength from that, too. He wasn't a little guy—we were a gang. We wanted to nail the crowd to the back wall, and we could do that as a unit. And our weapons were high-powered amplifiers.

We quickly began piling up our list of firsts. Not only had we gotten a professional nod from the Yardbirds, but we also went on our first "tour." We were to do three nights opening for the Byrds at the VIP, then were to accompany them down to Tucson and then back to do the Phoenix Coliseum.

We were impressed that the Byrds actually had a guy who did nothing but set up their amps. We immediately called on a friend, Mike Allen, who was already hanging around a lot, and asked him to be our honorary equipment mover. Although a quiet, passive fellow, Mike jumped right into the spirit of the band and started dressing weird—only, his concept of weird was *weird*. He wore a black turtleneck (copied from the TV spy show *The Man from U.N.C.L.E.*) and a velvet cape, and he always had a small pillow balanced on his shoulder. (Take that, Salvador Dalí.) We called him Amp Boy.

One day in 1966 Jack walked into our rehearsal and told us he'd arranged a recording session for us. "You have to choose an A-side and a B-side," he said.

When pressed for what we should do, Jack suggested the treacly love song that was all over the radio that year, Bob Lind's "Elusive Butterfly."

We naturally laughed like hyenas. Jack blushed.

When we finally settled down to think, Vince suggested Marvin Gaye's energetic soul groover "Hitch Hike." For the B-side, I urged the others to agree to "Why Don't You Love Me," by the Blackwells. It was a driving pop song with howling harmonicas, from a British movie about post-Beatles bands like Gerry and the Pacemakers called *Ferry Across the Mersey*.

A couple of afternoons later we were in the studio and John Speer pounded out the drum hook on "Why Don't You Love Me" with incredible force. We followed that with the best version of "Hitch Hike" ever recorded—if, of course, you don't count Gaye's original or the Rolling Stones' cover. It was the best version to come out of Phoenix, anyway. For all the friends and family who dutifully bought it, though, we couldn't sell two hundred copies.

"Elusive Butterfly," meanwhile, shot straight to No. 1 on the charts, and you couldn't get away from that song no matter where you went.

Sometimes you look at the dramatic turns that appear in your life and you think, There are no accidents. Fate really does want to smack you.

Now we come to Inspiration Event No. 3. When it came to inventing rock theater, our biggest revelation came in 1966, when we debuted at the Phoenix Star Theater in a road show version of the hit musical *Bye Bye Birdie*. Jack had arranged it—he knew that our exposure from doing the play would help him pack the VIP.

Bye Bye Birdie is a corny but entertaining musical about the disruptions in a middle-class town when a famous, dangerous Elvis-like rock-'n'-roll star, Conrad Birdie, comes to visit. We were to play his backup band, the Birdies. The show starred comedian Jan Murray as the exasperated dad.

We showed up for rehearsal and found ourselves getting manhandled by the choreographer, Michael Bennett. Years later, we'd have plenty of opportunities to remember this guy when, in the late 1970s and into the '80s, Bennett was the king of Broadway with revolutionary shows like *A Chorus Line* and *Dreamgirls*. The skinny fellow bossing us around in Phoenix would have been just twenty-three years old in 1966, but he had the fire of a guy going places fast. We couldn't have guessed then that it would be early burn-out and death by AIDS. Looking at him then, we just knew he was in charge.

With short black hair, black dance attire, and the nerve-jangling energy of a New Yorker, Bennett called us out to the stage and told us to join a line of gorgeous girl dancers. He counted out the steps and demonstrated a turn, which the real dancers picked up immediately. The Spiders proved that our athletic backgrounds meant nothing. We were stone klutzes.

"Timing! Timing!" Bennett yelled while clapping to the count. He watched us stagger around like a bunch of winos and gaped: "You guys are *musicians*?"

Everyone waited while Bennett froze, in deep thought.

"All right, I want a dancer on each of their arms." He waved, and two girls suddenly appeared at my elbows. Bennett showed us what he wanted by sashaying across the stage with an imaginary girl on each arm. When he called for action, the five Spiders and their gorgeous escorts almost collapsed.

"No, no, no, *stop*!" Bennett yelled. "Somebody's going to break a leg or something."

Again, everyone waited while he paced back and forth in deep, frustrated thought. My posture-conscious bookends stood gracefully, tits at attention.

While Speer looked as alert as a Marine recruit, Tatum was already smiling at his escorts with smooth familiarity. What was he thinking?

For a short piece of eternity, everyone in the theater stared solemnly at Bennett and wondered what the genius would come up with.

"Screw it," he said abruptly. "Cut the scene."

The girls dropped my arms as if they were a leper's pajamas and stalked off.

The rehearsals flashed by, and soon we had the numbers down cold. Our costumes for the play were our actual Spiders jackets and black turtlenecks. Having no costume changes was good, as our schedule had us finishing the show at night and streaking across town to play a late show at the VIP.

And how's this for luck? One of our scenes was a dream sequence complete with guillotine, coffin, and pallbearers.

Opening night arrived. The theater hummed like a beehive and smelled like a blend of perfume and cigar smoke. Vince and I sat on stools backstage and watched the bustling. Everyone seemed to have been sped up into a higher gear.

Vince pulled a harmonica out of his pocket and blew a bluesy riff, only to be quickly shushed by the prop manager. Another guy rushed up, pointed his finger, and said urgently, "Birdies! Your cue is coming up. Where are the other Birdies?"

"I'll get Tatum," Glen said. "I might have to pry him off that dancer girl, though."

Tatum walked out of the dressing room tucking in his shirttail, looking sharp in his black outfit and smiling the smile of a guy who'd just gotten lucky.

Vince said, "Let's get into character. We're the Birdies!"

This was one of those theater-in-the-round houses that were going up all over the country. Vince led us up the wooden walkway of Ramp No. 4, and we hit the stage to a huge outburst. Conrad, portrayed by actor Tom Hasson, pointed at Speer, who counted the downbeat. We tore into the song, and the Phoenix theatergoers got a gyrating dose of rock 'n' roll.

Corny? Yeah, but it was still a huge charge when Conrad pointed at a section of girls and they all screamed and fainted. And when he bumped his butt and hissed, "Suffer," every remaining girl screamed and dropped to the floor.

Yeah, we thought. Yeah.

It was a brief run, but our first exposure to the theater was powerful. We just soaked it up. We witnessed bickering among the actors, which was a theatrical experience in itself, and it was our first encounter with beautiful, half-dressed dancers.

After every Birdie show, we hurried to the VIP for a late set and threw in a couple of our new show tunes, "Honestly Sincere" and "One Last Kiss." Only, now our theatrical juices were flowing. We commanded *our* stage with our own set of rules, and we were feeling bolder, tougher, and more legitimate than ever before.

The theatrical vampire had bitten us and, to put it into words that anyone would understand, its eternal spirit drank deeply from the rivers of our souls.

Then we went home to our parents' houses and slept in our childhood bedrooms.

I saw the blonde again. It was at the Encanto Park Bandshell, the best-known park in Phoenix. We were watching the opening band, the Holy Grail, and I noted that the lanky drummer with the sun-bleached hair was the "Wipe Out" king himself, Neal Smith. Unlike his smiley surf band, the Laser Beats, there was some serious grit to the Holy Grail. They weren't afraid to go boogeying off the beaten path.

While the band covered the Paul Butterfield rouser "Shake Your Money Maker," some hard-faced members of the Phoenix police force gathered at the side of the bandshell. Evidently they had a problem with one of Neal's cymbals, which had a big red FUCK painted across it. When the police walked onstage, Neal surprised them by smashing his drums to smithereens.

While Neal was getting escorted away, I spied his lovely sister in the crowd. I got up my nerve and approached her. "Would you wear my hat while I'm onstage?" I said.

"I guess so," she replied with a puzzled look.

While we tuned up behind the shell, I said to the guys that we needed to come up with a finale that would outdo the Holy Grail's. We tossed around some ideas and decided to stage a fistfight and make everyone think the Spiders were breaking up. The only way it would work, I said, is if we did it with straight faces.

Staring into the sun, we rocked out to an enthusiastic crowd. When we got to our final song, John and Vince started yelling at each other. John ran to the front of the stage and grabbed Vince by the collar, and in a jiffy they were in a knock-down, drag-out fight. They stormed off the stage in different directions, while the rest of us shrugged and finished. We walked off in melodramatic concern.

Offstage, Glen was confronted by a couple who wanted the details. He put on a grave look and said, "John killed Vince, but they revived him at the hospital, so John gave him a bouquet of daisies and now they're married."

So it worked. Our fake fight did the trick and we upstaged the Holy Grail.

Neal's sister walked up to me with a derisive smile. "You guys just did that for attention," she said, fishing my hat out of her bag. "You're not really breaking up, are you?"

I was so awestruck by her beauty that I groped for something to say. Reaching deep into my suitcase of cultivated wit, I said, "It sure is hot today."

Her expression went flat. Once again, she walked away.

In the summer of 1966, in a move that he would later think about heavily, John Tatum up and quit the band. He was attracted to another group that knew how to play the song "Shotgun," so he took his great hair and rhythm guitar chords to them. When I saw him onstage with them, I had to admit that they did the song right. Even so, Glen, who considered Tatum a good friend, was really sore.

We were desperate to find a replacement. Vince, Glen, and I remembered a group we'd seen at a battle of the bands at a shopping mall. They were called the Trolls and looked like football linebackers imitating the Beatles. Glen sneered that they just did "girl songs," but I admired their tight harmonies. Their singing guitarist had left a strong impression on me. I had even made a note of his name: Michael Bruce.

Like the other Trolls, Michael played a big orange guitar. "It's like a Popsicle," Glen said, laughing.

I called Michael up and made a date. To show that there were no hard feelings, Tatum joined me, Glen, and Vince on the reconnoitering mission.

The Bruce home was a very nice house. Mrs. Bruce showed us to Michael's room, where we found big-shouldered Michael surrounded by football gear and barbells. Oh. A *football* jock. But at least he also had boxes of records.

Right off the bat, Michael wanted to make it clear that he was skeptical about joining the Spiders. His explanation boiled down to our lack of a clean-cut image.

I pointed out that we were the house band at the VIP. "And we get paid, too."

"And we don't play any girl songs," Glen chimed in.

If we had doubts, they drifted away when Michael showed us that not only did he own a reel-to-reel tape recorder but he had an equipment-hauling truck parked outside.

Vince leapt ahead in the negotiations and told Michael he had to buy Tatum's pin-striped pants.

"That's silly," Michael said.

"Who are you to talk?" I replied. "Your band has orange guitars!"

"Is this a band or a scam?" Michael said. He fished three fives out of his wallet and handed them over to Tatum.

"Practice tomorrow at three," Vince said. "At the VIP."

When we hit the sidewalk, Tatum laughed. "I can't believe he bought the fucking pants."

Vince looked up. "You know, we never actually asked him to join?"

When Michael showed up at the next rehearsal, he brought along his orange guitar and a nice Fender amplifier. As soon as we started jamming, it was clear that Michael and Glen would work well together. Both of them could play rhythm or lead. And Michael gave us another strong vocalist. On top of all that, he learned songs almost instantly.

As our band began to grow and add strengths, Michael brought us the determination to do our own stuff: We had gone down to Tucson to do an audition near the university, and on the drive back we killed time by tossing around some songs that we might cover. Mike shook his head and said, "Nah, let's write our own songs instead." He kept working on us till we realized we had to knuckle down and compose some originals.

As soon as we got back to Phoenix, Vince and I came up with a song called "Don't Blow Your Mind." The guys liked it. (Glen, of course, wanted to call it "Don't Blow Your Wad.") We began thinking it was good enough to record.

In the sixties, recording studios were like used cars—you never knew what you were getting into. Generally, the nicest-sounding studios were in the big cities, but even out in the sticks there were actually some cool places to record, like Sun Records in Memphis or Muscle Shoals in Alabama. When we lumbered into the Copper State Recording Studio in downtown Tucson, we had no idea what kind of ride this would be.

The studio owner, Forster S. Cayce, would be our producer. His assistant was a guy named Frank, who said, *"Achtung!"* after everything Cayce said. They led us into their dark soundproofed studio and held us captive to their unique method of production, best described as Taking Forever.

You hear about those legends, those rhythm and blues acts that recorded five albums before lunch. The Spiders had no such luck. We spent days watching Cayce move our equipment around the studio trying to find a good sound. Then we'd go across the street to Denny's and put the arm on Cayce for another round of grilled cheese sandwiches and Cokes. At night, we slept on the cold studio floor.

The days rolled by in a fog of grilled cheese sandwiches and *Achtungs!* One day we walked in to find Cayce swaying back and forth in front of the studio monitors while he played the Fortunes' song "You've Got Your Troubles (I've Got Mine)."

"Just listen to those horns!" Cayce barked. "What are they saying, fellas?"

Vince and I were clueless. Cayce just smiled. "They're saying, 'I don't give a damn.' Can you feel it? 'I just don't give a damn!'"

He wanted us to get that same "I just don't give a damn" emotion on "Don't Blow Your Mind."

Glen grumbled that if he had to sleep on the floor one more night, he really wouldn't give a damn.

"That's a good song," Michael pointed out, "but that's not really our cup of tea."

At lunch, Michael went down to the corner and bought the new Beatles single "Strawberry Fields Forever." He put it on Cayce's turntable.

Instead of swaying back and forth, Cayce stood still and listened intently through the whole song, all the way to the mysterious fade-out. His mind was not blown.

"Too thin," he snapped and walked out of the room.

Over the next week, we slowly got some tracks down. We did two-part harmonies, and Glen got to lay down some guitar with a buzzy fuzz tone over Vince's garage band vocals.

"Ain't too shabby," Glen said when he heard the final result. We decided maybe Cayce was a producer after all.

Santa Cruz Records released the single to radio play in Tucson and Phoenix. By the week ending October 27, 1966, "Don't Blow Your Mind" had reached No. 11 on KFIF Boss Radio charts. Not bad for schoolkids.

I figured we'd have a better chance at extending our stay at the VIP if we kept playing different songs all the time. Further, we felt we had to keep changing our image as often as we could. That way, people wouldn't get tired of us. Vince, Glen, Michael, John, and I agreed, and we threw ourselves into it like fiends.

We pounced on any idea, no matter how silly. The VIP kitchen became our main source of stage props. After the kitchen utensils, we incorporated napkins, straws, and spatulas into our act.

Charlie Carnal, our lighting technician, joined in on the extreme conceptualizing and added to our psychedelic transformation. He constructed what he called the Lobster Strobe. It was a metal munitions box he'd bought at an Army-Navy store, outfitted with a high-intensity light and reflective foil liner. An electric motor turned a metal disc with cutouts, creating a soothingly hypnotic, strobelike lighting effect.

Charlie also constructed the flasher lights, long wooden boxes of footlights that he placed at the front of the stage. Hinged flaps with vividly colored gelatins would drop in front of the lights, creating over us a panorama of impressively intense colors. Charlie operated all this with a keyboard he called the Light Organ. (A few years later, when we were seen in the movie *Diary of a Mad Housewife*, there is a quick shot of Charlie flashing the keys.)

Another lighting effect, created with a seven-foot plywood disc, was called the Light Wheel. But for the radio ads, Jack dubbed it the Electro-Lucent Mind Machine.

Charlie never seemed to mind when we stomped his flasher lights to smithereens at the end of a show. He'd calmly collect the pieces and rebuild them for the next show. He was such an artist, and his lights were such a vital part of the show, that we voted to give him a nice share of the pay.

As our ever-changing spectacle got more sophisticated, our shows became more thought-provoking and, indeed, borderline spectacular. If something bombed, it bombed. But if something worked, we'd find a way to extend it. People came to see what we'd do next. The changes didn't come from weekend to weekend; they happened from set to set.

Kids started telling their friends, and of course we were giving them shows that were easy to exaggerate about in the retelling. Vince loved this, and started making up rumors, just to see how they'd evolve and come back to us.

One day, we walked into the VIP and Jack Curtis said he had bad news. A Japanese group called the Spyders had released a new album. As we understood it, having an album out meant that they legally owned the name. When the initial shock wore off, we vowed to come up with a name that nobody else would ever think of in a bazillion years. After a flurry of suggestions, we settled on the Nazz. We got it from Glen's favorite new Yardbirds song, "The Nazz Are Blue."

By rehearsal's end, we had a new song to go with our new name. We also had plans to consummate the new name by growing mustaches and goatees.

My dad's reaction to my hair was tough. When we were kids, we'd get sudden haircuts at the kitchen table. But now his son was in a rock band, and he didn't have a whole lot of truck with that. Although his general outlook in life was "Learn for yourself," he felt strong enough about my so-called line of work to take me aside one day and give me the Talk.

By coincidence, I had in my back pocket a wad of cash I'd just picked up. I smoothed the money out on the table between us. He took a good look at it, nodded, and changed the subject. That was the last grief he ever gave me about being a musician.

With the money infusion, I went out and bought a cream white 1964 Ford Falcon with slicks and a tachometer. *It* was cool, therefore I thought *I* was cool. With this and Michael's van, we could start taking on some out-of-town bookings. We were rolling.

One of our favorite rides was actually in a baby-blue Mustang owned by a friend of the band, Michelle Mueller, who went by Toodie, the perfect nickname for a girl inflicted with chronic happiness. Even her sky-blue car beamed happiness. She became Vince's favorite mountain-climbing companion.

This is the other part of being in a band: Some of the people you attract just bring positive vibes. Toodie still does, actually.

Then we got it. Total perspective. Our position in the universe was finally revealed.

We were playing a hole-in-the-wall coffeehouse in Tucson called the Minus One when the door flew open and a troop of guys in full Nazi regalia marched in and stood at attention. Everyone stared in disbelief. We were staring, too, even as we stood on the "stage," which was a four-by-six sheet of plywood screwed to the bar.

One by one, customers got up and squeezed past the newcomers to get the hell out. After a lot of shouting and stomping, the Nazis seated themselves in military fashion.

Looking on with a mild curiosity was a girl who had been dancing by herself all through our show.

We had come down to this coffeehouse in the shadow of the University of Arizona in the hope of making a dime or two. A cup of coffee at the Minus One cost fifteen cents. They were used to gentle folkies here, but we had cleared the air by opening up with a lightning-fast version of Chuck Berry's "Nadine." Vince devoted the song to all the coffee fiends in the house.

The Nazis shouted, "*Sieg Heil!*" while the dancing girl waved her arms and spun around the room as if still in a beautiful dream.

After twenty unsettling minutes of this Tucson coffeehouse putsch, the troop snapped to attention and, with a great deal of ceremonious stomping, marched out the door.

We were shaking, but maybe it was all the free coffee we'd been knocking back. After three loud sets, Vince thanked what was left of the audience for coming. We were barely off the barstools when the owner put on Joan Baez's "Farewell, Angelina."

A kid approached our table. He explained that everyone hated the Nazis. Nodding toward the dancing girl, he said, "My friend wanted me to tell you she really liked the vibrations of your music. She's deaf and she dances in front of the speakers so she can feel the vibrations."

"Oh," Vince said. He borrowed a pencil from me and wrote a note on a napkin to the girl. It read, "We love how you dance."

The kid took the napkin over to the dancing girl. She smiled and waved at us and kept on dancing.

I wondered how we'd explain this gig. *Well, a bunch of Nazis and a deaf girl really liked us.*

Vince laughed. "It's a reflection of our wide range of appeal."

"We should bill ourselves as the band that appeals to everyone but the masses," I said.

Vince took on a noble expression and said, "When the weird people become the masses, we'll be famous."

3.

SUNSET STRIPPED

KEEP PLAYING TILL THEY BREAK UP THE CHAIRS

RIGHT FROM THE BEGINNING, the nature of our act had a way of provoking situations. We just had that magical wizard's dust that would turn a restless crowd into a dangerous mob. One night in Tucson we got a real taste of what we could unleash.

The Monterey Ice Rink, a small hall on the south end of Tucson, was half ice rink, half bowling alley. You could feel the icy cold seeping up and mixing with the desert heat.

The owner of the joint was a brash little round guy with a cigar stub jammed in the corner of his mouth. One look at us and he'd start snarling like a Rottweiler with issues. "The only rule here," he once barked, "is keep playing till they start breaking up the chairs, then get your asses in the back room."

We knew the fights were coming. We had played this place before and had seen the beady-eyed cowboys ready to grind us into hamburger.

The gangs all huddled in their private corners of the Monterey. Over by the jukebox were the greasers, which even then was an old term but it's what everyone still called the hot rodders. These guys were all striking moody Marlon Brando poses. It was 1966 and their Brylcreemed ducktails might have been a good ten years out of date, but *they* didn't know it. They thought they were the coolest thing on the block and were ready to rumble.

Another group ready to rumble was the Mexicans. And then there were the cowboys, who were always itching to hand out some prairie justice. After a long, hard week, the cowboys were looking for the chance to get in a brawl, even if it was with another cowboy whose only crime was not having his hat on straight. All it took was, "What are you looking at?" and fists would be flying. They just wanted something to brag about on Monday morning.

There were two other groups at this rickety club. The Indians just floated above it all, and the surfers were pretty laid back, too. Neither of them wanted to fight much. And don't ask me why there were surfers in Tucson, since the Sonoran Desert had a noticeable lack of big waves. These guys would drive to California or Baja once a year and then spend the rest of their time driving woodies around Arizona with surfboards tied to the roof, trying to pick up surfer chicks who wore white lipstick and said that everything was *real cherry* or *so bitchin'*.

You notice I haven't said anything about longhaired freaks. We definitely didn't have anybody on our side. Nobody tough, anyway. For the rest of the cliques, one issue could unite them all: These longhaired guys in the band, *these* were the guys to kill.

In the late afternoon sun, we were unloading our amps out of both cars outside the club, while the owner snarled at us for being late, when I looked around. We were on the edge of town, and the tank in my Falcon was nearly dry. I told the guys I was going on a gas run. Vince said, "I'll go with you."

By now we had gotten comfortable dressing on the wild side. Our little taste of stardom and adulation at the VIP Lounge had made us feel cocky. I had on a white silk shirt with tassels hanging all over it, like I was some stripper who'd hit the skids. By now our hair had gotten so long we might as well have worn walking billboards proclaiming, "Please Punch Me."

Vince and I got only as far as the first intersection when two cowboys pulled alongside us in a dusty pickup with rifles mounted in the rear-window rack. One cowboy yelled, "Hoooeee, are you a dude or an ugly little girlie?"

Vince, the good son of a preacher, never, ever swore. So I was really shocked when, for the first time, I saw him do something crude. He flipped them the bird.

"It's a red light!" I yelled, watching the cowboys fly out of their truck. *"Why'd you do that?!"*

Just in the nick of time, Vince tapped down the door lock. The cowboys banged away on our windows.

The light changed and we went barreling past the gas station and out into the desert.

Vince looked in the rearview mirror. "They're after us," he said.

We knew the stakes. The newspapers were always running lighthearted stories about some rancher who caught a hippie on his property, decided to give him a haircut with the sheep shears, and, darned the luck, cut off part of his ear, too.

I was looking down the road, getting frantic and thinking, There's not another gas station until Mexico. I had a four-barrel Holley carburetor on top of that Ford engine and it was just chugging down fuel. The gas gauge was practically coughing. They've got guns and they're going to kill us in the middle of the desert where nobody will find us, I thought.

Then I got this idea. I got way out ahead and spun a huge 180-degree Brodie turn out in the desert. The dust and dirt were flying. I zoomed back toward town and we passed the cowboys close enough to see their red faces in mid-scream.

I looked in the rearview mirror and saw them whipping around and getting on our tail again.

Okay, I'll double-bluff them, I thought. I did another big rooster tail one-eighty. We zoomed back past them again like this was all just a *Road Runner* cartoon. Finally we pulled over and sat there with the engine idling.

"I don't see them," Vince said. "I guess we scared them away." Typical Vince.

We got back to the club in time for the owner to chew out our asses again.

"Just play and you'll get paid," he growled. "Then everybody's happy."

The crowd looked like packs of restless animals in their respective sections of the large, dim rink. In the dressing room, Vince regaled the guys with the story of our chase, and somehow his new version was already twice as preposterous.

The guys just shook their heads.

Then we walked confidently out to the stage—but who do we see waiting up front? Those cowboys who'd just chased us into the desert.

The two of them stood there with their skanky grins, their boots and ten-gallon hats. About eye level with us, they gave us their best showdown stares and pounded fists into palms.

"You assholes are dead meat," they sneered. "*Dead meat.*" Some other rowdies joined in the chant.

We tried to ignore them and kicked off our set with our usual barn burner opener, "Route 66." But we couldn't ignore these clods right in front of us. They had a posse assembled, a lynch mob, a whole mess of folks glaring at us. They were all pounding their fists.

A cowgirl elbowed her way through the crowd and took the front position. And it was some position. There was no missing her. She was a big-breasted girl with a low-cut top to show off her Cadillac cleavage. With a loud voice, she joined this hillbilly chorus of revenge.

Glen was completely unperturbed. Onstage, he usually had this real back-alley indifference to the world. He also liked to smoke while he played, and he would stick his cigarette up in the guitar strings at the end of the neck.

We began to play "Baby Please Don't Go." While Vince wailed on his harmonica, Glen walked to the front of the stage and, with a haughty air, "ashed" his cigarette right down the front of the cowgirl's Cadillac cleavage.

My brain was screaming, *Why'd you do that?* But of course I knew why. Glen was always ready to step over the line.

So what happened? The cowboys started cheering! Glen was an

instant hero to them. The second he flicked the ashes, they wanted to be on *his* side. Even the girl with the big-time cleavage was cheering.

There you have the essence of Glen's magic. He just didn't care, he did crazy things, and he was loved for it.

As the room got hotter, so did the notion in the crowd of fighting for fun. Our third set wasn't even finished when we were taking refuge from the bedlam in the dressing room, pressed against the door with the hinges giving out while we divvied up the money.

Glen and I ended up in a cemetery that night. He had hooked up with the rink's bubble gum–popping ticket girl, and they were doing it on top of somebody's grave. Meanwhile, I was stretched out under a tree with a tall girl named Denice on top of me. She had removed my boots and was wiggling her toes against mine while her tongue explored my tonsils.

Driving back to Phoenix the next day, we were laughing about all that abuse from the cowboys. We knew one thing: They would be talking about us. We knew our act was working. Our intention had been to get attention. If the customers had something outrageous to tell their friends, then it was more likely those friends would come to see us, too.

It's kind of funny to think that it had been only two years since the Beatles hit America, on February 7, 1964, a date which will live in infamy. There were little hints of androgyny in the early days of rock. In the mid-fifties, Elvis Presley had that big, splashy wave of hair and those loud pink shirts. Big stuff. I'm sure it got him into a few fights down south. John Lennon grew up idolizing Elvis. When the Beatles came out, parents thought they were outrageous. Then the Rolling Stones came out, and the Beatles weren't outrageous anymore.

We were watching and studying, and we were convinced we could push the boundaries a little further. To this day I have no idea why we were so gung-ho. That night in Tucson wasn't the only time we escaped by inches.

We loved to brainstorm. Maybe that was the source of our creativity, our willingness to dive into abstract conversations, with everybody piling on zingers and trying to trump everyone else with batshit-crazy ideas.

In our minds we were designing a stage show fit for the Roman Colosseum. It didn't matter that that world existed only in our heads. We just knew that our fantasy was infinitely more fun than getting a job at the local car wash—which, by the way, Glen and I actually did for a week.

John, though—he didn't care for all this acrobatic discussion. He just wanted us to sit down and write garage band hit songs. Of course, he wanted *us* to write these songs. As the drummer, he didn't think that was his duty. It might actually have been a good idea to dumb it down like he wanted, but the rest of us were flying on some other plane.

It was around this time that I realized our two guitarists couldn't have been more different. Michael had the muscle-bound stance of the football player he'd once been. I liked him in our band. He was smart and likable but often had the obstinacy of a lineman. Meanwhile, Vince and I were runners. I like to think that experience gave us a leg up, so to speak. We were lean *and* kept moving forward no matter what. Glen was thin, but moved with an intense wariness. He always had a cool, aloof, self-contained air. You could drag Glen to the smoking gates of hell and he'd just look in and make some offhand insult. Glen and Michael were not too much alike as people, and when it came to playing styles, they were polar opposites. Yet when it came to *shaping* music, they made it work. Something good was happening.

The band needed a meeting place with a roof and no parents.

This was the decree from Dick Phillips, a friend who had produced our early recording of "Wonder Who's Loving Her Now" in a gunnysack. Dick was becoming a man of signficant influence in our lives. For one thing, he was consumed with our pursuit of musical originality. As our conversations unfolded, he dutifully wrote down everything we said, even ideas that, to us, should have slipped into the vapors by the next morning.

Charlie and Mike chipped in their ideas, too, but Dick (who would later change his name to Dick Christian) was the cosmic thinker. It seemed to us as if he'd seen everything in the world worth seeing, so we were happy to have him treat our mental dribblings as if they were mind-blasting concepts.

Dick really encouraged our androgynous look. When we looked at the other bands, we realized that if long hair shocked people, we were gonna have the longest hair of any band, ever.

Michael, still a jock at heart, didn't really want to hear about any gender-bending style at first. He had zero interest in wearing shiny fabrics and presenting himself as possibly not being straight. Big bruiser that he was, though, he wasn't thinking in terms of knuckle-dragging garage band music. He was a fan of simple, catchy pop songs. He probably would have been happy in a Carnaby Street coat doing upbeat tunes like the Buckinghams. He did have that pop sensibility.

So Michael kept resisting the clothes, but . . . the chicks dug them.

And wouldn't you know it? Once he started getting down with the weird clothes, he started pulling the most girls, too.

One day, Dick confronted us. He'd just been to the Sunset Strip and got a reckoning of the big time. "Do you guys want a shot at making it?" he thundered. "Or are you just happy sitting here in the middle of the desert?"

No, no, no, we protested. We weren't happy with our teensy-weensy slice of fame.

So the answer was clear. We had to hit the LA scene. Without making any plans or even packing lunch, we jumped in the van and took off. The Summer of Love 1967 was calling our names.

We were so idealistic. Reality was just this nuisance that reared its ugly head once in a while.

When we got to Los Angeles, we didn't know where to go. We went to Griffith Park and found the observatory where James Dean had the knife fight in *Rebel Without a Cause*. That night, we found ourselves bunking on park benches. At dawn, we saw a guy from a sandwich truck throwing out the old stuff, so we waylaid him for freebies.

Although we hadn't slept much, we were eager to get all decked out for Sunset Boulevard. Vince had his snakeskin jacket and feather boa; Charlie had his long hair down one side topped with a derby hat; Mike Allen had his cape with trademark pillow on the shoulder; Glen had his ripped jeans and his shirt buttoned right to the top; Michael had pulled on his fringed leather jacket; and I had my glow-in-the-dark skeleton pants. For us, there was no difference between stage gear and street clothes.

We hit Sunset Strip and thought we were on top of the world. We strutted down that packed street like we were a five-headed dragon.

We saw the clubs: Hullabaloo, Gazzarri's, the Whisky a Go Go. We saw the names on the marquees: Aretha Franklin, Johnny Rivers, Iron Butterfly, Buffalo Springfield, the Byrds, Love, even the Doors, whose song "Light My Fire" was clearly the song of the summer.

We couldn't afford admission, but we hardly noticed as we were so pop-eyed by the show on the street. People were coming from all over the country to take part in this scene. Hippies, freaks, flower children, runaways, big-busted babes, dealers—they all bopped, hustled, and scored in a big, flowing carnival. A human tidal wave poured down Sunset. The traffic was badly jammed, the cars on the boulevard weren't even moving. We looked around in a dazed condition, shell-shocked. This was the real thing.

"Look at the lungs on that specimen," Vince said.

"It's all silicone," Michael said.

I'd never even heard the word *silicone* before, but there it was in all its titillating glory. These babes were *out there*. I kept seeing women wearing see-through blouses with nothing underneath but a couple of big hellos.

That summer, free-floating madness reigned. Although we were dressed pretty crazily, in the Summer of Love you had a lot of leeway for crazy. The kids there clearly wanted to feel the love. But Vietnam had come down hard on the country, like a giant meat cleaver, and the Los Angeles police weren't really in a welcoming mood. Paddy wagons roared up and flocks of astonished kids got driven off. We saw one particularly outraged hippie, his face twisted in rage, get manhandled into a police car, screaming, "Pigs!" It was happening everywhere.

For bands, the competition was killer. We heard there were more than three thousand groups looking for work in Los Angeles. A garage band from Phoenix wasn't even going to get an audition. And to actually get a gig and get paid for it? Dream on.

After these visits to LA in the Summer of Love, we would drive back to Phoenix feeling pretty roughed up. For all the brainstorming we'd done, I suppose we were just a garage band with big airs.

Garage band music is raw and primal, kind of like the tribal dance before the virgin gets tossed into the volcano. There were other primitive yahoo bands out there, and some were getting on the charts with songs like the Standells' "Dirty Water" and Count Five's "Psychotic Reaction." Maybe we could have become big with that kind of music. We were good at it. But we said no. We wanted to do something nobody had ever heard before.

We started rehearsing ten hours a day and pushing the limits as far as we could. We would take our music to deep space. Our drummer, John, just wasn't happy, though. You could hardly blame him. We didn't even have food. John would fold his arms and say, "I don't want to jam anymore."

The rest of us didn't think we were just jamming—we were learning how to play, looking for an identity. In those days bands had their own style. Today, a lot of bands dress exactly the same: jeans and black shirts. But back then, an individual look and sound was critical. If ten bands played in a battle of the bands, you had ten totally different-looking bands.

Back at the VIP, our theatrical explorations got stranger and more unpredictable. We hauled in every prop we could lay our hands on.

"An audience wants to see a show," Vince said. "They can play the record at home if they just want to hear the music." He was pretty clear about this: Theatrics were mandatory if you wanted to hold the attention of the television generation. For me, it was about the need for artistic expression.

Vince and I began to imagine staging and lighting in conceptual terms. Soon, everyone was playing off our ideas. Even Michael, who at first seemed wary of our artsy shenanigans, began matching and topping us.

Michael, Glen, and I grew more experimental with our cover tunes. One of the great records of that year, 1966, was Paul Butterfield's *East-West*. They'd started as a blues band, but on that album they erupted in a thirteen-minute jazz-raga unlike anything we'd ever heard. We began stretching out on this number, but after twenty minutes, John Speer would drag us back to an orderly structure.

The experimentation did bring about one important change in the band: Our desire to learn another cover song was obliterated.

We couldn't stay away from LA.

In the fall, Dick turned to a friend of his named Doak to see if the band could get a short stay at his Hollywood apartment. Doak agreed but had no idea what he was getting into. We arrived and took over, and Doak was too polite to ask us to leave.

In short order, Doak's refrigerator held nothing more than half a box of yogurt. Mattresses covered the floors at night, and in the daytime we lined the walls with them, the better to contain our musical racket. We rehearsed like crazy and imagined audition possibilities. Doak stopped coming around.

One day, Charlie and Dick asked if I would like to drop acid. We were alone in the apartment while the guys were off at the Sunset Strip. I hesitated until I saw that the stuff seemed to be having only a mild effect on them, so I tried just a quarter of the amount they'd taken. It was on a tiny green square of paper.

Fifteen minutes, then twenty, rolled by and I felt nothing. I was just about to look for something else to do when I noticed Charlie was *slooooowwwwing-wing-wing* down and turning into Elastic Man. His arms reached all the way across the room and snapped back like in a frighteningly vivid cartoon. The walls, ceiling, and floor swelled and contracted like a breathing membrane.

I grew fixated on the ceiling lights, which shot out kaleidoscopes of rainbow colors. The visual turnabouts came rapidly and might have been nice, but emotionally I was on a roller coaster. One moment I felt supreme joy and then catapulted over the edge into some sinister depths. I had a sure feeling of danger, that I might slip irretrievably into some hellish dimension.

Then, in a blink, a smile expanded on my face till it seemed to stretch beyond my cheeks. I asked Dick if Vince was back yet. I wanted Vince there because he would be my link to reality.

Then Michael Bruce appeared. In his hand was a sack of tacos.

"You're stoned, stoned, stoned, stoned," he said.

He handed me a taco, but his reaching arm took on the perspective of a pipeline that curved back to a distant mountain range, which I realized was only Michael's shoulders.

I stared at the taco and saw the lettuce, tomatoes, and cheese writhing like snakes.

Hours passed—or at least *seemed* to pass—when Vince suddenly appeared. He was staggering drunk.

"You don't drink!" I said.

"I just forgot how to walk."

He laughed, and suddenly everything was hilarious, as if the carnival had come to town. Drunk or not—it didn't matter. Just being there, Vince created an eye of calm in the storm. I felt safer with him around.

The geometric patterns rolled past. The flashing rushes came in waves that slid away like an outgoing tide.

What had I seen? What was all it about? When I got my bearings later, I clearly remembered the accelerating blasts of color and the rubbery hallucinations. It had been an eye-opening spectacle, to be sure, but the sinister bouts of teeth-clenching fear made it a serious matter.

Beyond the hallucinations was the realization that this world, this individual's world, is limited to perceptions. If someone is crazy, or dreaming, then that is his or her reality at that moment.

Stumbling along, I found a new appreciation for my straight mind's ability to perceive things without the dangerous, amusement park view of hell. But I also realized that our mortal world isn't the only game in town. Most of us go through life without ever seeing beyond the limits of our senses. With the acid, I saw that my imagination was capable of tapping into an infinity of new horizons. Yet there is a safer way to get there, through meditation, books, and music. Who needs a light show with high anxiety and fatal dangers?

We landed a gig at the Hullabaloo, following the great Aretha Franklin. The Hullabaloo was a grand old theater on Sunset Boulevard, just east of Vine. In older Hollywood days, an impresario named Earl Carroll filled the place, then called the Earl Carroll Theater, with showgirls who spun around an enormous revolving stage. That landmark was renamed the Hullabaloo, and it was now packing in the hip young crowd with nonstop shows into the night. (Today it's called the Nickelodeon Theater.)

After Aretha's backup band did a nice warm-up, her backup singers did a set. Finally, at 2:00 a.m., the Queen of Soul delivered a powerhouse show to a packed house. Her voice rose and fell in emotional swoops with the drama of a lady on a flying trapeze. You could feel the whole room's spirits being lifted by her gospel squalls. Then she brought it down so effortlessly that it was as if the amazing crescendo hadn't happened at all.

The audience went wild, and she did encore after encore before finally waving and strutting off the stage like a queen who'd just conquered Egypt. Then the big stage revolved, and out from behind the giant curtain rolled our little band.

How would *you* like to follow a triumphant Aretha Franklin? At three in the morning? We nervously plowed into "Don't Blow Your Mind" and followed it with "Everything Is Orange"—to a rapidly emptying room.

Afterward, the guys were all humbled. "Look on the bright side," I said. "Now we can say that Aretha Franklin opened for us."

It was a great era for rock venues. Clubs and theaters in every city had opened up to the rush of kids who were itching to get out and boogey somewhere. Tickets were usually very cheap—and the clubs' owners were also usually very cheap. But at least rock 'n' roll was happening live and in your face.

One of the bigger scenes happening in southern California then was right off the beach, near Santa Monica, in the ancient amusement park Pacific Ocean Park. A hulking old theater called the Cheetah groaned alongside the water. Like the Hullabaloo, the Cheetah had once been something else entirely. The mighty Pacific had been lapping against its pilings ever since the 1930s, when it was the Aragon Ballroom.

Now it was aging fast, and having a last fling before it burned down in a few years. The surf made the cavernous room creak like an old ship. The ornate, hand-painted beams had been darkened from years of exposure to salty air and cigarette smoke. In an attempt to modernize it, a giant stainless steel curtain had been hung around the dance area. On the ceiling, merry-go-round lights radiated on tentacles.

First we had to audition. A red-haired firecracker of a gal named Sherry Cottle booked the acts. One afternoon we met her in the empty ballroom. "There are hundreds of bands who would die to play the Cheetah," she said. "What have you got that they haven't got?"

We tore through four songs while the catlike Sherry walked around and smoked.

"That's good," she said, signalling for us to stop. "I like your enthusiasm." She flashed a big smile and said, "I need two one-hour sets."

The Cheetah's poster for August 27, 1967, lets you know what kind of nutsy variety you could find in the hip joints that summer. The hitmaking Doors were the headliners. They were preceded by the stomping soul-funk of the Watts 103rd Street Rhythm Band. Opening the show was our band, the Nazz, with our still-strange music of the spheres.

We kicked off the afternoon set and then returned late to close the final show, meaning we staggered offstage at 2:00 a.m.

Based on Sherry's promise of future bookings, we rented a house nearby, on Beethoven Street in Venice Beach. It had a garage with room for us to play loud. Exciting ideas popped up during our improvisations, then dissipated like veiled dreams.

Although we were living on a shoestring, we were living large during our increasingly free-form rehearsals. Naturally, John Speer had to express his dissatisfaction. He especially didn't like it when some dealer like Gill the Pill dropped in and dispensed uppers and downers. John was adamantly against drugs. Vince also avoided drugs, but drank beer and maintained a "do your own thing" attitude.

John's own thing was to refuse to play and to storm out the door. We'd just grimace and keep on jamming.

The next time we were in Phoenix, we drove to the outskirts of town to a place called Thunderbird Park. Once, Vince, John, and I had run in cross-country meets there. It's surrounded by suburban houses now, but at that time it was high, wide, and empty.

There was a line of telephone poles going through this forgotten space, and on the bottom of the last splintery pole we found an electrical outlet. I'd spotted that outlet once during a picnic and had never forgotten that you could plug something in way out at the edge of the desert. So late one night we set up a couple of Fender amps on a cement table that was still toasty warm from the day's sun. The amps were glowing thanks to a power line that stretched all the way back to Phoenix.

John decided not to join us on this adventure. He explained that he already knew how to play. But Neal Smith tagged along. Neal had left his band, the Holy Grail, in San Francisco, as they'd gotten too deeply into drugs and Neal didn't want to be part of that. Just for kicks, we'd invited him along. Neal brought along a snare, a hi-hat, and, most refreshingly, a fun attitude.

We were stoked. Michael had a new volume pedal that he used to create big, sweeping swells. Glen had a new fuzz tone pedal that he would use to annoy every living thing within screaming distance. And I imagined that my bass rattled some ancient burial bones.

That evening Neal started with a marching cadence that sounded like the coming of Spanish horsemen. With that foundation, the guitars began to speak in a language that none of us had ever heard before. A vivid story unfolded. It spoke of anger and crying, of voyages to nonexistent places. Just when we thought it was all over, Michael dropped in some magical chords that ushered in a new story.

The skies were clear on the outskirts of Phoenix and you could see the vastness of the Milky Way. Our only audience was a band of feral cats roaming in the dark. We would see these eyes moving out there in the inky black.

That night, we weren't thinking about where we were going; we just traveled. Neal's syncopated snare matched our explorations perfectly. With a steady roll or a sharp hit at a crescendo, he was right there. Our energy combined perfectly.

The jam faded down to a soft, satisfying conclusion, followed by silence. As reality eased back in, we looked at one another and smiled.

"Neal, that was pretty damn good," Glen said. "Not too shabby for an Akron boy with one fucking drum."

"None of my bands ever played for fun like that," Neal said.

It wasn't the last night we played out there. Soon, word of our desert jams began to spread around Phoenix. Our intimate solitude became interrupted by party crashers. People showed up with hot dogs, marshmallows, and bags of peyote. We'd come there looking for inspiration, but folks were combing the night skies for UFOs.

Glen and I wanted to check out the competition, so one day we drove two hours to Tucson to see a concert featuring the Young Rascals, the Animals, and the Yardbirds. The Rascals were riding high on the hit "Good Lovin'," and they did an incredible performance. Afterward, Glen and I went backstage and struck up a conversation with Eric Burdon, the Animals' lead singer, outside the Yardbirds' dressing room. He looked at us with his intense gaze. When Glen brought up the Tucson cowboys who wanted to kick our ass, Burdon assured us that his hometown, Newcastle, in the north of England, was no stroll through the park. He seemed to take an interest in us and fired off some financial advice.

"Always jot down the amount you make at each gig," he said, pretending to hold a notebook tight against his chest like some skinflint bookkeeper in a Dickens novel. "And later, check that against your actual earnings."

It was then that I saw her again, the blonde, Neal's sister Cindy, knocking on the door to the Yardbirds' dressing room. I left Burdon and rushed over. The door cracked open.

"Hi," she said to a guy inside, "could you tell Jim that Cindy Smith is here?"

The door opened for Cindy and I followed her inside.

The first one I saw was Jeff Beck, and he was looking at me sharply. "Who's this bloke?" he said.

Cindy turned and gave me an annoyed look. "Oh, he's all right. He's in a band."

It was so cramped in there that the guys had to point their guitar necks up so they could tune up without stabbing one another. I made myself small in the corner and watched them divvy up their money and prepare to take the stage. I looked at the bass player. He was a new guy. I asked why he used black nylon strings.

"I saw a picture of them on the *For Your Love* album cover," I said, "so I tried a set and they sounded dead."

"I don't know," he said. "I've never played bass before." He stuck out his hand. "I'm Jimmy Page. I'm actually a guitar player."

I couldn't help but flash back to that conversation I had a year before with Keith Relf, when he said, "Jeff Beck? You should have seen the guy we had before him."

Glen and I caught the show from the first row, where we stood directly in front of Beck's Vox amplifier. Beck and Page teamed up like brothers and threw down a fireball set.

It was the best concert we had ever seen. Afterward, walking back to the car, Glen looked awestruck and said, "Ain't nobody better than that."

Driving back to Phoenix, I fretted about having made yet another dopey impression on Cindy Smith. Glen admitted he wouldn't kick her out of the sack.

"I've got bad luck with her," I said, moping. "Did you see what I did, following her like that?"

"If she likes ya, it won't matter."

"Geez, she must think I'm an idiot."

"At least you know she's good at judging people."

Our Phoenix sabbatical was over and we headed back to LA with freshly laundered clothes and a plate of my mom's spicy gumdrop cake.

When we hit the rehearsal room in our Venice Beach house, we felt the same old tension with John. Nothing had changed. After passing a joint around, we began improvising on a spacey riff, but John just sat there with his arms folded, steaming mad.

John was not just anti-drugs, he was doggedly against druggy-sounding music, not to mention all our majestic thinking.

"You're all wasting your time," he said. "We need a hit."

"Take a hit, then," Glen said, holding out a joint.

After our glum rehearsal, John went outside. The rest of us stood in the kitchen and agreed that something had to change.

"I'll tell him," Vince said. This was uncharacteristic of him. Vince always avoided confrontation—it was a key part of his makeup. But not when John stormed in and slammed the door.

"If you guys don't get it together," John seethed, "I'm quitting."

"Okay," Vince said.

The room was silent. Vince had spoken. John looked surprised, but he was in no mood to back down. The rest of us joined in, and soon John was in the back, packing his things.

Since Neal Smith was already staying at our house, it made the whole affair look premeditated. But it wasn't. One drum kit was removed and another hauled in.

Once Neal was set up, I said, "We've gotta play 'Wipe-Out.'"

Glen kicked his Twin Reverb to get the crackling sound, and we barreled through the song like a freight train.

Now Neal was in the band and we became *the five guys,* the unit. Aided by our brain trust of Charlie and Mike, we became as one: five guys who rode each other hard with verbal chainsaws, but still five guys who just agreed on outraging the world.

By now we were damn near the house band at the Cheetah. At least we could (barely) afford the rent on this house. When Neal first showed up, I told him he could stay in my bedroom, although *bedroom* might be a grand term for a little garage workshop with a mattress on the floor.

One day, out of the blue, that sweet girl Denice showed up at the door. This was the girl whom I'd made out with in the cemetery in Tucson. And here she was with a twinkle in her eye. I thought, All right! Cool! This is *nice*.

Well, Neal's band had been plowing the same turf we had, and he knew this girl, too. So she ended up with Neal.

Adding to the insult, we were all in the same bed. I can't *believe* this, I thought. But it was the free love era, we were in a band, and we were united, and that's what mattered.

4.

THREADBARE, BROKE, AND SPACEY

GLEN HAD BEEN TELLING us stories for years about this faraway place called Akron, Ohio. We could barely believe this warped picture he painted. But when Neal arrived, we had two Akroners regaling us with stories of dopey guys in their "highwater pants" (pegged Levis that ended above their socks). They knew about the same characters: Gibby Hornets, Linda Dickey, or that patch-haired kid who played the spoons while doing the Chicken Dance. Neal and Glen became instant buddies.

Musically, we felt like instant buddies with Neal. He had speed and finesse. Compared with John and his amazingly heavy, two-handed broadsword, Neal had the sleek quickness of a fencing rapier. His approach was sending us in promising directions.

We were free to start shaping our secret world. Every day marked a new trip into unknown regions of chord changes, leads, cadences, melodies, and harmonies.

While all this came from our hearts, our radicalized songwriting didn't exactly cohere into snappy ditties. Each of us had a million ideas, and we were trying to cram five bridges into one song. Tempos fluctuated like rainstorms. If a song had any semblance of normalcy, we altered it or threw it out.

One day after practice, totally famished and with nothing in the fridge but a jar of relish, we got a ride into Hollywood to a small Mexican place called Top Taco, where you could eat plenty for spare change.

Our thrift store clothes were threadbare, but we figured we had a conquering style. Neal had quickly adapted to this style with some Mexican bandito pants and turquoise bracelets. He had the hair going, too, and was in contention for longest hair in the world.

On our way to Top Taco, we clomped past the Mercury Recording Studio. We couldn't go past without remembering the time we auditioned there back when Speer was in the group. Michael had stopped us and said, "Let's go in and get a record deal."

Well, why not? We barged on in and met with a wall of freezing cold and darkness. Michael stuck his head in the control room and saw two guys looking bored.

"Is this where great bands audition?" Michael asked.

One guy looked at us. "This is your lucky day," he said, sounding as if his luck had run out long ago. "The equipment is already set up in the studio. Go on in."

"Right now?" Michael asked, astonished.

The guy shrugged. "It's now or never."

We trooped in and tried not to act shocked. Guitars were set up on stands. I picked up the bass—it was cold to the touch, but the red lights were glowing and the amps were humming. After some discussion, we lit into a song we'd played at the VIP, "Talk Talk," by Music Machine, because we knew it had been recorded there.

After two minutes of that, the engineer's voice cut in. "Hold it, that's enough."

The studio assistant walked out and pointed at Michael. "He wants to talk with the guitar player."

Michael went to the booth and in a few minutes came back with a quirky smile. "Good news and bad news," he said. "He wants the band but not the singer. They'll give us two days to decide."

We didn't need that. In Vince's presence, we rejected the deal on the spot and marched off to Top Taco.

With the combination plates on order, Michael approached me for a secret powwow. He reported that the studio had a song, and everything was lined up. Later in the afternoon, more private discussions were held. While we hated to walk away from a real deal, we were united in turning it down.

I felt strongly that none of us would have made it as far as we had without one another's input. Maybe we weren't the most accomplished musicians, but we were different from any other band, and that suited me fine.

I believed in what we were doing. We were going to make a statement that had never been made. Sure, I wanted a record deal so bad I could taste it, but friendship meant more. There was no way I could turn my back on Vince for my own gain.

Years later, Vince would finally record "Talk Talk," but it was with a new band, the one that replaced us.

In 1967, record executives were still pretty much old-school guys. They might have been ready to make a bunch of money off rock music for "the kids," but their hearts were still waltzing in the gym to the Tommy Dorsey Orchestra.

We had an interesting face-to-face with that attitude at our next tryout. Michael arranged a meeting at a record company in downtown Los Angeles. To prepare, we went to our garage and recorded a demo on a cassette tape.

The next day, we get to this towering black building where the security guard gives us a "What in hell?" look. We found the record company on the top floor and Groucho-walked through the door.

"We're from the IRS," Vince cracked. The receptionist managed to thaw out her face with a brief smile. After she notified her boss, we were allowed to go back into a chilly room lined with black granite. It was like a mausoleum.

On the far side of a massive desk sat the executive. His facial expression was so severe he should have been called Mr. Death. There we were in our thrift-store regalia. There he was with platinum cuff links shooting out of the sleeves of his black suit. His tan was the shade of a tainted orange. His shirt, tie, and glasses were all black. Judging from his expression, so was his heart.

Michael handed our cassette to Mr. Death, who got up and slid over to a tape player that looked like a Lincoln Continental. He returned to his massive black leather chair and sat down. The chair emitted a resplendent fart. We might have laughed, but all of us were imagining ourselves being outfitted with cement overshoes.

Mr. Death bowed his head and clasped his hands as if he were praying. He seemed to be sleeping—or dead.

Our songs boomed out. In that forbidding, sepulchral office, the songs seemed extra-crazy, but at least the high fidelity made them sound terrific. I got a feeling we were about to land a record deal. All we had to do was rouse Mr. Death from his frozen prayer.

After the final note of our masterpiece, Mr. Death remained silent. A slight chair fart shook the room.

Michael broke the ice. "So, what do you think?"

Mr. Death's hands lowered slowly. "You want to know what I *think*?" he said. "You want to know what I *think*?"

He got up and ripped our cassette out of the Lincoln Continental and held it over his black granite wastebasket. He grabbed a black granite cigarette lighter from his desk and set our tape on fire. He dropped the flaming cassette into the abyss of his wastebasket.

The smell of burning plastic was in the air. Nobody spoke. We filed out like a chain gang.

When the revolving door swept us out into the glaring sunshine of the street, Neal turned to give the building the finger. I was in disbelief that someone would destroy our music. "There were a lot of spontaneous moments on that tape," I said. "Now it's lost for good."

Vince announced that he was going to treat this rejection with a stiff bottle of denial. We blew the rest of the afternoon at a table full of beers.

We weren't the only ones making spacey music that year. Sherry Cottle booked Pink Floyd into the Cheetah. It was their first trip to

America, and with nowhere to go, they hung out at our house on Beethoven Street.

Roger Waters burst into laughter when he opened our refrigerator and saw nothing but one bag of carrots. His laughter died down when Michael told him that it was indeed all we had to eat.

It probably doesn't need mentioning that we were pretty skinny guys.

We all seemed to be alarmingly indecisive about how to get some food when Pink Floyd's roadie, a beaming Englishman named Les Braden, jumped into gear and got a list going for takeout. We would see a lot more of Mr. Braden's speed in action over the next year.

I sat down in the kitchen and started talking to Syd Barrett. I'd heard he was the founder of the group. On the cover of their album *Piper at the Gates of Dawn,* he had the striking looks and distant gaze of a Byronic hero. He seemed to be interested in what I was saying, but when I asked him a question, he didn't respond. His gaze was fixed.

Thinking he was stoned, I went to check out his guitar. It was propped up in a corner with no case. When I saw the rusty strings and the twisted neck, I sensed something was wrong.

"Syd loses his guitar," Les explained nonchalantly, as if Syd weren't sitting right there. "It fell off the back of a truck once and I found it in the street, in the rain. We have to follow him around to make sure he doesn't get lost himself. It's quite sad, isn't it?"

Syd sat as motionless as a mannequin.

Les and I continued to talk about our groups. Then Syd stood up abruptly and left the room. I went over to see where he had gone and found him in the living room facing a far corner.

"Just don't let him get out of the house," Les said quietly.

A new guitarist, David Gilmour, joined the group in December to replace Syd. Like the others, he had a powerful empathy for Syd. They were all reserved, polite, and engaging. But Syd's behavior was unsettling.

I don't know if the term *acid casualty* was in our vocabularies then. Some of us had been dabbling in drugs for only a year, so it was startling to come across somebody whose drug use might well have sent him into a dimension from which he could make no return.

Later, it was recognized just how much Syd's early burst of mind-blasting music was so enormously influential. Shortly after this Los Angeles trip, he would leave the band and go into seclusion. He recorded a couple of solo albums over the years, and then retired to a life of painting. The guys in Pink Floyd never seemed to stop loving him, and they did a beautiful song in tribute to him called "Shine On You Crazy Diamond."

One day we had an audition at a hot club on the Sunset Strip called Gazzarri's. We invited the guys in Pink Floyd to come along. While they sat at the club tables, we ripped through a full-tilt set that was augmented by Vince horsing around with long feather boas. After whipping us with the boas, he ended up stuffing them down his pants. By this time, the club owner had lammed out of the joint.

We walked over to Pink Floyd's table and asked what they thought.

"It looks like a lot of fun," Roger Waters said helpfully. The rest politely agreed. Then they turned their attention to what might be done about Syd.

Musicians have to get used to a life on the road, even if it comes from getting kicked to the curb. We got evicted from the house on Beethoven Street and moved into a battered old house on Crenshaw Boulevard in a rough area of South Central LA. There was still heavy tension in the air there, left over from the 1965 Watts Riots, a huge, six-day standoff with the police that tore up the neighborhood. But we had an ally in Lester Chambers, the lead singer of the Chambers Brothers, who lived in the house before us. He put the word out in the neighborhood that the freaky-looking white guys were all right.

The Chambers Brothers were also on a path to something new. A powerful group, they mixed their gospel voices with a driving soul beat and stirred the pot with psychedelia. They got big, but they should have been huge.

Lester told us that we would have a bluesman named Long Gone Miles living upstairs. We rarely saw Miles, but we sure knew he was there. One of their roadies had installed small speakers all through the house, and every afternoon at three, Long Gone would do a broadcast from his room. His mournful howl was accompanied by a guitar that sounded as old and story-worn as he was. He was the star of every song: Long Gone Miles got a Cadillac. Long Gone tied on a good one. Long Gone landed in jail. We could hear his foot tapping through the ceiling. We soon realized how cool it was to have an authentic bluesman spilling out his feelings from the room above.

Glen and I felt we should see him and pay tribute. So one day, we stomped up the dark, wooden stairs, introduced ourselves, and said we wanted to give him a present. Glen held out a bottle of Ripple wine.

Long Gone smiled like the Cheshire cat. "Sit yourselves down right over there," he said. We dropped down on a single bed with squeaking springs.

He unscrewed the cap, took a swig, and passed the bottle to Glen. Ripple, a cheap, sweet wine fortified with a high alcoholic content, was favored by street lushes all over. Hell, it was all we could afford. When Glen asked him if he liked it, Long Gone smiled beatifically.

"The guitar can do the talkin'."

He started twangin', slightly out of tune, and we knew that Long Gone's musical train was about to leave the station. He closed his eyes and wailed, "Ohhhhhh, Lordy Ripple Ripple wine gonna start a fire in Long Gone's head!"

When the bottle got around to him again, it stayed with him. He'd take another swig, and his foot would stomp even louder. He was off, and there was no end in sight. The blues had turned into a boogie.

It was a good house for feeling funky. The bathtub drip-drip-dripped, and unless you bailed it out regularly, it would overflow. The Chambers Brothers had created a practice room in the house, but you had to go down a ladder to a hole in the basement to get there. Once inside, we would find ourselves covered by the fluffy pink fiberglass soundproofing stuff that dropped in a steady rain of itchy particles and stuck to our sweaty skin.

One day Sherry showed up with a couple of LPs, the first albums by the Jimi Hendrix Experience and the Doors. We retired to the room shared by Neal and Vince, who had a cheap portable turntable set up between their metal cots. We gathered around the turntable and listened to the albums over and over.

The Experience album was earth-shattering. When it was over, Vince, ever the font of pop information, told us that Hendrix had set his guitar ablaze at the Monterey Pop Festival last spring, then run off stage, and hadn't been seen since.

The Doors record had a deeper, more psychological significance. It struck me as lumbering, almost dull, at first. But its effect was like a narcotic. By the third listen, I judged it to be the perfect soundtrack for LA.

On Crenshaw Boulevard, somehow they weren't thinking much about the Summer of Love. The nights were heavy with the sound of speeches coming through megaphones. One day a bunch of protesters followed us into the house, barged through the kitchen door, and started helping themselves to our groceries. They went through our pathetic cupboards and talked among themselves as if we weren't there.

We needed a change. Mike Allen grabbed a newspaper and combed through the classifieds for rentals. One house looked like a good prospect: It was on the far north side of LA. We jumped in the van and headed for a place called Topanga Canyon.

We were still the Nazz at this point. But then we heard about a band out of Philadelphia called Todd Rundgren and the Nazz. They had an album out, and according to that unspoken rule, they now owned the name. So for a third time we were back searching for another name. We were devastated.

For three weeks we fired back and forth every crazy band name we could think of. Then, one night, we were in Phoenix, hanging out at Lorena Weed's house. She fronted an all-girl trio called the Weeds of Idleness. We were sitting at the table firing off ridiculous names.

"Kissin' the Pussycat," I said.

"Frontal Lobotomy," Glen offered. "Bottle in Front of Me?"

Everyone laughed, but Vince just calmly said, "Alice Cooper."

Everything stopped. You could almost hear the tires screeching. *What?*

"Yeah," he said. "It would be like Lizzie Borden, the innocent girl who conceals a hatchet behind her back."

The rest of us were doubtful. If people were trying to kill us now, what would happen when we used a transgender name like that? No way. So we moved on.

But every name we came up with after that just paled. Alice Cooper? Yeah, it sounded wrong, and yeah, it sounded like an individual, but it was such a showstopper.

I was still wrestling with the name when I walked into my parents' house later that night. They asked what I was doing. I explained that we were working on a new band name. When I said "Alice Cooper," their faces froze. "*What?*" they said in horrified unison. Their reaction convinced me that we were on the right track.

When I saw the fellows the next night at Lorena's, I was on Vince's side. I was such a crusader. When I got inspired, I never let up.

Lorena got out a Ouija board and presented it with the name question. Vince and Dick held the plastic pointer as it moved around the board until "Alice Cooper" was spelled out. Well, ha. I'm sure *nobody* was helping.

Nevertheless, the Ouija board story did gain traction in years to come, and it's curious how some people remember the story backward. I can tell you, it was Vince, not the Ouija board, who came up with Alice first.

We moved forward instantly. We all agreed—even Vince—that this would be the name of the band and not an individual. That was our agreement.

The one thing we didn't imagine, though, was that the name would raise false expectations for what we were. We'd show up for a gig and some club owner would say, "Oh, no, no, where's the girl folk singer?"

In the early days, if somebody called any one of us Alice, we were happy to ignore them. It was our little in-joke. We'd think, "This jerk isn't hip to what we're doing." Vince wouldn't even look at them.

But as more and more people started calling him Alice, we decided, okay, it'll be both things. You'll be Alice, and the band will be called Alice Cooper. It would be like the British band Manfred Mann: Each guy in the group was called Manfred Mann.

He was still Vince, though, at least for a while. I started calling him Alice before anyone else. He had a chameonlike way of turning into new characters. This was a new character.

And Vince needed a new character. Something was wrong with our live shows. While the rehearsals always went well, the shows just felt different. Since we were no longer imitating other bands, Vince's imagined shield of confidence was missing. He was no longer borrowing the confidence of Mick Jagger or Paul Butterfield. He'd even taken to turning his back on the audience and facing Neal.

It was weird. I concluded that Vince should act out the songs.

I brought up this idea at our rehearsal. We had a song called "Nobody Likes Me." I said, "Vince, every song we do, you will be a different character. So it'll be like we have a whole bunch of lead singers. With 'Nobody Likes Me,' you are a little kid in his room who feels lonely and all your friends are putting you down."

We constructed that character. We got a screen door, knocked the window out, and put a curtain in it, and Vince would look out with a pitiful look and sing about nobody liking him.

The song "Levity Ball" was inspired by the movie *Carnival of Souls*, so we imagined the stage was a big ballroom with ghosts dancing. We said, Okay, Vince, on this song, you can see the ghosts and things that the audience can't see. That gimmick became a perpetual part of his act, where he looks with big, wide eyes at unseen things.

Our darkest, heaviest song was "Fields of Regret." It had some religious connotations and this sinister section where Vince narrated dark, sermon-like verses. For this, we told Vince to be a scary, evil character, and he really got into it with menacing gusto.

Now when we did a gig, Vince had his courage back. He was being someone other than himself. He could act out the part. This versatility is what eased the transition in my mind from thinking of him as Vince, my old pal, to seeing him as Alice, our Frankenstein's monster.

So it started as a joke, became a friendly salute among pals, and gradually became his name, his identity. We never forgot, however, that "Alice Cooper" was actually five people united as one.

In the telling of this story, it is here that Vince's identity will slowly transition into that of Alice. It was gradual.

The new band name provided one more good reason for people to get teed off at us. By now we were driving people out of the room. They would get one look at us onstage and start yelling insults as they scrambled for the exits.

Curiously, though, we began to develop a fan base. The people who actually stayed to the end of our shows were calling out for "Fields of Regret." If we didn't play it, they'd be going, "Fields! Fields!" I'm certain it was our most popular song because, for that number, Alice had developed a dark, commanding attitude. It really worked.

When the guys talked about dropping the song from the act, I said, "No, no, no. As a matter of fact, we need to do *more* songs like 'Fields of Regret.' Alice should become that character for every song." I was determined we were going to write more dark songs.

5.

TOPANGA

WE NEVER SAW the nudist colony that was said to be somewhere in Topanga Canyon. Nor did we see any witches or wizards. We did, however, stumble over what might be called disciples of free love. You were never short of wild 'n' loose times way out there on the western edge of LA, overlooking the sea, in the sunny Topanga hills.

We hadn't been looking for California's latest den of sin and iniquity. We'd just had to get the hell out of South Central. Mike Allen had circled a lot of rental houses in the Wanted ads, and this one had sounded okay. We took off in the van and headed up the Pacific Coast Highway. When Neal spotted the bikini-clad girls on the beach, he barked out, "I don't give a fuck what this house looks like. We're taking it."

We banged a right at the Topanga Canyon Boulevard turnoff and snaked our way up a canyon pass lined with rocks, dirt, and shrubs.

Mike parked in the dirt driveway, and we all piled out. The house was pitched downward, as if ready to slide off the cliff.

"We'll take it," Neal said. "Now let's go to the beach and get to know our new neighbors."

On moving day, we swarmed into the place like worker bees. The television was the first priority. Glen plugged it in, and Vince fidgeted with the tinfoil rabbit ears until a picture appeared. From that moment on, the TV was on permanently.

In addition to our road crew of Mike Allen, Charlie Carnal, and Dick (Christian) Phillips, the band had found a new roadie handyman: Les Braden. Les had resigned as Pink Floyd's roadie so he could hang out in California. British and proud of it, he was soft-spoken, kind-hearted, and an engaging conversationalist. Les and Michael shared an upstairs room. They quickly got to work decorating the room with black lights, fluorescent posters, guitars—and Ringo Starr's drum head, which Les had "borrowed" from Abbey Road Studios when Floyd recorded there.

Les got things done at lightning speed. After gathering everyone in the living room, he yanked a white sheet off a giant portrait of Lawrence Welk, the bandleader who called himself the "champagne music" maker. Only a few days before, Alice had admired that painting on the backstage wall at the Cheetah. (Welk got his start there when it was called the Aragon Ballroom.) Now here it was. Alice went right to work and cut tiny stars in Mr. Welk's pupils and then backlit them so his eyes took on a demonic gleam.

Neal, his sister, Cindy, and Mike Allen slept in a triple-decker army bunk. Alice slept in the same room, in a homemade coffin. Les installed stereo speakers in the coffin so Alice could listen to music whenever he laid his head on the blood-red velvet pillow.

"It's the best stereo sound I've ever heard!" Alice yelled, louder than he realized.

Glen and I claimed a downstairs room just off the band's practice room.

Charlie, our lighting guy, was reduced to putting his bed at one end of the rehearsal room. The three of us became consumed with the idea of turning this into the "crooked room." The slanted house gave us a big head start. We tilted all the photographs. Charlie shortened the legs on one side of his bed, the chairs, and the end table. The whole room was cockeyed.

While admiring our handiwork, we heard Michael announce, "We have some visitors from San Francisco."

This was the Topanga specialty: the sudden appearance of oddball folks with irresponsible smiles. A guy with a leather headband stuck out his hand and initiated the interlocking-thumbs handshake. He said he dug our digs. A girl wearing rattling beads said the house was far out.

We weren't above being social with them, so we took them to our practice room. Bead Girl was instantly upset. "Something looks weird in here," she said.

The guy in the leather vest said he was a drummer. His name was Joey Covington and he later played with the Jefferson Airplane. He sat down at Neal's drums and started slapping them with his bare hands. He called them the Trippy Traps. *Trippity trippity trippity trap . . .*

Bead Girl said, "This room is giving me the creeps."

"I think you're stoned," Glen said.

"No, really," she protested. "I'm freaking out. This room has real bad vibes."

Trippity trippity trap. The girl asked me to help her. When we got outside, it was dark. A car came swinging into the driveway, and I heard the familiar voice of Glen's girlfriend, Djinn, calling, "Hi, cats and jammers."

I introduced her to Bead Girl, whose awestruck manner contrasted starkly with Djinn's sarcastic Hollywood style.

"Sooner," Djinn said and went inside.

I informed Bead Girl that "Sooner" was Djinn's way of saying "Later."

Bead Girl rummaged through her bag and came up with a bottle of Southern Comfort. She took a big swig and then put the bottle to my lips. Then she revealed that there was another girl in her party.

"She's in that room upstairs balling your other guitar player," she said. Grabbing my hand, she guided it to her blouse. She poured more Southern Comfort down my throat, wrapped a leg around my waist, and said, "I feel like balling."

"Well, my room's in there."

"The creepy room?"

"No, but we'll have to go through the creepy room."

She pulled my hand off her breast and marched me in, past Trippy Traps and into the bedroom where Glen and Djinn had already cozied up in the top bunk.

"Smells like booze and patchouli," Glen taunted.

Bead Girl handed the bottle to Djinn, who cried out, "Southern Comfort! You *are* from San Francisco, aren't cha, darlin'?"

"A girl after my own heart," Glen said, sighing.

I'd been seduced in my life. I'd been made love to, and I'd simply had sex. But I had never been *balled* before.

The difference was evident: Bead Girl did all the work. In a flash, she had stripped down to her beads and had me into her action in one slick operation that left no doubt that I was filling a gap that others had. She took charge so thoroughly, I felt like a tool—a big dildo, perhaps.

Glen's voice came from the bunk above. "Do I hear fucking? Who's fucking in my room? Is that you, Dunaway? Who gave you permission to fuck in my room? Stop it right now."

Djinn laughed. Glen cackled.

Bead Girl continued balling her pretty little brains out. I could hear thumping sounds from the ceiling—things were happening in Michael's room, too. Then Glen's bunk started creaking.

To avoid premature humiliation, I put aside the usual baseball statistics and imagined how the house would look sliding into the canyon. The combined weight of all these bodies, plus the humping—it was going to be too much for the creaky foundations.

Bead Girl maintained a sprinter's pace. So I imagined skinny little Alice being the final straw to bring the place down. I saw headlines in the morning paper: "Unknown Band and Bead Girl Slide to Demise."

Bead Girl continued with no sign of letup.

While our biggest battle was just getting a little food on the table, elsewhere in the country, real wars were happening. We had to run back to Phoenix and face the draft.

I met Vince on the sidewalk in front of the induction center. We were such a team that it was barely surprising to us that we had been called in on the very same day. The warm morning air meant that Phoenix was in for a scorcher. I wore my white satin shirt with white tassels all over it. Vince wore a colorful poncho shirt and had his hair in a puffy Afro.

"We've got about twenty minutes," I said. "Wanna walk around before we go in?"

We walked down the block. Uncharacteristically, Vince remained as quiet as I. At the end of the block, he said, "We'd better get back." We did an about-face.

"I don't get why they're fighting in Vietnam," I said.

"Me neither," Vince said.

"You're the last person I would pick for the army," I said. "I mean, I don't want to go, but if they take me, I'll go. But *you*, you're even skinnier than I am, and I could never imagine you hurting anyone."

Back at the induction center, we came upon a group of guys standing in a circle smoking and talking about how they were going to kill people. They gave us hard looks as they threw their cigarettes on the ground and joined the flock of teenagers through the big gray doors. Inside, a bulldog-faced guy instructed everyone to sit down and keep quiet. None of us knew what was in store, not even the guys who wanted to kill people.

Somebody whispered something, and the bulldog guy barked, *"Do you think this is all a big joke?"* I knew the answer but didn't raise my hand.

We found our assigned lockers, stripped down to our underwear, and stood in line. Vince looked like he would have blown away if anyone sneezed. Now that all the draftees had stripped down, it was clear we were all in the same boat. Suddenly I couldn't hear, I was blind in both eyes, and I couldn't pee in a cup. I didn't want to appear fit enough to go.

At the end of the day, the draft board medical guy informed me that I would be classified 4-F because of a hernia, which I didn't realize I had. He said, "Notify us as soon as you get that taken care of." Unfortunately, I couldn't hear him.

Vince was to receive his 4-F classification by mail. I think he was underweight and claimed religious objections, although he told people that he was classified 1-A and that he went back for several more physicals before he finally convinced them to fail him for reasons of questionable sanity.

A few weeks later, Glen took his physical. Due to chronic allergies, he also was classified 4-F.

Michael's residence kept switching back and forth between California and Arizona, and eventually Michigan, each time postponing his physical due to sluggish red tape. Uncle Sam finally caught up with him in Michigan, where he was inducted and put on board a blue bus to boot camp. In transit, however, he freaked out on a multidrug overdose. They pumped his stomach and changed his classification.

Neal's story takes a bit more explaining.

On April 12, 1968, Uncle Sam notified Neal to report to the induction center, so he decided to get drunk first. Mike Allen and Vince's sister, Nickie, were the only sober people on the ride. The other passengers were Vince, Neal, and two six-packs of Budweiser. In their inebriated wisdom, they had decided to drive into the desert for some moonlight target shooting.

"This place looks as good as any," Vince said.

Nickie slammed on the brakes, and a cloud of dust engulfed the car. Neal unfolded his six-foot-three frame and got out of the car. He handed the .22 rifle to Vince and said in his best Gabby Hayes voice, "Wait here, Roy. I'm gonna piss on that thar cactus over yonder. Don't you peek, Dale." Dale Evans was Roy Rogers's wife, and Gabby Hayes was their old-timer sidekick.

Nickie laughed and said, "Nothin' to see."

Neal took a long pee.

Vince said, "You're gonna kill the cactus."

Neal finished and said, still in his Gabby voice, "I'll go set up some empty cans. I'd better do some target shootin' if I'm goin' off to that thar Viet Nam."

Neal heaved two cans into the air and yelled, "Shoot 'em, Roy." Neal stumbled backward into a ditch. "I hope there ain't no Gila monsters here. You don't want one of them thar Gila monsters to get hold of yer dick. Cover yer ears, Dale!" Neal climbed onto the hood of the car and leaned his back against the windshield. Vince got out of the car and climbed up beside him. The car started rolling ever so slowly.

Two jackrabbits darted across the road. Neal snatched the .22 out of Vince's hands, aimed, and fired.

Nickie stopped the car's forward motion. "Did you get it?"

"I don't know," Neal said. He handed the rifle to Vince, grabbed a flashlight, and ran down the road swinging the light around. "Where the hell did it go?"

Crack! The .22 fired again. Nobody looked as surprised as Vince.

"I've been hit," Neal yelled. "I'm shot. My ankle's shot." A warm stream of blood filled his boot. "You stupid idiot, you fucking shot me. Fuck!"

Vince slid off the hood, laid the rifle in the road, and ran up to Neal. "I'm sorry," he yelped. "I didn't mean to shoot. Are you all right?"

"No, I'm not fucking all right. You shot my fucking ankle. Fuck! Ow!"

It's a good thing that Mike Allen (practical and sober) was there to help Vince (sorrowful and drunk) load Neal (bleeding and swearing) into the car so they could rush him to the hospital.

Once there, Neal had instructions: "Don't anybody say a thing," he said. "I'll do all the talking." The pain worsened as the numbness wore off.

In the emergency room, a cop confronted them.

"It was an accident," Neal said. "I shot myself."

"No, you didn't," the cop replied.

Neal hopped up and down on one leg, aiming an imaginary rifle toward the wound. "I shot myself," he insisted.

The cop took a long look at Neal, then Nickie, then Mike Allen, and when he got to Vince, he pointed authoritatively and said, "He did it."

Vince sat speechless.

The cop said, "Nobody's filing any charges, so it looks like you girls are getting off lucky this time."

Nickie said, "Thank you."

The cop looked at Neal and said, "Next time, shoot yourself in the head."

Since there was no insurance coverage, Neal's mother paid the bills totaling $498.95. And thanks to that chunk of lead in his body, the U.S. Army deemed Neal ineligible for service.

When people heard our band's new name, there would be a pause. Then some people would smile, some would look disgusted, and some would get pissed off—but everyone reacted. Love it or hate it, the name couldn't be ignored, which suited us just fine. Now we could inspire a backlash just by saying our name.

Vince had done good. Vince had done real good.

Word of our new name spread through Phoenix like a cloud of locusts. We were hated overnight. Most of our fans felt alienated, and called us everything from pansies to Hollywood fag asses who were begging to get our faces smashed in. The band bonded in defiance.

The first time we heard an announcer say our name was in Santa Barbara, California, on March 16, 1968. The poster had billed us as the Nazz, opening up for the Nitty Gritty Dirt Band and Blue Cheer. We looked out at the daytime crowd at the Earl Warren Showgrounds and—well, we didn't see mutiny in the eyes of this uncaring world.

Our crazy new name left no room for mediocrity. Neal certainly wasn't that—leg cast and all. He attacked his drums with alarming energy. We had never seen him play so assertively.

As Vince and I stood on the sidelines and watched Blue Cheer lay down their Godzilla riffs, we noted that they wore jeans, the same as every other band. It looked dull. How were we different? Okay, Glen's jeans were so tattered they were held together by safety pins. Between Blue Cheer's songs, when we could hear one another, the band made a pact never to wear jeans onstage again.

We sat in a circle on the warm pavement in my parents' driveway. In early 1968, we still went home for gigs. Vince blew his harp to Cannonball Adderley's "Work Song," from the Paul Butterfield Blues Band, a song we all loved. Neal tapped his sticks on the driveway.

We were waiting for Mike Allen to show up in the van with our equipment so we could make the haul to LA.

"Show me your new hot rod," Neal said.

I opened the door of my '64 Ford Falcon, and Neal climbed into the driver's seat.

I showed him where I had run a wire from the radio to the backseat. "I just shove my bass cabinet into the backseat, plug the wire in, and I get loud music."

"Maybe you'll start a new trend," Neal said.

The faded green van with one dim headlight pulled up.

"Ahhh," Neal said. "I love the smell of overheated radiator."

"Why is the van leaning to one side?" I asked.

Mike Allen said, "Would you boys like to invest in a new set of shock absorbers?"

"I like it just like that," Vince said. "It gives it character."

I was surprised to see a washing machine in the van. Michael said we would need it. We loaded the drums, guitars, amps, and suitcases as flat as possible and put in the mattress that Michael had brought on top. Then we threw in the sleeping bags.

My mom and dad came out of the house and told us to be careful and said they wished they were going with us.

"That would be interesting," Glen mumbled.

I hugged them goodbye and jumped in the van.

"Ya might wanna get some new shocks on that thing," my dad said.

"Bye. Be careful." Mom kept waving as the van rolled away.

Through the Arizona desert we went. Conversation died. All that remained was the sound of the grumbling engine and the sand whipping the van. The wind intensified as we passed through Palm Springs. The faintest hint of daybreak lit the sky.

I asked Mike if he wanted me to take the wheel.

"I'm fine," he said. "You can go to sleep."

I slumped forward on my folded jacket, and before I knew it I'd eased into a dream where I was riding a white horse with an extremely long tail. A tiny green hummingbird fluttered up to my ear and spoke high-pitched whistling words. The horse's mane flapped around me as its long strides lifted me up to the heavens where stardust slithered across the sky . . .

A honking horn and severe swerving startled me back to consciousness. Mike Allen was fighting to regain control of the van through a sharp turn on the Los Angeles freeway. Rush-hour traffic pressed in on all sides as we swerved. Then the van tipped sickeningly and, as if being pushed by unseen forces, it rolled over.

Vince and I couldn't help falling against each other. Mike's head flipped out the side window and then back in just before the window slammed against the asphalt. I heard screeching tires, blaring horns, and a thud as my head hit the van's ceiling.

Then the van flipped back up and over again, bodies and equipment tumbling. I collided with Vince and then bashed into Mike Allen again.

On the fourth roll, the van landed upside down and the windshield burst like a shotgun blast. Vince was now to my left, and Mike Allen was gone.

As the van slid toward the curb, I struggled to lift my head out of harm's way. A fierce scraping sound echoed from the roof. Car horns were blaring.

Then everything stopped.

Vince looked over at me, our faces only inches apart.

"Are you all right, Den?" he said.

"Yeah, I think so. Are you?"

"Where's Mike?"

"He's gone."

From the back of the van we heard a muffled "I'm okay."

Then: "Me, too."

At last Neal's voice broke through: "Can somebody get this shit offa me?"

Vince tried to avoid getting cut on the shattered glass as he crawled out the van's side window. I followed. We looked at one another in disbelief.

In the accident, Mike Allen had been ejected from the van, seat and all. He was upright in his seat, still strapped in and sitting in the median.

Vince and I yanked on the van's back doors. We dragged some gear out, and then dragged Charlie and Neal out. Michael crawled out, and then Glen emerged, holding his head. I asked if he was hurt.

"I had a dream that we were in a wreck," he replied.

Neal hobbled over to the cement median in front of the van's steaming hood and lay down. In a daze, Mike Allen dragged the mattress over and laid it on top of him. "I think he's in shock so we should keep him warm," he explained.

The traffic looked like it was backed up to Albuquerque, so Michael started directing cars to go around. Mike Allen explained to a guy in a suit that a driver had cut him off, which had forced him to swerve sharply.

"Let me get this straight," Glen said. "You drove all night, our shock absorbers were shot, the truck was overloaded, there was a sharp turn plus a dip in the road, the traffic was going eighty miles per hour, and some asshole cut us off! Gee! I wonder why we flipped?"

Our voices were drowned out by the *whap-whap-whap* of an approaching helicopter. Sirens screamed as swarms of cops arrived.

In the wreckage, I could see my bass—with a broken neck. Neal's drums had been smashed to smithereens. Our lack of injuries seemed pretty miraculous.

Glen said gravely, "I think we took a wrong turn into the Twilight Zone."

Neal hobbled across the blizzard of broken glass and asked if anyone had seen his boot. He picked up shattered pieces of his drum kit.

"So, Neal," Glen asked. "How do you like being in the band so far?"

"First you guys shoot me, then ya try to mangle me. This is my kind of band."

When we got back to the house in Topanga Canyon, Michael called an emergency meeting.

"The band can't continue without a van," he said. "I think it's time to pack it in, unless . . ."

"Unless *what*, Michael?" Neal said.

"Unless Dennis sells his Falcon and loans the money to the band," Michael said, aiming his most heartfelt, earnest look at me. "We'll pay you back as soon as we get back on our feet."

Everyone was quiet. I looked around the room and wondered if anyone else would have made the same sacrifice.

"Look at us," I said. "What else are we going to do? I mean, *look at us*. Music is the only thing we know how to do. This seems bleak, but giving up seems a lot bleaker."

6.

YOUR MUSIC IS KILLING MY WIFE'S PETUNIAS

HEADLIGHTS SWEPT ACROSS the dark curtains. Alice stepped over and parted them to peek outside. A caravan of cars had pulled into the driveway. The Doors had arrived. A scream went echoing down the canyon. It couldn't have been from anyone else but Jim Morrison.

We could hear the Doors slamming their doors.

Only a year before, the Doors had been just like us, another struggling band in LA, gigging wherever. We'd run into them at the Cheetah, the Whisky, and other places. Then, in June 1967, their song "Light My Fire" became the sort of monster hit that really puts a band on wheels. No matter where you turned, you heard that song. It was a headline in every newspaper, whether the subject was free love or race riots.

One year later, they were cranking out their third album, doing big tours, getting on *The Ed Sullivan Show*, and then getting told by Sullivan that they'd never work in this town again. They'd barely tasted fame before they were awash in *notoriety*.

But they still had time to hang out with the musicians in Topanga. This was good at first, especially for Morrison. He'd always wanted to be an infamous character, but now that he was, the attention of his fans was getting him a trifle unglued. There were stories of him turning over chairs in nightclubs, but we knew him as a bright guy ready for conversation.

An old friend Norma Green had gotten to be friends with Doors drummer John Densmore's girlfriend, Peggy, who had a best friend named Pam Kath. She was with Terry Kath, guitarist for the band Chicago. Pam and Norma swung by one day and informed us that the Doors would be coming over for a party. Peggy had promised to lure them over by, if necessary, withholding sex.

"Come on, everybody," Norma said, clapping her hands. "Let's all pitch in and straighten up the house."

Alice looked around at the unholy squalor. "We'll need hydraulic jacks to straighten up this house."

Still, the Doors were coming. We went to work. As night came on, Alice looked around at our spruced-up digs. "The house looks weird this clean," he said. "It just isn't natural."

Then a vehicle's headlights lit up the curtain and our guests trooped in. Pam and Peggy couldn't have been bouncier if they'd been on Pogo sticks. The Doors and their producer, Paul Rothchild, walked in and looked around, followed by David Crosby and Arthur Lee. David had recently been fired from the Byrds, and while Arthur's band, Love, had done some deeply eclectic and interesting albums, he wasn't very happy.

Pamela clapped her hands together and said, "Let's get this bitchin' party going." She grabbed Peggy's hand and they danced around the room singing "Hello, I Love You."

Jim Morrison leaned against the television, blocking the screen. No one complained. Doors guitarist Robby Krieger's attention was seized by the twinkling eyes on the Lawrence Welk portrait. "Fascinating home décor," he offered.

Morrison sat on the floor and stared at our unusual "coffee table." Les had built it in homage to what he thought Arizona folks would like. Its glass top and screened sides held a cage of scorpions and lizards. Morrison gazed at it with fixed intensity.

"Lizards," he said.

Les noted his interest. "That's Lizzy, and the other is Borden," he said. "The white tarantula is Blackie."

Neal reached into the cage and coaxed the tarantula onto his hand. He brought it out and maneuvered it onto Morrison's hand.

"Where did you get it?" he asked.

"We were on our way to a gig in Fort Huachuca, Arizona, and all of a sudden the whole fucking desert was crawling with tarantulas."

"They looked like monkey paws," I said, "all crawling away from the sunset."

"The whole desert was moving," Neal said. "I spotted this white one and stopped to look at it."

"That sounds cool," Morrison said.

Tink, tink, tink. Norma tapped her spoon against a wineglass. "I've got an announcement to make. The party is moving downstairs for a séance."

Glen and I looked at Alice, who looked at Neal, who looked at Michael. We were all thinking the same thing: Séance?

Downstairs in the basement, Norma had chalked in a large pentangle on the wooden floor and placed a candle in the center. Morrison joined Norma and several others in the circle and sat between Alice and Michael. Everyone in the circle joined hands. Norma asked everyone to quietly concentrate. The flickering candle sent spooky shadows dancing on the walls.

"We want to speak to the spirit of the house!" Norma called.

Outside the circle stood the skeptics. Arthur Lee flashed a sarcastic peace sign to David Crosby. Neal smiled and took a big gulp of beer.

Morrison, however, was deep into the ceremony. He gripped Michael's hand. Alice was in deep concentration, too, but it seemed more like prayer. Everyone got so quiet that I could hear my heart beat.

"Spirit, we feel your presence. Will you answer us?"

A long, powerful silence was shattered by Norma's abrupt shriek. Chills shot up my spine. Norma's eyes popped open wide and she sat up straight, pointing a finger straight at Morrison. After an intense minute, a low, grave voice came out of her.

"This is my house," said the gruff Norma. "Some here do not believe, but their presence will be tolerated . . . I am from the dark past . . . I have lost loved ones here . . . in this house . . . I seek the truth . . . I must communicate . . . I cannot find rest . . ."

Then Norma fell forward and writhed about. Her long hair flopped into the candle. Everyone remained stock-still as she lay limp on the floor. Even the skeptics were dead silent. Like me, they were baffled by the absence of detectible fakery.

She revived slowly, then shook her head, and a smile appeared. She seemed to be the same old Norma again. People took that as a cue for sighs of relief. She really didn't know what had happened to her? She had seemed very convincing.

Suddenly, the ceiling gave way with a tremendous noise as a body came crashing down into the circle. Everybody leaped back in total fright. This was real. As we stared with popping eyes and ashen-faced fear, we saw the figure unfold himself in the circle. It was Glen.

"What the fuck, man!" he barked as he rolled over. "Who left the fucking trap door open?"

I looked up at the open trap door and burst out laughing. The door was cut through the floor of an upstairs closet. Glen grumbled that at least he hadn't spilled an ounce from his flask. The solemn mood returned, although by now everyone had teeth marks on their hearts.

Morrison believed that the whole bone-chilling episode was authentic. Even in Hollywood, where every man, woman, child, and dog was an actor, if Norma was faking it, it was still a riveting performance.

The party picked up again, and Alice's charismatic social skills kept him in the limelight, as usual. But it was clear that a bond was forming between Glen, Robby, and Jim. In the wee hours, guests began to file out and go home. But Glen and Jim kept hanging together in the doorway.

Glen started bragging about how we would often "hoof it" all the way to Hollywood. Now, most LA people didn't believe such a journey was possible on foot. The twenty-mile hike required you to go down the snake-twisty Topanga Canyon, march along the busy Pacific Coast

Highway, and then turn inland through the armed fortresses of Beverly Hills. But we were old track guys; we had the legs.

Unfortunately, we didn't have the shoes. I had a pair of thrift-store loafers that I had painted kelly green. (Jimi Hendrix would later tell me he thought they were cool.) All the miles I'd walked had caused the nails to poke through the insides of the heels, so I regularly put cardboard inserts in for padding.

Morrison listened to our tales of marching bravado and took it as a challenge. He would up the ante, in fact, and do the journey *barefoot,* he said. He told the others to go on without him. And just like that, he pulled his boots off and walked over to the edge of the cliff and hurled them into the distance. Then he strolled off into the darkness.

The others seemed accustomed to going on without him.

Glen, Djinn, and I plonked down on a sofa. Glen had retrieved a jug of Mountain Red Burgundy from his secret stash, so we had that. I fell back for a moment, and when I opened my eyes again, it was morning.

Stumbling out into the driveway, I saw Glen and Alice. We were all dazed and hungover, but almost as one we got the idea to walk down to Hollywood. Maybe we should go hang out at the Doors' business office and see if there were any spare contracts hanging around.

We took off at once, marching single file, with Alice in the lead. Glen kept up. Although he had spent the majority of his life in an armchair or in bed, and his only forms of exercise were jumping around onstage or humping girls, Glen could move.

"The Doors are pretty cool," he said as we walked down the canyon road.

"Of *course* they're cool," Alice snarled.

"No, I mean really cool."

Fourteen miles later, as we crossed Santa Monica Boulevard and headed for the Doors' office, we heard someone yell at us. We turned and saw a silhouette of a lone man walking up the old, dormant streetcar tracks. It was Jim Morrison, stepping over the railway ties and heading our way.

"Jim!" Alice called out.

He walked up to us, pointed to his feet, and grinned, "I did it. I hoofed it all the way barefoot, man."

"Wow," Alice said. "I'm impressed."

"Barefoot is easy," Glen said. "Try wearing my goddamn boots." We looked down at Glen's pointy-toe boots, which he said were better for stomping on the feet of Hare Krishna disciples at the airport.

Jim looked at us wonderingly. "What are you guys doing here?"

"What are *you* doing here?"

"That's my office right there."

"Have you been walking all night?" I asked.

"I fell asleep on the beach." He smiled. "But I hoofed it all the way! So what are you guys doing here?"

"We're just scroungin' around for some lonesome pussy," Glen said.

"Yeah, well, so am I," Jim said. "But first I need some boots. Do you know where I can buy some?"

"Buster Brown is right up the street," Alice said authoritatively.

Jim looked at him. "You're kidding, right?"

We marched up to the store, and Jim Morrison went in to try on some Buster Browns that Alice had suggested. When he came out, Glen flicked open his switchblade and said, "Want me to cut the buckles off?"

Jim flashed a big smile.

Alice and I badly wanted a pile of tacos. Glen and Jim were locked in a deep conversation about a young lady about town, Pam Zarubica—"Suzy Creamcheese" in Frank Zappa's world. We left them there and headed for Top Taco.

I didn't see Glen again until the next day. He explained to us that he and Jim had gone off to a Mexican restaurant where they drank all day and most of the night.

"Yeah, I taught him how to drink," Glen said.

Alice listened to this, nodded, and said negligently, "So what? We had Top Taco."

This was only the beginning of many all-night drinking binges for

Glen and Jim. During one on July 8, 1968, at around four or so in the morning, Jim remembered that the Doors had an early photo shoot. This would be for the cover of the album *Waiting for the Sun*.

"Jim started freaking out because the band wanted a picture of them at dawn and he didn't have enough time to go home and get his clothes," Glen explained. "So I took my black sweater off and told him to try it on. He liked it and left for the shoot."

For all the cheap highs and lust in Topanga Canyon, at least we played music. One day, Neal unveiled a new drum kit. He'd painted it powder pink and stuck on decals of bunnies and flowers. It looked like some 1940s baby's crib. The paint job made it look like a consistent kit, but the various drums were a mishmash of bargain-basement odds and ends.

He sat down and began playing in a cool jazz style. Alice started snapping his fingers like a hipster, and Glen and Michael picked up their guitars and added their most sophisticated chords.

We couldn't let well enough alone, though, and Neal and I started chanting, "Death!" Vince tore into a lengthy harmonica solo that led us down into the dark precincts of "Fields of Regret."

We were wailing hard when the door suddenly burst open. In the doorway was the silhouette of a large man.

Our playing dribbled to a stop. The big man stood there in menacing silence like Clint Eastwood. His eyes zeroed in on Glen and all the loose paraphernalia dangling from his shirt. The man suppressed an icy fury.

"I don't care if you wear shit all over your shirt," he said evenly, "but you've got to turn that racket down. Your music is killing my wife's petunias."

He gave us all a final hard look then turned and marched out.

We had groupies before we had income. It started in Arizona, and initially it was an innocent thing. We were actually surprised that we were attracting groupies—Hey! Girls *like* the androgynous look! But we were treading water financially for a number of years there, and still the young ladies came around with big, bright eyes and hopeful looks.

You know about groupies. Some were just pixieish sprites out for a craven good time, but many had skills in music, marketing, fashion, or something, and they liked to make things happen.

Then there were the GTOs: Girls Together Outrageously. This group of rock-'n'-roll wenches had become the queens of the Sunset Strip. We were used to gawking at celebrities—Alice would stare openly at anything that moved—but the first time we saw the GTOs, walking on a side street in Hollywood, with their ultra-vivid, crazy clothes glaring in the noonday sun, we were all agape. We immediately went over to talk to them. They took one look at us and invited us to a party, which, they said, was already in full swing.

Alice explained that we didn't have a car. The GTOs said they didn't have one, either, so we all walked up the hill into Laurel Canyon.

The GTO named Miss Christine took charge of introducing us around to the other Misses. They were all named Miss Something-or-other. Miss Christine had a very slight, Olive Oyl–type frame that she wrapped in layers of vintage clothing. Her billowing dark hair and whispery voice conveyed a distant naïveté. I could see Alice taking a devout interest in her.

Then we were introduced to Miss Mercy, who sat on top of the television with one boot propped on a chair. She seemed to be unaware that she was shooting us a beaver as panoramic as the Grand Canyon. Her mascara was smeared like a Jackson Pollock painting, but it didn't concern her. In clothes of a thousand clashing colors, she looked like a homeless gypsy. When she talked, she spewed profanity like a Marine drill sergeant.

For all the *Outer Limits* ecstasy of their clothes, they seemed to have some nostalgia for the 1920s silent screen starlets. Miss Christine had a Lillian Gish thing going. Miss Pamela, who would become Pamela Des Barres, would write a book, *I'm with the Band (Confessions of a Groupie)*, in which she really nails Miss Mercy's presentation: ". . . a plump version of Theda Bara wrapped in layers and layers of torn rags, an exotic bag girl with black raccoon eye makeup . . ."

Miss Pamela presented quite a contrast. Once a ballerina, she had moon-white, curly blonde hair and always wore sheer dresses that proudly displayed her braless boobies. Whenever she caught anyone staring at them, her eyes twinkled and she smiled like sunshine.

The Coops, as we were called, found these girls, and the other four members of the GTOs, to be kindred spirits. We took to hanging out with them every time we ventured into Hollywood.

Alice, in fact, got in deep with Miss Christine. They became hand-holding fashion clones. They not only wore each other's clothes, but you might say they wore each other. Miss Christine meticulously primped Alice's hairdo so it fluffed out like a black poodle's. Now their hair matched. Both had the same sort of slumping posture, and from behind, you saw these two question marks and you had to figure out who was who.

Okay, they *looked* avant-garde. But their romance was as simple as Mickey and Minnie's.

The GTOs' place of residence said everything. They were lodged in the basement of Frank Zappa's Laurel Canyon fortress. The historic old house, built by cowboy star Tom Mix from the silent movie days, was known as the Log Cabin. Alongside the row of rooms occupied by the girls was a single bowling lane.

One day Alice and I were lounging around the basement, helping Miss Christine baby-sit the littlest Zappa, Moon Unit. Zappa and his band, the Mothers of Invention, were off touring. Their records *Freak Out!* and *Absolutely Free* were getting a lot of attention, especially with those who liked it freaky.

You could look at Zappa and see nothing but a clownish character, and hear nothing but a dense sound collage. But as Alice would later point out, the guy was a maestro—and he was not a little intimidating.

So Alice was playing with the baby when he turned to kiss Miss Christine's hand and said imploringly, "Can you get Zappa to give us a record deal?"

She laughed nervously.

"Pretty, pretty, pretty, pretty please with sugar on it?" Alice continued, working his old magic.

"Good God," Miss Christine said. "I'll ask Mr. Zappa if he'll come to hear you play at the Cheetah."

Mister Zappa? Okay! Alice and I walked all the way back to Topanga Canyon talking nonstop about our breakthrough.

The band was stoked, too. We worked up a dozen new notions for an unforgettable show. Les came up with that trick where you wrap up a plastic dry cleaning bag into a rope, hang it up, and set it on fire so that flaming drops whiz down to the ground. But Les brightened the trick up with some colorful plastic flags that he had "borrowed" from a car dealership. Some brainstorming led us to the "Cage of Fire" concept. Alice was to stand inside a cage while singing "Fields of Regret."

We tried it out at our next performance, at the old Wrigley Field in downtown Los Angeles. It was June 27, 1968, and the afternoon concert was billed as "Phantasamagoria: The Community Effort." It was a benefit for a free medical clinic.

We walked into the locker room and were surprised to see Zappa sitting on the floor playing a stream of remarkable licks on his unplugged Les Paul.

"Hi, Frank," Alice said. "We didn't know the Mothers were playing here."

"I'm just the emcee," Zappa said. "And so we finally meet."

Alice enthusiastically started pitching our Cage of Fire act, but Zappa said he couldn't stay. He walked out to his car, and Alice went with him, talking us up.

In a quiet room I found an iron bench and sat down with my bass to warm up. Out of the blue, a girl with long brown hair came up and stood in front of me smiling. She said she liked my long hair and, without any warning, straddled my lap, facing me.

She began gyrating ever so subtly, although it sure didn't seem subtle to me. She now had my complete attention.

Then Michael walked into the room, riffing on his guitar. When

Alice and Glen followed, the girl licked my cheek and whispered, "Too bad for you. I guess I'll be seeing ya." Then she left.

"Don't you just hate this job?" Glen said, watching her go. "Music and pussy, music and pussy. Does it ever end?"

I groaned. "Thanks for the privacy, you pervs."

"We just saved you from getting the clap," Neal said.

The show went off about as well as my seduction scene. The stage was way out there in the baseball diamond's centerfield. The stiff breeze made it hard for Les to light the plastic flags. No one could see the "flames" in the afternoon sunlight anyway, so we toppled the contraption into the diamond and set the whole thing ablaze. It was just a charcoal skeleton smoking by second base.

"How will we ever top this?" Alice said as we slouched toward the dugout. "A bathtub full of scorpions?"

Meeting Zappa really emboldened Alice. He kept working on Miss Christine. Even though she was worried that Mr. Zappa was always very busy, one day she said, "I'll ask him if it's all right for you to come over tomorrow."

Alice immediately interpreted "*Ask* him if it's all right" as "*Yes!* You have an appointment!"

He was now on fire. "He'll *have* to love us," he said as we walked along Ocean Beach Parkway through Malibu, "because he's as crazy as we are."

I was dubious. I couldn't remember Miss Christine saying anything about our bringing instruments for the meeting, which Alice assumed was nine in the morning. It seemed a doubtful hour for a nighthawk like Zappa.

We stayed up all night working on our song list. We boiled our guitar strings to refresh their brilliance. We worked up some cool remarks for Zappa.

Norma rounded up a car for us, and the next morning, bright and early, we were hauling our gear up Zappa's steep driveway. Michael knocked on the Log Cabin's door until a sleepyheaded Miss Christine peered out. After one flabbergasted look, she shushed us and whispered, "What are you doing here? I haven't even asked him yet!"

But the wheels were already in motion. We barged right in. Miss Christine frantically ran ahead of us to block a door down the hall. When we began setting up our equipment in the hallway, she threw her hands in the air and said, "Fuck!"

As soon as we were ready, we started playing "No Longer Umpire" to Zappa's bedroom door. Within a minute, the door cracked open and a hand emerged motioning for us to stop.

We stopped. Zappa stuck his head out. In a calm voice, he said, "Just let me get some coffee and then I'll listen."

Miss Christine hurried to the kitchen. Zappa emerged, quietly closed the bedroom door behind him, and leaned against it.

"Good morning, Frank," Alice said. Zappa nodded and remained quiet. He did have a slight smile, however, so it seemed he appreciated our boldness. We hoped.

Miss Christine returned with a jumbo mug of black coffee and a saucer of cookies. Mike Allen set up a card table, and Zappa sat down and blew into his steaming cup. At last he said, "Let's hear it."

So the Alice Cooper assault ensued. Even in the confined hallway, we managed to jump around a bit. After the fourth song, Zappa again signaled us to stop. He had an encouraging gleam in his eyes.

"You guys play things that I couldn't get the Mothers to play," he said.

I knew that couldn't be true, but it was a great compliment.

"I have my own record label called Bizarre," he said. "If we can work it out, I would like to record you guys."

Even Alice and Michael stood speechless. Miss Christine smiled in relief.

"Do you have a manager?" Zappa asked.

We all said, "Nope."

"You'll have to find one. If you can't, then my manager might do it, but it would be better if you found your own."

We showered him with thanks and departed. As our car snaked

down Laurel Canyon, Neal said, "Where the fuck are we gonna find a manager?"

Neal's sister, Cindy, had moved into Hollywood a few months previous to earn money to help support the band. She landed a job at the Inside Outside boutique on Santa Monica Boulevard, where she designed and made shirts. One day, two guys came in the store and she struck up a conversation with them. She asked if they had anything to do with bands.

"We manage a band," said Joe Greenberg. "I'm sure you've heard of the Left Banke. 'Walk Away Renée'?"

"My brother has a band," Cindy replied. "You should hear them. They're *really* good."

"What's the name of the band?" asked the other guy, Shep Gordon.

"Alice Cooper."

Joe smiled. "Does she look anything like you?"

"It's five guys," Cindy said. And when she told them that Frank Zappa was going to produce them, she saw a lighbulb go on over their heads.

When they left, Cindy ran to the phone.

"Get 'em up here right away!" said Neal. "And good goin', baby sis."

The next day, Shep and Joe pulled up at the store in their ride, a Cadillac hearse, and took Cindy up to Topanga.

They were barely in the door when Alice was all over them explaining our song "Refrigerator Heaven."

"It's about cryogenics," Alice said with assurance. "Freezing your body after you die so you can come back in the future."

"Salvador Dalí wants to do that," I pitched in.

"Far out," said Joe.

"We'd offer you guys some food," Neal said, "but we only have ketchup."

Glen shook his head. "It's all gone. I used it to make Bloody Marys last night."

Someone lit a perfect dovetail and passed it around. To avoid getting foggy-minded, I did fake inhales.

Michael sure wasn't foggy. "Enough small talk," he said. "I know what *we* can do for *you,* but what can *you* do for *us?*"

The tap dance began. Joe was able to call on his streetwise chutzpah and razzle-dazzle us, while Shep offered what seemed to be sound, methodical wisdom.

"If you want to make it, you can't fake it," Joe said. "You need a manager, and with us, you get two for the price of one." He held up two fingers in the peace sign.

"What cut do you want?" Michael asked.

"If we decide to manage your careers," Shep said, "Joe and I get twenty percent."

"If we sign with you," Michael continued, "how do we know you'll stick with us for the long haul?"

Shep's response was actually about himself, but it sounded impressive: "I'm going to be a millionaire by the time I'm thirty. That's at least twenty percent of what you'll be making." He shrugged. "Figure it out."

The math was beyond me, but it certainly sounded better than our situation. We'd had enough of sprinkling ketchup and Parmesan on toast and calling it pizza.

Despite the smokescreens, the cartwheels, the sleights of hand, the pounding drum that was supposed to bring rain, it was clear that everyone in the room really needed some sort of deal. We'd find out later that the business about managing Left Banke had been pulled out of thin air—they knew a guy who knew a guy. But by now, they could smell a deal, something real. They were confused by our name, but agreed it was catchy.

"We're playing the Cheetah this Saturday," Alice told them. "It's the Lenny Bruce Memorial Birthday Party show. Zappa will be there. We'll put you on the list."

"We'll be there," Shep said, twirling a lock of his hair.

As their Cadillac hearse motored away, Michael took the lyric sheet to "Refrigerator Heaven," flipped it over, and started writing a list of contractual needs.

"We don't have time to find anyone else," Alice said. "Besides, they seem like good managers."

I was worried that our career seemed to hinge on this one meeting, but as Glen said, what else were we gonna do?

We considered the Cheetah our turf, but its grandeur was fading fast, like a heavily made up dowager walking out in bright sunlight. An additional stage had been set up outside, on the beach, for the Lenny Bruce memorial show, and milling around was a crazy-quilt crowd of hippies, beachcombers, freaks, girls in bikinis, and of course loads of cops.

The headliners were the Doors and the Paul Butterfield Blues Band. When we arrived, Iron Butterfly had just finished playing "In-a-Gadda-da-Vida" to waves of people on the beach.

When it came time for our set inside the Cheetah, the GTOs gathered in front of the stage. Miss Christine waved to Zappa, whom we'd spotted in the back of the room.

"TESTES. TESTES." Michael's voice boomed out as he tested the microphone. Alice walked out in a white ruffled shirt with a pink feather boa. His microphone was dead.

This didn't stop the announcer from hailing us with a big "Here they are! Alice Cooper!" After some stumbling around, Neal kicked us off on "No Longer Umpire"—only Alice couldn't be heard. Michael's harmony had to carry us.

When the song ended, Alice said in a sultry voice, "Can someone turn this mic up? I'm not Janis Joplin."

From there, things only unraveled further. During "Reflected," Glen's fury built and he swung his guitar at me, so I retaliated in a mock battle. Alice crashed into Neal's cymbal with the mic stand, then jumped up and down and egged on the audience.

The audience was having none of this, and started trooping for the exits. They were leaving so fast that I looked behind us to see if there was a fire or something. As we thumped into "10 Minutes Before the Worm," our performance had become as chaotic as a runaway circus train. This only annoyed the crowd even more. The few people who remained seemed to have stayed just to heckle us. The GTOs' screams and our fans who'd stayed to hear "Fields of Regret" were our only signs of hope.

We thought we saw Zappa laughing as he headed for the door.

Afterward, Shep was all grins. "Wow!" he said. "It takes a powerful force to clear a room that fast. We've got to turn this around and make it work for you." Already he was scheming like a mad scientist.

Miss Christine chimed in that Frank had *lovvvvvvved* it. She said it had been a lame audience.

"They couldn't hear the lead singer," Glen said. "I would've walked, too."

Michael lamented that we needed new equipment to keep it going.

Joe snapped, "Whatever it takes."

That was good to hear.

Then a guy walked up to Alice and asked if he'd do an interview. Alice said, "Sure."

"The audience left," the interviewer began. "What was that all about?"

Alice was instantly authoritative. "The audience left because they couldn't take the sexuality of the group's performance," he said. "Alice Cooper is launching a mental revolution."

"Do you really believe people like you can start a revolution?"

"You can't fight progress."

Shep watched this and smiled. "Amazing," he said.

The band drove back to Topanga that night wondering if the show had been a success or a disaster.

We had to move to Hollywood. Topanga just wasn't doing it for us. We were stepping up rehearsals, planning new costumes, pushing our phone bill over the top.

Once again, Cindy came to the rescue. One day in the Inside Outside boutique, she overheard a musician from Rhinoceros mention that the band was moving out of LA. She immediately told Joe and Shep.

The place they were vacating was a mansion in the Hollywood Hills. From one angle it looked like Zorro's hacienda. From another, like a Tijuana jail.

Our landlord was the actor John Phillip Law. We liked that. He'd played the blind angel in the futuristic French film *Barbarella*, which served as a huge inspiration for our increasingly bizarro costumes.

Since Cindy had offered to make our stage costumes, Neal invited her to live in the house, too. Cindy had first decided to make the move to California after the van accident, when she heard her brother sounding so lost. She'd been attending a fashion college in Texas, but she knew she had to get to the Coast. Living with the band, she swiftly got to know just about everything that went on, and she took steps to make things right.

Neal and Cindy had grown up without a father, in the "cool house" of the neighborhood. Cindy liked the way her mother made their place feel open. There were lively records on the phonograph, and kids always wanted to hang out at the Smith house. Cindy wanted that for the rest of her life, and she brought that good vibe to the band house.

Figuring out the "bedrooms" was not easy. Charlie Carnal and I split a big room, but I chose a closet, which was, conveniently, the size of a mattress. I figured if a girl came to my room, she'd be in my bed right away. Good theory, anyway.

Cindy created a bedroom out of the unused dining room. Well, it was unused till somebody walked through on his way to the kitchen. Speaking of which, Cindy wasn't going to put up with our miserable vittles. Suddenly we had tuna casserole coming out of our ears.

I found myself gazing at Cindy more and more. She was so striking to look at, and radiated such a sense of fun. Creativity just shot from her fingertips. Who wouldn't have looked?

Oh, I wasn't the only guy checking her out, but I was determined to get to know her. I would look at her and wonder if Neal would mind if I got next to her.

Late one night, I was quietly going through her room to the kitchen in the hope of finding a morsel of food. She was at the table, so we started to talk. (Later, she'd joke about this moment and say that her first thought was, Great, he's either stoned or horny or both.) Things seemed to get easier between us. It was our first real conversation, and it was nice.

Finally, she said she had to get to bed. She slipped under the covers, and I just stood there. It's not like we had run out of things to talk about, so I sat on the edge of the bed so we could be at ease.

She liked me. I felt warm. Moonily, I told her I wasn't leaving till she gave me a good night kiss. She didn't know what to think. At last I moved in. We kissed.

Lightning, shooting stars, worlds aflame. Something happened that I'd never known, a tremendous physical reaction. Just from a kiss.

There was no denying the nuclear moment. From then on, we began to seek each other out at every opportunity. It was so comforting that our physical fire was equaled by our artistic temperaments. Some days we would just lie in bed together reading, drawing, or dreaming aloud. We didn't want anybody else to see us together, but nothing felt so right as when we were near each other.

But how was I going to break this news to Neal without it jeopardizing the band? I didn't have to. When finally she knew Neal was getting wind of it, Cindy took him aside privately and assured him that our feelings were mutual. She said we'd tread lightly.

As time went on, and success and constant traveling separated us, we each sowed a few wild oats—as she said, I had to "set my chickens free"—but we kept coming back together stronger and stronger.

I eventually came to know what she knew: that we belonged to each other and no one else.

Among the million things she shared with me was a beautiful memory. I once heard her tell a friend, "I knew it was him the first time I kissed him."

It was time to sign contracts. The only thing was, you needed to be over twenty-one to sign legally, and that left out three-fifths of our band. So we made an occasion of it and invited the Buxtons, the Bruces, and the Furniers out to pen the contracts. Shep scraped up the money to buy a turkey, so we could have an extravagant dinner, complete with mashed potatoes, corn, green beans, and cranberries. The house smelled wonderful as we all sat down for an afternoon meal.

First, Mr. Furnier said grace. Then the assault began. The parents watched in amazement as we tore into the food like jackals.

Afterward, we moved to the living room, where the contracts were spread out on a cabinet. The Buxtons' stone-faced expressions made it clear they were in no mood to sign anything. Glen needs to finish college, they said. Needs to get a job with a sound future. Mr. Buxton said he'd get Glen a good-paying job in Phoenix at AiResearch.

Glen's expression said, *Dead end.*

Deflated, Mr. and Mrs. Buxton began reading the management contract.

Alice had already worked his parents over. The Bruces just threw up their hands and watched as Michael swung into action like a crusading district attorney, drilling Joe and Shep on point after point.

I had some questions, too. Such as, what if Zappa's deal fell apart? What if we lost our house? What if nobody bought our record? The others waved off my questions as silly—but of course all these things would later come to pass.

I'm pretty sure Joe and Shep had no full understanding of what a professional contract should entail, but they sure did possess that New York energy, along with a skill for weaving charmingly creative bullshit. It all boiled down to blind faith and necessity.

The ballpoint pens came out. Neal and I signed on, and so did the parents. Done deal.

After a brief celebration, in which the parents pretended to enjoy sipping budget champagne from plastic glasses, we hustled them out and prepared for a real party. Soon we had the house crawling with musicians from Steppenwolf and the Mothers of Invention, plus neighbors, friends, and assorted Hollywood lowlifes. The GTOs were in full song.

I was alone at the kitchen table, having a pensive moment, when Suzy Creamcheese came in and sat down.

"You don't know what you've got, do you?" she said. "Frank didn't." She took a long pause and looked at me with testing eyes and inviting cleavage. "He had no idea what he had when he recorded *Freak Out!* He didn't know until after it was released. I had to tell him."

She was in that moment letting me know she was doing the woman's duty of defining us. I nodded silently.

"I see," she said. "So you're the quiet one. Are you the wise one?"

I couldn't think of an answer, so I remained silent and hoped it would be taken for wisdom.

"We shall see," she said, her look piercing.

Behind her psychological probing there was a charming, likable person. But, oh, she was quite the handful.

Glen must have performed more favorably in his interview with her, because he started visiting Suzy in her separate cabin on Zappa's property. He said not to tell Michael, because they were both visiting the cabin.

On September 16, 1968, it was official. Joe and Shep negotiated our contract with Zappa's Bizarre Records and we signed it.

When we all piled into Zappa's house for a photo session, we found the great man stretched out in the basement, talking on the phone. The space was crammed with road cases, a purple Hammond organ, a statue with a gas mask.

When he was done, Zappa hailed us merrily. "Hello, Alice Cookies!"

He paused and studied our reaction, which I'm sure was deathlike.

"Each song," he continued, "will have its own little record, the size of a cookie, and the cookies will come in a can. The cans will be stacked on the counter at the record store with a sign that says, 'Get Yer Alice Cookies Here!' The kids will have to open them with a can opener to get the records out. The band will be called Alice Cookies!"

We all coughed modestly, to disguise the sound of our imminent death rattles. Still, Frank's excitement seemed genuine, so we actually discussed his idea. As Frank sipped his coffee, his eyes twinkled with enthusiasm as he added, "You can toss your cookies into the audience."

You have to know this about Frank Zappa: The man emanated intellectual energy. For all his carny sideshow appearances, he was brilliant. *But putting our records in cookie cans?*

We were still in a daze about this turn of events when Zappa's album cover artist, Cal Schenkel, took us out to the backyard for the photo shoot. By nightfall we were adamantly against the cookies concept.

The next day, Frank's manager, Herbie Cohen, shot down the idea instantly. Records in a cookies can would be too expensive. We were to remain Alice Cooper.

7.

PRETTIES FOR YOU—
THE ACCIDENTAL ALBUM

IN OUR WORLD, "moonlighting" took on a different cast; it meant we would start recording at midnight and get booted out at dawn. Glen was fine with that. The rest of us were just thrilled to be walking into a bona fide recording studio with carpets and recorders and tweakers and boosters or whatever they were. Whitney Studio in Burbank might have been an insignificant little dump, but to us it shone like Mission Control.

For our first session, Zappa didn't look happy. He'd walked in clutching his gut. "I think I've got the flu," he said, drooping like a dog. It was not a good omen.

The album we were making, *Pretties for You*, doesn't have the vividness that characterizes our later, successful albums. There's a good reason for that. If the album sounds spooky and experimental—well, there was a lot of that going around in 1969. And having Frank Zappa meant no commercial harness was going to be inflicted on our spacey collage.

Frank had us set up our gear but not put up any baffles. These are the portable sound guards that prevent stray sounds from going into the wrong microphones. "Pretend you're just rehearsing in a garage," he said. "I want it to sound like I'm driving by in my car."

We were still setting up when Frank said, "Run through the songs so we can adjust the levels."

Caught off guard, we blasted through three songs. We were still tuning up along the way and were ready to do another when Frank's raspy voice came in over the studio intercom. "Come in for a listen," he said. "It sounds great. We've got some takes."

Some takes? Who was doing any official takes?

We filed into the sound booth and had a listen. "There were some clams in there," Glen said.

"We can fix it in the mix," Frank responded blithely before retreating to the bathroom.

Just then, a jarring blast of patchouli oil scent entered the booth. A guy in a tie-dyed T-shirt walked in and held up a perfectly rolled dovetail joint. "Hey, man," he said, "I'm delivering a good-luck gift from the Jefferson Airplane. Zappa told them all about you dudes. They wanted to wish you a groovy session."

We had been feeling so low, lonely, and unknown for so long that getting a token of encouragement from one of the world's top bands struck us as a very good omen. Still, we discreetly took our good-luck amulet outside. Miss Christine had warned us how much Zappa disapproved of all drugs. He'd fire anyone in his band who was getting high.

Stoned or not, Michael was on top of the situation. If any of the next takes were going bad, he ordered us, "Just stop playing, so they'll have to take it over from the beginning."

In the very next song, my pick broke, so I stopped. We all crashed to a halt. Frank's raspy voice boomed over the studio talk-back. "What's the matter! Are you stoned?"

Okay, now we're all tense. But the next songs had a little more energy as we were warmed up and actually *knew* we were recording. I promised myself I'd never record under the influence of anything ever again.

The next time we went into the control room to listen to the takes, Frank was off in the bathroom. In the chaotic-sounding playback, you could hear more of Michael's guitar through Neal's drum mic than his own mic. Our songs had so much of this "leakage" that they might have been recorded at the bottom of a lake.

Zappa staggered out of the can and said he had to go home. That was not what we wanted to hear. He was obviously ill and needed to leave, but we had been counting on his help to make a great record.

So it was up to Ian Underwood to salvage the carnage. Ian played piano and woodwinds in the Mothers and, like all those guys, seemed to be a musical whiz kid. We scrambled on through the night.

The next night: No Frank. Again. But Ian had a fresh pot of coffee going.

"Frank was a little tough on you guys yesterday," he said, "but he has his reasons. He thinks his phones are tapped. He thinks they're out to bust him because of his political views."

Ian played our previous night's take of "Reflected," and my heart sank. The recording quality was so amateurish. Suddenly, the recording studio had lost its glamour. Suddenly, the carpets were dirty, the lighting was cheesy, and the equipment was outdated.

"There are things we might be able to fix," Ian said, "but some things, we're just stuck with."

Alice clapped his hands and stood up. "We've got to make the best of it. Let's go!"

In the studio, Michael noted that the album could use a little more texture. He glanced at the enormous studio organ with its three tiers of keyboards. "This looks like it came from the *Titanic*," he said.

Michael began to play and, in moments, had a glorious, haunting melody going. It was what he thought the organist on the *Titanic* would have been playing as the ship went down. He notified Ian that he wanted this recorded, and we soon had a take.

It went like that. When we recorded "Sing Low, Sweet Cheerio," Alice and Michael traded off vocals and actually fell into a musical pocket. Thanks to the final roach from the Jefferson Airplane gift, Glen was inspired to come up with a guitar part that would have done Quicksilver Messenger Service proud.

High school buddies Vince and Dennis acting natural in a photo booth.
(Dennis Dunaway private collection)

Glen Buxton, John Tatum, Vince Furnier, Dennis Dunaway, and John Speer (not in view) in the Spiders Sanctum at the VIP Lounge in Phoenix, Arizona.
(Thomas J. Buxton)

Dennis Dunaway, Neal Smith, Michael Bruce (with a hammer), Alice Cooper, and Glen Buxton on the roof of Zappa's garage following their first meeting as signed artists. *(Cal Schenkel)*

Alice gets a surprise.
(Dennis Dunaway)

Michael Bruce with a tuning fork, lounging in the living room at the band's Pontiac Farm in Michigan. *(Dennis Dunaway)*

Cindy Smith and the Frog that greeted Bob Ezrin on his first visit to the band's farm. The Frog only said "Ribbit" until Cindy kissed it, and then it turned into Dennis. *(Cindy Smith Dunaway)*

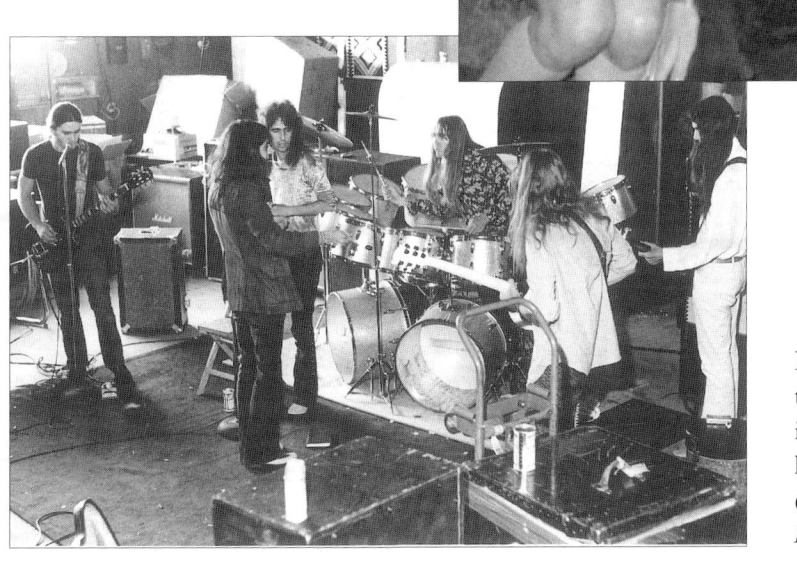

Bob Ezrin passes through a trial by fire in the Alice Cooper rehearsal room in Pontiac. *(Photo by Ric Siegel © Paul Brenton)*

Dennis mans his Green Gibson EB-0 Frog Bass as a kid is welcome to sit in the Electric Chair.
(Photo by Ric Siegel © Paul Brenton)

Dennis creating bass lines.
(Photo by Ric Siegel © Paul Brenton)

Alice swings the hypnotic watch as Glen Buxton plays slide spoon on "Black Juju." *(Photo by Ric Siegel © Paul Brenton)*

Alice climbs on top of the Electric Chair in Charlie Carnal's eerie lighting as the group's dramatic Feather Storm begins. *(Photo by Ric Siegel © Paul Brenton)*

Alice Cooper surrounding Charlie Carnal at the Warner Bros. Bastille Day Bash at the Ambassador Hotel. *(Monica Lauer)*

(Above) Dennis warming up for a show in Paris. Mirrors reflect Neal Smith and Bob Ezrin. *(Bob Ezrin)*

(Left) Dennis and Glen conjure up their sinister stage attitudes at the Olympen, Lund, Sweden, November 21, 1972. *(Photo by Stephan Lindblad © Anders Mossberg)*

(Below) Cindy Smith, Dennis Dunaway, and Michael Bruce recuperating between shows at One 5th Avenue in New York City. *(© Len Delessio / www.delessio.com)*

Neal Smith, Glen Buxton, Alice Cooper, Michael Bruce, and Dennis Dunaway just after writing "Generation Landslide" in the Canary Islands. *(Cindy Smith Dunaway)*

Neal Smith sitting on top of the world. *(David Cluett, Jr.)*

The Billion Dollar Babies Holiday Tour. *(© Bob Gruen / www.bobgruen.com)*

(Above) Glen Buxton playing guitar at the Chateau Marmont in 1974. Glen always stayed in the room that Jim Morrison recommended. *(David Cluett, Jr.)*

(Below) Dennis and Cindy just before tying the knot at the Town Hall in Greenwich, Connecticut, where Lucy and Desi got married. *(David Cluett, Jr.)*

PRETTIES FOR YOU—THE ACCIDENTAL ALBUM / 117

Now we were moving along. "Fields of Regret" became an operatic nightmare—and it's an important song, because this is the foundation of Alice's stage character.

Ian was open to our inclination for experimentation. Alice's harmonica was cool, so Ian had us record a second layer on top of it in full stereo effect. I played a slinky bass slide while Glen unearthed some tingly sounds by picking the strings behind the bridge. At the three-and-a-half-minute mark, Glen erupted in a solo that sounded like angry hornets devouring a city.

Many years later, Glen would be named by *Rolling Stone* magazine on its list of the one hundred greatest guitarists. If anybody should question that, just point them to the originality of that solo. It's not a solo; it's a psychotic crime spree.

Alice did a voice-over after that in which you can really hear the marks of his being a minister's son. Masterfully, with a biblical tone, his lyrics warned of eternal fate.

As our session time dwindled, we decided to fool around with an informal recording of "Levity Ball" that we had made during a rehearsal at the Cheetah. At the club, we had set up microphones far and wide, and the dim floor provided a perfect setting for imagining dancing ghosts.

The recording, however, was on an old tape that had been used many times over. The machine's worn erase heads hadn't completely removed the previous recordings, so native voices from the 1950 film *King Solomon's Mines* leaked through. We loved it. We knew our "production values" might get criticized, but as Glen said, "It's got the feel, so why not use it?"

Zappa had said that what made our band so unique was the ability of the five of us to agree on such abstract concepts.

The album art had to be suitably out-of-kilter, so for the back cover, photographer Ed Caraeff took our portrait at a Hollywood art gallery, surrounded by kinetic sculptures of chromed automobile parts. I kept the motif going with a chrome shirt that Cindy had made for me. Alice's "shirt" was actually a sequined majorette's uniform, complete with green fringe. Miss Christine had bleached his hair dishwater blond just for the shoot, mostly because too many people were calling him Tiny Tim.

"Here, read this," Joe Greenberg said one day. "It's your new biography."

Just to make sure not one living soul would ever regard us as folk singers, we had concocted a press kit that detailed the fate of a sixteenth-century witch named Alice Cooper whose sister had been burned at the stake. According to the story, I was a reincarnated artist of the court, Glen was a fiery warrior, and so on.

Glen looked up and said, "It beats reading about a bunch of dopes that showed up from the desert."

I nodded. "We're reincarnated dopes."

Little did we know that this bit of fiction would follow us for years.

The front cover of the album was a highly risqué painting by Edward Beardsley, a piece of art from Zappa's home. It showed a girl lifting her skirt above her panties at a funeral. We didn't stop to wonder if this would be helpful in getting the record into stores. But we knew that our image on the back cover, with all our way-too-long hair, would be regarded by most red-blooded males of the time as a real sock in the face.

Whatever else it did, the album established us as the forerunners of glitter rock, although later artists would get credit for inventing it.

It was during our only paying gig in December of 1968 that I saw that Alice was getting a valid grasp of the dramatics. It was at a big concert at the Shrine Auditorium and Exposition Hall in LA. Zappa's Mothers of Invention dominated the show, along with Frank's old friend Captain Beefheart, but the real stars were the audience: a Day-Glo sea of freaks. They had transformed the crusty old auditorium into a costume ball from hell.

For "Fields of Regret," Alice did an impressive Jekyll-and-Hyde transformation. He became a different entity. Folks in the audience were bug-eyed.

Backstage, Alice got into an interview with a reporter. "Most groups are too hung up on applause," he explained. "We're looking for an effect—any kind of effect. If someone throws up, that's an effect."

Glen leaned into the reporter and cracked, "I guess this clears up that no-applause mess."

On New Year's Day 1969, we landed a five-day stand at the Whisky a Go Go, opening for Led Zeppelin. We actually didn't know all that much about them, other than they were an outgrowth of our old heroes the Yardbirds. The bass player I'd talked to backstage in Tucson, Jimmy Page, was now Zeppelin's guitarist. They were still six months away from becoming sensations. All we knew was that it was a rare paying gig for us: one hundred bucks a night!

The Whisky was just as lubricious a theater for the bands as it was for the gawkers. Driving up the Sunset Strip on the first night, we saw the girls in hip-huggers and sheer blouses clustered on the boulevard like sprays of orchids. Longhaired hippies and freaks hung out, too, as if they were sure this was the place to be. The LA Sheriff's finest observed it all through military sunglasses.

We parked our car in an illegal spot up the hill. As I got to the stage door, out came Robert Plant, surrounded by groupies.

The bouncer put his palm on my chest. He was your usual iron-brained gargantuan with a brick jaw. "Where do you think you're going?"

"I'm in the band."

"Sure you are."

"He's telling the truth!" piped up a girl with a Betty Boop voice. "Would he dress like that if he wasn't in the band?"

Ah, the ladies of the Whisky. Anyone who ever got near them has to sigh at the merest recollection. As a tradition, the groupies lined the Whisky entrance so they could rub their breasts against chosen celebrities. It was a memorable pleasure.

Once Mr. Iron Brains let me inside, I immediately spotted Robby Krieger leaning against the bar. I gave him a cool nod. He gave me a cool nod and toasted me with his cool beer.

In that Los Angeles moment, the Whisky was the place to be seen. If an off-duty guitarist from the Doors like Krieger would go there, you knew that producers, directors, ultra-hip showboaters, and folks hungry for a break would also pile in. And once you got tired of searching out famous faces, you had only to look up at the balcony, where the girls leaned over to display their talents to the crowd below.

The walk to the stage is where nervous energy converts into stage energy. It's when you suppress your anxieties and convince yourself that you're in total control. That night, we knew we couldn't just play to the audience, we had to *seduce* them. Conquer the Whisky and you've conquered LA.

Alice stopped at the end of the hallway and puffed up his hair. "Stick with me, boys," he said, "and I'll have you wearing diamonds as big as scrub buckets."

Thus charged up, we found an even higher level of energy onstage. With the feather boas, the theatrics, and a drum solo from Neal that went between thunder and slapstick comedy and ended with him falling off the stage backward and landing on the GTOs, we went right up to the edge of a smashing finish, and then went over it.

We bid the crowd farewell in a waterfall of cheers and applause. Mike Allen and Charlie hauled our equipment off the stage, and Led Zeppelin's crew pushed theirs into place.

Nobody would have wanted to follow the show we'd just laid down. Zeppelin canceled the last five days of their engagement. There were rumors that they all had the flu. Let's hope it wasn't brought on by having to follow us. A hundred bucks a night, split among the band, the crew, and now the managers? Who cared? We'd just tasted a new high. Playing well at the Whisky meant you were at the receiving end of a smorgasbord of sex and drugs, Hollywood rock-'n'-roll style.

In LA, there were a lot of groupies who were not necessarily interested in getting laid but in being seen with a band member. It was a matter of appearance. It was a matter of whom you walked into the Whisky with, making all your peers jealous as hell. That was a big deal.

The best seats in the Whisky were the booths. The girls at the Whisky knew that the cream of the crop were in those booths. And you never felt secure in them, because if somebody bigger walked in and needed a booth, you might get kicked out of yours. Everybody was a star there—but a bigger star was always on his way.

One night I escorted a groupie into the Whisky and quickly came to feel like *she* was escorting *me*. I was instantly aware of how the girls had a ranking system going. She paraded me through to make sure everybody knew whom she was with. I suddenly felt like we had a bit of status. Not so long ago, I could hardly get into the Whisky. Now here I was being *shown off* in it.

After the parade, she took me upstairs and dragged me into the ladies' room. I muttered, "Shouldn't I be in the other—?"

She said no, it was fine. From inside a stall a girl's loud voice sailed out, "It's okay, darling, we've seen it all before."

That was LA.

Joe and Shep were as down and dirty as we were. College buddies who had come out to LA, they were doing some kind of business out of their apartment. So the timing was perfect: We all wanted to make something happen. And don't get the idea that we were skulking around. We were all equally ambitious and sharing this zeal was kind of fun.

They were bunked at the Landmark Motor Hotel, on Franklin Avenue. It was off the beaten track. That's why Janis Joplin, Jimi Hendrix, the Chambers Brothers, and other bands liked staying there. If you drove past it, you'd never think in a million years that anybody important would go there.

The Landmark was a basic motel, a horseshoe of rooms built around a swimming pool. Janis was known to go skinny-dipping in the pool. It seemed like we always got there right after that happened.

We might have been getting our first few offers of free pleasure from the rock fans, but Janis was getting a *lot* of offers. And she was taking them. To see her huge persona, you wouldn't think that in 1969 she was only a few years past being a street person in Frisco.

On October 4, 1970, she would die of a heroin overdose in her room at the Landmark. It gave the joint such awful infamy that they had to change its name.

When we saw her, though, she was just a Texas girl skipping around, not afraid if the world saw flashes of her nakedness. She was sailing on sunbeams.

Our old friends the Chambers Brothers were always in and out. Their song "Time" was a gigantic hit in LA, and getting a lot of play around the world, too. It was a great, infectious song with its cowbell banging away. It was always a *major* climax to their show, and the chords would ring out forever.

Hendrix was at the Landmark a lot, too. We dressed as crazy as anyone in LA, but when we saw Jimi, we had a running joke about making fun of his clothes. He thought that was funny.

Jimi was a mild-mannered, soft-spoken fellow with a great sense of humor. He laughed a lot. He liked people, and he would initiate conversations with anyone who looked interested. He noticed what people wore, and if he thought something was cool, he'd say so. Peace and love all the way. He was a charismatic charmer without even trying. His air of "not trying" was actually part of his appeal. There was no question he had a big heart. He was just under six feet tall, but seemed over eleven feet. And when you were in a room with him, you got the Jimi you hoped for. That's what women fell for, his kind and caring demeanor. Of course, he was also a handsome guy.

Damn, he loved to play guitar. He would go down to that club Thee Experience, on Sunset. Surrounding the front door was a giant blowup of his face, so he had reason to feel at home there. No matter who was playing, he'd walk on stage, plug in, and start jamming. What was anybody supposed to do?

One time after Jimi had played a concert in Phoenix, Neal and I showed up backstage. The crowd in front was so big that he begged us to get him out of there.

Back in the hotel room, Jimi sprawled out on the bed, playing his guitar through a small Fender amp. He wondered what the coin slot next to the bed was for. When he realized it was a Magic Fingers vibrating bed, he shoved all the quarters he had into it and got the bed pleasantly shaking.

His bandmates Mitch Mitchell and Noel Redding wandered in, and Jimi called out, "Go get some more quarters!" By now, we were all sitting on the vibrating bed like it was a carnival ride.

In a few minutes, Noel and Mitch returned with a brick of weed wrapped in red cellophane. I don't know where they'd gotten the stuff, but it could have been from Dr. Frankenstein's lab. We giggled our way into the purple dimension.

There was a reason all these musicians visited Joe and Shep's apartment. The two always had pot, so whenever we went over for a meeting, there were all these joints flying around. But that was hardly a shocking reversal on any room where musicians gathered.

Joe was very New York City street smart. We had never really known anybody like him. He could talk anybody into anything—or at least die trying. Without feeling guilty at all, he'd call up some record company execs and give them a big pile o' bullshit. It would just be a cold call, too. He'd manage to get someone on the line, and then lay a high-octane spiel on them, convincing them that they'd better get busy and listen to this band that was creating such a sensation.

In the midst of these calls, he'd look at us, arch his eyebrows in mock disgust, cover up the receiver, and make all kinds of remarks about the schlemiels on the other end. He respected them, but he just wanted to make us laugh. He'd do this through a hundred phone calls.

Shep was more the thinker. He was the guy who was planning how to make something big happen. That fit in perfectly with us. Our stage act was bold and about trying to get attention. Shep didn't know from our gender-bender style, but he sure had the instincts of an old vaudeville guy who knew how to get fannies in the seats.

Shep often talked about Colonel Tom Parker, who managed Elvis and had built him into an icon. I would later realize that with Parker, it was all about Elvis, and the band was replaceable.

Shep was determined to get us some press. On St. Patrick's Day in 1969 we were playing at Thee Experience. Cindy had made us all pants out of clear plastic. While the rest of us pulled them on over our jeans, Michael put his over only his Jockey briefs. It was pretty funny. Then Shep called the cops and told them that there was a band playing in clear plastic clothing and they'd better get down and arrest us! His ploy didn't really work. But that was Shep's instinct for gaining press and notoriety. He wanted to move past the rock rags and get into the mainstream press.

Joe's sensibility was more practical. He could walk into any room or venue and tell you exactly how many people it would hold. He'd also make sure we had a guy with a counter recording how many paying customers came in the door. He and Shep got very good at hounding club owners for proper payment—*before* we went onstage.

Joe and Shep were greenhorns, but ready to join the carnival. Maybe if they'd been old hands at the game, they would have tried to mold us into something more acceptable. As it was, they were totally open to our craziness.

They saw the outrage and repulsion we created. But they also saw we were building a base of some very committed fans. Shep believed that if we could just tap that energy we could rule the world. Joe often verbalized the commitment they shared with us: "Whatever it takes, man. Whatever it takes."

Meanwhile, it took six months for *Pretties for You* to hit the stores, a length of time that made us think it had been shelved.

8.
SO FINE IN '69

ANYBODY WITH A RECORD COLLECTION will tell you that 1969 was a pretty good year for rock. In the two years after *Sgt. Pepper* laid waste to all preconceptions, the major labels had gotten mighty accommodating of music they once would've thrown out on the street. This was especially true for Frank Zappa's label. Our baby *Pretties for You* hit the stores, and the long road of touring began.

Every performance of ours was an original—one show was nothing like the one before. Zappa got us another stand at the Whisky, and we did everything we could to make it something you'd remember: We snaked our way through the tables to the stage, plugged in, and spewed out a speedy rendition of "No Longer Umpire." Alice was just as slinky and seductive as ever, twirling an umbrella fringed with rubber rats hanging from little nooses. It was working, but the show still felt like a bunch of guys trying to rope an octopus.

In July 1968, two of the biggest record company honchos ever to bang the table, Mo Ostin and Joe Smith of Warner Bros., had come to see us play. Word came back to us afterward that they had actually listened to most of our set but had walked out shaking their heads. One of them was heard to say, "How do we go back to the Board of Directors and tell them that we want to sign a bunch of cross-dressing guys called Alice Cooper?"

They were right. Our show was impossible to explain. Alice tried gamely to make sense of it to anyone who'd listen, but of course the show he'd describe would soon be superseded by the next bizarro show.

Then we found out that Woolworths, still a major store chain, had banned *Pretties for You* over its cover. In 1969, censorship of this sort was still in force. Bizarre Records scrambled to have censor stickers placed over the girl's lack of humility. Alice thought that was just great. An adolescent male's imagination, he crowed, was more powerful than cartoon panties anyway.

The critics seemed unmoved. One guy reviewed the album as containing "Songs Disney had sense enough to leave in the can." That one stabbed me right in the heart.

Glen read the review and snarled, "That guy's a critic because he doesn't know shit about music."

"He's just a big fuckin' loser with a typewriter," Neal said.

"And he's got a free copy of our album," Michael said.

"I can't believe he didn't like the music," I said. "It's the most original record ever made."

"You're all crazy," Alice said, holding up the newspaper. "This is a *great* review!"

We had thought the album was going to set the world on fire. Instead, we made it to 110 on the charts. I think Joe and Shep made more money selling copies out of the trunk of their old Cadillac.

The album that helped our careers the most at this stage wasn't even our own. We walked into the office one day and Joe handed me an album with a cheap white cardboard cover. Shep was grinning.

"What is it?" I asked.

Joe smiled and said, "It's food on the table."

It was *Great White Wonder*, which they were about to help make the most famous bootleg record ever. (We hadn't even *heard* of bootlegs at this point.) Joe and Shep had gotten hold of thousands of copies of this record of pirated backroom recordings of Bob Dylan. Since Dylan was the reigning wizard of folk rock, these unreleased songs had incalculable value.

And Joe and Shep had carloads of them. By selling those records on the side, they ensured our survival. Food on the table.

These were golden times when it came to a wide-open music scene. The whole business was open to any kind of absurd cross-pollination. One night we were playing Thee Experience, and the other acts on the bill were bluesman Slim Harpo and avant-garde saxophonist Pharoah Sanders. (Maybe the owner of the club, Marshall Brevitz, who liked us a lot and let us rehearse in the back room of his head shop on Sunset and Vine, the Psychedelic Supermarket, knew we were an experimental band. So, why not?)

We met Slim backstage and told him how much we liked his songs "I'm a King Bee" and "The Scratch (Baby, Scratch My Back)," two real sneaky-sexy R&B songs. Glen offered him some whisky from his flask. Slim laughed and said, "You scratch my back and I'll scratch yours."

Alice volunteered that he'd learned "King Bee" through the Rolling Stones cover, and Slim just smiled and said it was good to work with musicians whose "thing" was so different from his.

He didn't know the half of it. The three acts couldn't have been more at odds, a genuine blues great followed by Alice Cooper, with the night closed by the most abstract saxophone player in the cosmos. Psychedelic Supermarket, indeed.

We were getting the gigs, but we weren't exactly thriving: $1,300 for the month of March, which doubled what we had earned in February, but still wasn't much. We had expenses. Let's see now, for five musicians, a light show guy, a roadie, and two managers, we had to buy gasoline, guitar strings, clear plastic for pants, harmonicas, drum heads, Budweiser, several jugs of Mountain Red Burgundy, canned tuna fish, cottage cheese, saltines, and rubbers, and pay the rent.

Oh, yeah. The rent.

One day, we returned from a road trip to find we'd been moved out of the Tijuana hacienda/jail and into a place Cindy had found for us.

"Joe and Shep didn't want to keep paying the rent while you were gone," Cindy said. "Plus it rained for two weeks straight, and the house was leaking so bad that the stucco walls were falling apart. I made five vests and five pairs of pants, but I had to keep running through the house emptying pans of water. I couldn't even sleep."

Our new apartment building, at 2001 Ivar, was positioned right against a bend in the elevated Hollywood Freeway. An endless stream of traffic hurtled past. Closed curtains didn't blot out the rumbling noise or the vibrations from the passing semis that threatened to crash into my second-floor room.

Cindy had the only ground-floor room. For convenience's sake—not hers; everyone else's—the band's heavy equipment was stacked to the ceiling in her room.

One day we were having a band meeting in Neal's room when we sprang the news to the rest of the group that Cindy and I were an item.

"So that's it!" Michael said, beaming. "I wondered why Dennis was talking so much and being so outgoing!"

On occasions when Cindy didn't spend the night upstairs in my room, Glen had company in his insomnia until the early morning traffic lull, which seemed to last from 4:45 a.m. until 4:49 a.m., when it was just quiet enough for me to doze off.

We began to call the place Freeway Purgatory. Cindy and I were happy, but the band was gasping for air.

We traveled. Vancouver. Utah. An army base in Colorado, and then over to Aspen (back before it was glitzy). Finally we hit Cincinnati. Hard rock territory. The midwestern crowds loved high-energy bands.

One evening Neal and I got bored in our motel room. He threw a pillow at me and nailed me in the back, so I grabbed one and whacked him. Blow by blow, the battle escalated. Soon, feathers were flying out of a hole in his pillow. He was in hysterics and ripping the pillow open until the room was filled with a lofty snowstorm.

"Wouldn't this be great onstage?" I said.

By this point we were incorporating just about anything we had on hand into the show—anvils, petticoats, tires, whatever. So, Neal and I could have been hurling bean sprouts at each other and wondering about their stage potential.

Naturally I brought a pillow to our next show. It was at the Kinetic Playground in Chicago. Michael got an idea and snatched a fire extinguisher from the backstage area to add to the mayhem.

When we walked onstage, a heckler began shouting things about our looking like girls. Alice ignored him. A girl threw her bra onstage, and Alice picked it up and held it up to his chest. Surprisingly, the heckler shut up.

At the end of the set, Alice tore the pillow open and Michael used the fire extinguisher to spray the feathers to kingdom come. Charlie's flashing lights added a wild, erratic strobe effect, as if the whole room were engulfed in a vivid rainbow-colored snowstorm.

From that night on, janitors joined the list of people who hated us.

Speaking of hate, we didn't feel too much love in New York City. In the Midwest, we got the audiences roaring. In the fleshpots of Manhattan, however, we got a distinct chill. For a week in July of 1969 we played the hipster's paradise, Steve Paul's The Scene, along with the McCoys. Their guitarist, Rick Derringer, took us out for our first Nathan's hot dogs. Then we did the psychedelic arena in the East Village, the Electric Circus; there was trash strewn all over the floor when we arrived, but that was nothing compared to how it looked when we left.

We were bunked in a freezing East Village dump we called the Ratty Hotel. I was pondering another night between its questionable sheets when two beautiful girls in freakish outfits invited me to a party downtown. I didn't have to think twice and jumped into a piss-yellow taxi with them. I'll call them Ogleooma and Nippleina.

The party? I guess it was like any ol' charming downtown party where a guy with a throbbing vein in his temple pulls a knife on you, someone else burns your arm with a cigarette, and you escape with your life in a taxi amid an echoing call of "Fuuuuck youuu, youuuu fuckinnnng whorrrrrrrrrre."

These girls had reputations. I was rattled by what had just taken place at the party, but the girls cuddled each other and seemed very pleased. We reached their place, and Ogleooma said, "You're coming up, aren't you?"

"I'd better get back to the hotel," I said.

"Don't be a bore. Come up for some fun." The *Vogue*-worthy Nippleina batted her smudged eyes.

The prospect of two girls at once in New York City led me upstairs. Unlike the girls, the apartment had zero decoration. The phone was ringing when we walked in, but they ignored it. The two of them plopped into bed at once. Ogleooma invitingly patted the narrow crevice between their two bodies.

I sat at the bottom of the bed for a moment and pondered the view between the stockings.

Ogleooma fingered her cleavage and produced a folded piece of paper, which signaled Nippleina to roll up a twenty-dollar bill. The girls leaned their heads together and took turns snorting.

Ogleooma said, "Do you want some H?"

Smack? The phone rang again and it was like an alarm bell in my head.

"No, thanks," I said. "Gotta go now."

The girls didn't even look up as I left. Once down on the street, I breathed a big sigh of relief.

What if I had decided, *Why the hell not?*

In the fall of 1969, Joe and Shep had convinced movie director Frank Perry to give us a part in his new movie, *Diary of a Mad Housewife*. Perry's wife, Eleanor, had written the screenplay, about a self-centered husband (Richard Benjamin) and his fed-up wife (Carrie Snodgress). She meets an egotistical writer (Frank Langella), and despite their mutual dislike, they end up having an affair. Later, husband and wife attend a wild Manhattan party where a hip band (Alice Cooper) is playing.

Perry contracted Mars Bonfire for the musical score, so we had to choose one of his songs. We settled for a tune called "Ride with Me, Baby." Without telling anyone, we decided to alter the arrangement to include our chaotic sound collage from "Lay Down and Die, Goodbye."

Two days before they shot our scene, Frank Perry told us to arrive bright and early the next morning for makeup. Early morning is a cursed time of day for musicians. Naturally we showed up looking like the all-night trash.

"Wear your weird clothes," Perry had said, "and make sure you don't tell anyone why you're here."

The set was built to look like a hip Manhattan nightclub. For three long days, we showed up, got a cosmetic overhaul, drank coffee, and sat around being mysterious. By the second day, the irresistibly cute Carrie Snodgress guessed that we were to play the party band.

On the third morning, several cases of champagne arrived, which the extras popped open and sucked down. Charlie coordinated our lighting with Perry's lighting crew. And per our request, the prop manager brought in a fire extinguisher, mannequins, and plenty of feather pillows.

Perry gathered the band into a private huddle and said, "We've got fifty pillows. The crew will shake all those feathers down from the catwalk." And to make the feathers stick, he said he had several cases of olive oil for Alice and the crew to pour on the crowd.

We got ready on the stage. Cindy had designed the band's stage costumes, including Alice's rainbow-striped metallic pants and a matching top with one shoulder bare. Michael's costume featured a satin cape that attached to each wrist. Glen wore silver metallic pants and a dirty white leotard top with a cluster of mirrors on the chest. Neal's gold pants had conches down the sides. I wore a silver sleeveless shirt and silver pants. I played my mirrored green Gibson EB-0 "Frog" bass, which, in my opinion, served as another fashion accessory.

Wearing his brown derby hat and velvet poncho, Charlie sat cross-legged onstage. He played keyboards, but rather than making sounds, each key controlled a flashing light. And since he played his Light Organ with the focused dedication of a musician, Perry instructed one cameraman to make sure to capture Charlie's performance.

Perry, sitting high in a director's perch with wife Eleanor beside him, addressed the crowd with an electronic megaphone.

"I'm sure you've all noticed the weird-looking guys that have been hanging around the set for the past few days. These gentlemen are in a band called Alice Cooper, and we're all in for a musical treat.

"Are we ready? Okay, everybody, get ready for a wild ride. This is one take only. Aaaaand *ACTION*!"

The champagne-buzzed extras began to gyrate with exaggerated delight. Alice sauntered across the stage mussing his hair and singing while Perry pointed the cameramen toward every delicious bit. But only Perry and the guys in the rafters knew about our surprise.

Two verses passed, which meant we had met the film's contractual requirement to do the Mars Bonfire song. Then, suddenly, without warning, Michael's guitar began to whine like a cat, Glen's rhythm chugged, my bass howled, and the music transformed into a disturbing wall of noise. The dancers became erratic as our frantic onstage bashing erupted.

Alice brought out a nude mannequin, poured olive oil on it, and tossed it into the crowd. He emptied a second bottle onto a girl's white blouse, which made her hidden talents pop out like a wish come true. More oil began to splash down from the rafters. Michael leaned his guitar against his speaker cabinet and let the feedback roar while he grabbed the fire extinguisher and prepared for all hell to break loose. Alice gave the signal, and a ton of feathers rained down from the rafters. In seconds, before all vision was obscured, the camera got a shot of the well-oiled audience, who by then looked like a crowd of dancing chickens.

Glen leaned against his amplifier and his pink guitar wailed teeth-grinding feedback. I lunged toward him, then jumped backward into my amp and fell to the floor kicking my feet in the air. Michael rolled across the floor as if the fire extinguisher were out of control. Neal's arms flailed violently. The extras looked very surprised. And Perry looked very pleased.

The song came to an abrupt end, but the extras continued dancing until Perry yelled, *"Cut!"*

The dancing stopped and the room filled with cheers and woozy laughter.

"Thank you, everybody!" Perry yelled. "That's a wrap!"

Up to her knees in feathers, the extra in the well-oiled white blouse jokingly asked Alice what he was going to do about her cleaning bill.

He glanced at her nipples and said the blouse had been improved.

The next day, we were allowed into a screening room to view a rush print of the party scene. Perry's crew had really captured the visual absurdity of our performance with full impact.

Alice nudged me and said, "We're even crazier than I thought we were. We should always use that many feathers."

The movie ended up getting a nice bit of serious attention, not least of which came from Neil Young. When he saw the movie, he fell in love with Carrie Snodgress. He was moved enough to write a very romantic song about her, "A Man Needs a Maid." They became lovers and had a son, Zeke.

We had one last incident surrounding the filming of *Diary of a Mad Housewife*, on our final morning at the Ratty Hotel when Glen woke up to discover that his guitar was gone. It had been nabbed from under his bed by a thief who had been desperate enough to sneak into adjoining rooms occupied by nine guys.

Glen stomped across the lobby to the front desk. He let his suitcase drop to the floor, pounded the service bell, and began yelling about his stolen guitar. When the desk clerk showed little interest, Glen turned and said very loudly, "The beds have crabs!"

Now the bystanders took notice. Glen hammered the bell a few more times and then reached for his suitcase.

It had vanished.

Exploding, Glen kicked the ashtray stand across the room, where it clanked against the wall. Neal joined in and tossed a stack of stationery into the air. During this visit, Glen had lost everything except the shirt on his back, which he had borrowed from Neal.

We hopped in the car, and Joe Greenberg drove us around as we looked for someone carrying Glen's guitar. Glen was quiet.

"Look on the bright side," Alice said. "Somewhere in Manhattan there's a wino with green velvet pants and a pink Les Paul."

Everyone laughed but Glen.

Joe stopped in front of Manny's Music and told Glen to go in and pick out a guitar and that he would come in and pay for it. Glen walked out of Manny's with a red-sunburst Rickenbacker, but even that didn't pull him out of the dumps. He was so low that he wasn't even complaining. He just flicked his cigarette ash on the car floor.

It's worth saying again that Glen really, really treasured his guitars. He was always fiddling around with them and giving them love and attention. Even later, when we were living the life and getting set up in fine hotel rooms, Glen would transport a soldering iron and screwdrivers from place to place so he could doctor the pickups.

He also loved playing guitar. Once we did a two-nighter at a military base in Colorado. Glen and I were killing time playing eight-ball in the hotel rec room, and he got completely absorbed by a song on the jukebox, Simon and Garfunkel's mournful "Homeward Bound." He grabbed up all the dimes he could and fed them into the jukebox. Then he sat down on the floor and listened to the song over and over until he had the chords worked out. He was completely sappy over it (even if he changed some of the lyrics to being about having some warm pussy waiting at home). Music and guitar filled his soul.

Losing a Gibson Les Paul to some thief—that was bad. His two earliest guitar heroes were Chet Atkins and Les Paul. For all our wisecracks, we felt for him. So despite the success of the movie shoot, once again the Alice Cooper group left Manhattan feeling beaten up.

"When are we going to get something happening?" Alice said.

"Zappa's too busy doing his own thing," Michael responded. "He forgot about us."

In the band's view, Bizarre Records' support had fizzled out. An album was due, but no studio time had been booked. We were used to rejection, but this was our *record company* doing the rejecting. We weren't up to our usual bouncing back in defiance.

Our shows had developed into a string of disjointed "happenings." We maintained a sense of humor, but the solemn sincerity of our delivery suggested hidden significance. Our audiences seemed bewildered, enlightened, upset, or any of a gamut of emotions. They had to ponder if there was a profound reason for Alice to put the brassiere on the suitcase and stab it with a sword. Was there some hidden meaning in Neal's having a woman's face painted on the crotch of his white pants? How does one explain why I sprayed pine fragrance over the audience? It was our version of Dada, and it was fun.

Due to our androgynous looks and reputation, the band lived in a world of negative reactions, even in Hollywood. When we were rushed into Sunwest Studios in Hollywood, we were met by a producer who clearly shared the popular opinion of us. David Briggs had just come from producing an album with his close friend Neil Young, and was still in the thrall of Neil's elegant simplicity. He scoffed at our clothes, scowled at my baby-blue boots, and looked like he deeply resented merely being there.

We really needed another month to write songs for the album, but Joe and Shep wanted to fulfill our contract with Bizarre and move on, so there we were in the studio. Maybe our lack of preparation irritated Briggs.

It was also not very uplifting to listen to the playback of our first song, "Mr. and Mrs. Misdemeanor." We didn't realize how disjointed it was. We quickly steered it to a more relatable treatment. Glen was under the influence of his friend Doors guitarist Robby Krieger when he played the slide guitar part, except Glen did the slide with a spoon.

With the threat of censorship over our heads, our lyrics were juiced up with double entendre. Alice whipped up our contribution to that genre with "Shoe Salesman." Glen responded instantly to the happy melody and added some lovely Chet Atkins–style chords. With Alice and Michael harmonizing, it created such a pleasant, carefree mood that even Briggs's ears pricked up. He came into the studio with us and added a nice piano part. Alice and Michael kept their vocal harmonies simple because we wanted the light, bubbly mood to mask the heavy subject matter. But unlike "Puff the Magic Dragon," our lighthearted treatment did nothing to disguise the song's lyrical drug reference.

Michael wrote "Below Your Means." As we had all agreed on a more relatable musical direction, and even though we hadn't had time to bring it to full realization, the song actually fell into a groove. On this rare occasion, Michael and Glen used similar distortion on their guitars. Neal and I locked in pretty well.

We resurrected "Lay Down and Die, Goodbye" from our Nazz days, but our new recording would be radically different from our original Nazz single. Charlie had influenced the song's new direction by repeatedly playing an avant-garde album by Karlheinz Stockhausen. The German electronic music composer had created "Song of the Youths" from a tape recording of a German boys' choir that he had chopped into hundreds of pieces (the tape, not the choir). Then he spliced the bits back together into a disturbing collage. Stockhausen's complete disregard for traditional musical structure was a big influence on our song. (When Zappa had found out that we admired Stockhausen, he spent an afternoon playing his favorite rare electronic recordings for me and Alice.)

David Briggs looked like he just wanted to be put out of his misery. "Let's record the psychedelic garbage," he said.

Onstage, "Lay Down and Die, Goodbye" had a different mood every time we played it. Sometimes Alice played a squalling harmonica part, and other times he clinked a crystal glass with Glen's slide spoon. Sometimes he shoved the microphone into the monitors for a shrill, ear-shrieking feedback, or scraped the microphone against Michael's guitar strings to create a sound like grinding teeth. Those sounds weren't entirely random; he experimented with them. Other popular enhancements included erotic moaning noises and heavy breathing by Michael. The exploration was the fun of it.

But it was just psychedelic shit to Briggs, and the *Easy Action* album ended up with a pretty flat atmosphere, especially when compared to the graphically intense shows we were doing at the time.

Easy Action made a modest charge on the charts and then whimpered out. We were still hungry for something that wasn't on the menu.

So we hit the road.

If you like the smell of stale beer and cigarettes, start a band and book some bars. If you like being a target for flying beer bottles, book bars. If you like being cheated out of your pay, or getting punched by a jealous drunk because your eye wandered down to his girlfriend's cleavage . . . bars.

Being booked into every dive in the country (not to mention the cockroach-infested rat dens that posed as motels) made us bona fide experts on the subject. If we weren't in those joints, we were all piled into a station wagon that smelled of stale beer and cigarettes.

Back and forth across the country we went, driving and playing, driving and playing. Sleeping with groupies and then driving. Real sleep was a fleeting luxury.

If our "Lay Down and Die, Goodbye" fever dream was a bit much for Briggs, imagine the reception it got in a cowboy bar in Scottsdale, Arizona. JD's was a joint run by Waylon Jennings. Somehow we got booked into the main cowboy bar instead of the Riverbottom Room downstairs, the normal venue for abnormal rock acts.

Fortunately Neal showed he could do drunken cowboy as well as anybody. He swung his legs up into the ceiling rafters and hung upside down pounding his drums. The cowboys in JD's were so amused that they plumb forgot to hate us. Our psychedelia was the furthest thing from the whining country tunes the good ol' boys had come to cry in their Coors over, but Neal had them toasting their bottles and laughing their asses off.

Then there was the Saugatuck Pop Festival, the festival from hell. Alice remembers it now for giving us a shot of energy. That's not what we felt when we arrived, though. The air loomed heavy, the kind of air that could stir up a black funnel in a heartbeat. The Michigan festival site was in the middle of nowhere. Trampled hills rolled up each side of the crowded valley that stretched out in front of the stage. It didn't take a cat's blink to tell us the bikers were rowdy. Motorcycles roared down each hill, through the parting crowd, and up the hill on the opposing side.

A man stood on another hill, behind the stage, with jittery-red heat lightning flashing behind him. He had a shotgun.

MC5 and the Stooges were on the bill, but the headliner was the Crazy World of Arthur Brown. Brown's 1968 single "Fire" had gotten a lot of airplay.

Brown ran out singing "Fire" with his head ablaze, or at least his metal hat had flames lashing out of the top. But even that couldn't grab the crowd's attention. The violence had gained a momentum of its own.

A biker roared down one hill dragging someone behind him on a rope. He pulled the guy through a bonfire that spat orange embers into the air. The hilltop erupted with cheers of "El Toro!" The biker released the rope, and the person rolled to a stop.

"It's our turn," Neal said. "Let's play and get the fuck outta here."

One after the other, we climbed the rickety ladder to the tall, creaky stage. From there we had an unsettling view. I could barely make out anyone save for the folks standing near the bonfires, which were a prime target for the bikers. The whole wicked scene resembled a Hieronymus Bosch painting.

Moments after we began playing, a thud jarred the stage. I adjusted my footing and saw Glen reach back to steady his amp. The bikers had everyone's attention, including ours.

Then the stage took another jolt. This time I could see a bunch of guys down below using a telephone pole as a battering ram.

Now we could see, out in the ugly dimness, two bikers riding down the hill holding a length of chain between them. The chain snagged on a stump and was yanked from their hands.

Things were clearly out of control. I asked Neal if he thought we should stop. Just then the stage shifted back. I braced myself for a fall, but it creaked to a halt. Alice said, "That's it." Glen and I unplugged and climbed down the ladder behind Neal. Michael took his time as if it were no big deal.

Our roadies, Leo Fenn, Ronnie Volz, and Mike Roswell, managed to get the equipment clear before the stage slowly collapsed. Onlookers and stoned-out people mobbed the backstage area. One guy with a crazed looked darted up and asked if he could be in our band.

We packed up our guitars, jumped in the station wagon, and made our creeping-slow escape through the crowd. Neal looked back and said he hoped they'd save his drums.

Alice hunkered down in the car seat: "That was the worst one yet."

9.

BLOOD, SWEAT, AND TOLEDO

WE DIDN'T PLAY WOODSTOCK. When we confronted Zappa and asked why we weren't there, he just said, "Because we don't want to be."

We did see a little history made, however, at the Toronto Rock 'n' Roll Revival a month later, on September 13, 1969. The festival featured a lot of old greats from the '50s, but the event became famous thanks to the mystery headliners: John Lennon, Yoko Ono, and the just-formed Plastic Ono Band. Lennon managed to corral Eric Clapton for the gig, too. Their appearance earned such a hoo-hah (including a documentary and an album) that it gave Lennon the courage to leave the Beatles a short time later.

Like I say, a big event.

We sure as hell didn't belong on that roster. We looked down at names like Chuck Berry and Bo Diddley and felt utterly miscast. But the brilliant creativity on our managers' part had gotten us there. To help us earn our keep, Joe and Shep organized the event and arranged for us to do two performances—our own show and then, validating our place on the bill, backing up Gene Vincent.

We were thrilled with that. Back in the '50s, Gene Vincent had had a lurid reputation of his own. He wore a black leather suit onstage, and the press wrote of him as if he had a dark, sexual force. A man after our own hearts.

The day we met him in a motel room to rehearse, though, we were just wearing jeans and T-shirts. We brought over a small practice amp.

Gene was nervous, and confessed that he hadn't performed in a while and was feeling apprehensive. We poured on the charm and told him how much we loved him. Alice said he especially liked Gene's jumpy classic "Woman Love." The trapped-animal look on Gene's face started to relax.

The hallmark of Gene's hits was a booming, echoey sound, so Glen and Michael got busy plugging a microphone into Glen's Echoplex effects pedal.

Gene tested the mic. His tap repeated in a ghostly reverb. He smiled.

When Glen asked him what song he'd like to do first, Gene stepped up to the mic, closed his eyes, and began to sing, "*Wellllllll . . .*"

Aw, we knew instantly the opening call of "Be-Bop-a-Lula." We'd heard it croon out of a million jukeboxes. And there we were playing it with its originator! I could feel the hair on the back of my neck stand up. Our rehearsal went beautifully, and I couldn't wait for the show.

A beautiful sunset cast an amber glow over the jam-packed Varsity Stadium. While we were preparing to go on, commotion and flashbulbs announced John and Yoko's arrival for a press conference. Everyone with a clearance badge crushed into the backstage dressing room.

Soon, some flunky bopped into our room to get our feather pillow because, he explained, John had said the locker room benches were "too fookin' hard."

We thought that was pretty cool—that is, until it was time for our show and Lennon wouldn't give our stage prop back. We had monstrous plans for that feather pillow. Numerous volunteers went to get it, but they all came back saying John was refusing to give it up.

"What's more important?" Glen said, "our show or Lennon's ass?"

It wasn't like we didn't have any other props. We made big things happen with our tiny budget. For example, we had giant weather balloons to toss into the crowd. Still, Alice masterfully milked the idea of a standoff with Lennon over the pillow, and the press ate it up.

The crowd was getting antsy when a festival worker saved the day by showing up with feather pillows from his nearby home.

The guitars chimed out. I stuck near Neal to make sure I could hear the drums. All my nervous energy went straight down to my stomping foot. As we all kept time, I could feel the wooden stage moving with the beat of the song. Our erratic music was a far cry from our rock 'n' roll, but those roots were still there in the compulsive way we felt the beat. All that energy, with extreme volume, will carry along everyone in its wake, and we soon had the audience rolling like an ocean of floating wallpaper.

Alice crawled to the front of the stage, and the crowd nearly pulled him over the edge. I felt a tug on my guitar cord and saw Michael nearly fall. His boot was snagged, but he managed to stay upright and cue the ending of the song.

Alice staggered back to the drums rubbing his arm. I asked if he was okay.

"Yeah," he said. "Where's my watermelon?"

Neal raised his goggles and said, "I'd like some of those melons in the front row."

I looked at his goofy expression and asked if he was stoned.

"I dropped a tab of Sunshine, and that girl's tits keep swelling up like balloons." Alice and I looked at the girl's tits.

Hissing at jet engine intensity, Neal's cymbals drowned out his voice in what appeared to be a blood-curdling scream.

Provided with a watermelon, Alice heaved it into the crowd. And when it hit, that was our cue. Musically and visually, all hell broke loose. Neal's bass drum thundered like stampeding buffalo. Glen's guitar sounded like a siren, while Michael's squealed for help. Bashing my bass on the stage floor created a low resonating vibration that threatened to pop my eyeballs out of my head. Alice ran back and forth across the stage in a sped-up panic.

For years, it's been repeated over and over that someone in the audience threw the chicken onstage, but that chicken was ours. The chicken idea had originated at a gig at the Eastown Theatre in Detroit. One of Glen's guitar parts reminded me of cackling chickens, so I thought it would be funny to have a couple of them roosting on top of his amp. Thanks to our incredible crew and a Detroit guy named Larry, who got the chickens, we made it happen. The chickens would appear out of nowhere and pose on Glen's amp.

The idea worked so well that we had to take our fine feathered friends on the road. Glen kept them in his bathroom at the motels, where they had plenty of food, water, and attention. They were treated like pets. Glen named one chicken Larry and the other one Pecker.

In a D. A. Pennebaker film of the show, *Sweet Toronto*, you can see Michael falling down with a fire extinguisher and Alice pulling a chicken from a pillowcase. The pillow feathers are flying, the strobe lights are flashing, and the giant weather balloons are crashing on to the stage.

In the stormy confusion, Alice pulled Pecker out of the pillowcase and tossed him skyward. But instead of flying away, like Alice had imagined, Pecker flailed down into the crowd—where he was pulled apart.

This disturbing turn of events passed quickly in the blistering pace of our playing. The lights became blinding as the song climbed higher and higher toward its final crescendo. And when the intensity couldn't scream any louder, our gigantic chords ended in a final resolve.

Feathers still hung in the air as the stadium's applause reflected the crowd's reaction. They were in shock, especially the people in the front, who'd gotten splattered with watermelon and chicken blood.

We were almost in shock ourselves, totally sweaty, covered in feathers, and exhausted from the performance. As we were about to stagger offstage, a guy ran on and ordered us to stay because Gene Vincent was coming on.

Gene Vincent? *Now?* He was scheduled to appear later in the show, but the promoters wanted to validate why we were on the bill, so they'd thrust Vincent out onstage.

The timing couldn't have been worse. We had had every intention of being his faithful backup players, in jeans, T-shirts, and sunglasses. We had wanted to *honor* him, a star we idolized.

Gene walked out onstage and appeared rattled, if not petrified. Who wouldn't have been, after Pecker's bloody demise? And the last time he'd seen us, we were just ordinary guys—not glitter-flaked zombies from Planet Zorg. He looked at us as if to say, *Where in the hell did you guys come from? And what the hell are you wearing?* Although the odds were against him—and not for the first time in his unusual career—the old pro found it within himself to deliver a good set.

While the audience treated him warmly, the stadium was still buzzing about the chicken, and still was when we left. As for the story of the audience throwing a chicken onstage, that was concocted to get us off the hook with animal protection organizations, who, after the "Chicken Incident," showed up at every Alice Cooper gig to prevent our murdering chickens, which we never did!

What did people see in us onstage? Alice Cooper didn't fit into any existing category, so the critics invented categories to put us in. "Glitter rock," "theatrical rock," and "shock rock" were the ones that stuck.

Even in the earliest days, my mom made my stage shirts out of satin because I liked how the material reflected the lights. And Alice's mom joined in by making matching gold corduroy jackets for the Earwigs and sharp-looking black jackets for the Spiders.

But it was Cindy who'd designed the striking clothes that set Alice Cooper apart. She was the one who drew designs, hunted down unusual fabrics, created her own patterns, and constructed most of what we wore. She usually did all this overnight, and always on a tight budget. So, unless you count perhaps Liberace, Little Richard, or maybe Elvis in his gold suit, Cindy was the originator of that chrome, sparkly look.

We were punks in shabby, ripped, sequined clothes held together with safety pins. Our hair now went to our waists, accessorized with bent forks, chicken claws, and rearview mirrors. We looked ambiguously sexual and sinister. Any parent would have thought we were a threat to their children.

One night, when we were set to play the Eastown Theatre in Detroit, Joe and Shep announced that we now had a budget for new costumes. Cindy said, "Fine, get me some fabric. I'll make some jumpsuits."

For the Eastown show, we brought in a shiny, corrugated aluminum background, and from that we got the idea of putting up mirrors and other shiny things to reflect the light back at the audience. Cindy went out and got a bolt of cloth in silver stretch Mylar. But who had a sewing machine? Alice's then girlfriend, Cindy Lang, had parents in the Detroit suburbs, and they had a sewing machine in their rec room. So my Cindy hustled over there and took over the rec room and stayed up all night stitching together our Costumes from Another Planet. The girl knew how to get the job done. It was just breathtaking to see her in action. When we walked on to the stage, the audience beheld Cindy's dancing mind as much as ours.

When we went touring in "these United States" in 1969, we found that they weren't so united after all. Things changed fast every time you crossed state lines.

It was in the industrial towns of the Midwest where the action was most intense. When we hit a big outdoor festival at Raceway Park in Toledo, Ohio, we saw an unruly crowd and a stage where no one seemed in charge. This was a situation we both loved and feared.

"So this is the Big Mahops," Glen said, looking out over the crowd. He'd use that made-up word only if a crowd was truly *big*.

With nowhere else to go, we sat in our station wagon to tune up, only to see a body slam into the windshield. The body slid off, leaving a sweaty blotch. It had started as a football skirmish, but now guys were just shoving each other for the hell of it.

"We're in Toledo, all right," Michael said.

Alice slid his hand into a leather glove, made a fist, and said, "Let's hit the stage, boys."

No sooner were we onstage than a volley of beer cans flew through the air and exploded at our feet.

Michael looked at Glen and said, "Just making nice, huh?"

Alice tried to gain control, but the crowd had a will of its own. He ducked a flying beer can, which hit my bass and burst open.

One maniac managed to get his hands on our fire extinguisher and hurl it into Neal's drum set. Another guy was grabbing my pants. As I kicked at these jokers, they got mad and began to climb onstage to really get us. The roadies Mike Roswell and Ron Volz raced out to shove them back. This only prompted more flying missiles.

I heard Glen moan, and turned to see him fall to the stage writhing in pain. He had been hit in the knee with a hammer. This was so serious that we stopped playing. The lack of music only seemed to magnify the violent nature of the scene. The crowd was out of control.

Roswell helped Glen limp behind his amplifier for shelter, and then he went to call an ambulance. Michael was the last to join the rest of us behind the amps. A glass jug hit my amp and shattered all over the stage. Glen's leg was soaked with blood, so Ron cut the seam of Glen's pants and wound a guitar cord around his leg for a makeshift tourniquet.

"Did anybody see that motherfucker?" Glen said.

"He's a fucking retarded redneck," Neal said.

"A retarded redneck from Toledo," Glen said. "What a fucking loser."

The pelting continued, with no sign of letup. We heard a distant siren. Glen had his arm over his face when the paramedics finally arrived. His face looked frost white as they carried him off on a stretcher. Sirens blasting, the ambulance inched its way out through the turmoil.

When we got everyone else back into the questionable safety of the station wagon, crazy people began yelling and pounding on its sides. Ron drove slowly up a dirt road to the exit, only to see a guy standing there with a baseball bat.

"Hang on, we're not stopping," Ron said, and gunned our wagon through the gates and to freedom.

So, ah-hum, Om, and *Ommmmmmmm*, how do you compare the Toledo audience with what we saw in San Francisco? Alice Cooper actually played a Love-In. It was a free show held at Speedway Meadow, in San Francisco's Golden Gate Park, only a very stoned throw from Haight-Ashbury.

We were still recovering from Toledo—the bandage on Glen's leg was brown with bloodstains. And there we were, outdoors again, with a soothing wind blowing as low, gray clouds rolled over. Occasionally the fleecy clouds parted for a moment and let a wash of amber sunlight pour through.

The stage was a wobbly old wagon that creaked like an ancient ship. Alice beat on a cowbell with a hammer, and Neal joined in with his bass drum. A few people climbed aboard the wagon, but the vibes were peaceful.

A smiling hippie girl stepped in front of me and cupped her hands over my nose. A strong aroma like smelling salts filled my head, and I felt like fainting. In the far distance I could hear a fading voice say, "It's a popper, *maaaaaannnn* . . ."

My heart racing, I fell against my amp and tumbled off the back of the wagon. By the time I regained my senses, some guys had heaved me and my amp back up and I was playing, barely in control. Glen smiled rosily.

My gaze turned to a girl standing in the grass. She looked like Grace Slick. The top of her blouse had dropped to her waist, showcasing a delightful set of free love boobs. Nearby, other girls straddled guys' shoulders and waved their tops in the breeze.

Boobs bounced. The wagon bounced. Everything bounced.

A bearded guy reached up to Alice with a ceramic jug and told him to have a hit of electric Kool-Aid. Alice blew into the spout like a jug band player and banged it with his hammer, causing it to shatter and its contents to splatter. Nobody scattered, because by that point nothing really mattered.

By November 1969, the euphoria of the pothead days had come undone. Taking gentle trips had been replaced by shooting speed and watching friends overdose. A certain loveliness had gone away.

The overlord of the San Francisco music scene back then was Bill Graham, and he just didn't like us. Maybe he was quick in catching what Alice would later claim: We were the band that drove the stake through the heart of the Love Generation. Graham was probably seething about that very thing when he was forced to book us for four days at the Fillmore West. On a typically arcane bill of the day, we were to headline over It's a Beautiful Day and the Ike and Tina Turner Revue.

Graham's sentiments toward us weren't all that sentimental. "Get those motherfuckers off my motherfucking stage. Either they play motherfucking music or they motherfucking act, because they ain't motherfucking doing both!" (Three years later, he'd tell us how much he loved us. "That stuff from before? I was kidding!")

In the Fillmore, loyal San Francisco partisans hooted at us, but some Hells Angels at the perimeter told them to knock it off. Backstage, the Fillmore groupies seemed hell-bent on living up to their reputation for balling the band members' brains out. Some looked earthy, some looked like biker chicks, while others wore bustiers and garters, which fit in well with the old saloon feel of the Fillmore.

Graham was famous among musicians for his personal generosity, but he drew the line at us. We'd find out later from one of his staffers that he had given them strict orders: no drinks or food for those guys.

It's possible that Graham just didn't like our managers. Maybe among the hippie bands he was dealing with, he wasn't coming across too many ballsy New York guys like Joe and Shep.

Shep had a certain style. He could charm people, and he'd talk in this very soothing voice and be very matter-of-fact and gentle about everything. If the people he was trying to convince didn't go for it, he'd shift gears a little bit—still charming them, but with a certain matter-of-factness. Then, when he got to a point where he knew the charm wasn't working, he would *explode*.

With Bill Graham, there were a lot of these explosions. He was probably used to bands bending their rules a bit to please him, but we just weren't caving. Joe and Shep definitely wanted that payment in their hands before we went onstage.

We had a funny run-in with Graham a while later, when we had a gig headlining at the Cow Palace, a cavernous arena better suited to rodeos and basketball. When Graham caught wind of a concert in *his* town, he announced a free concert at the very same time, featuring every damned band in San Francisco. Thanks, Bill. Just the same, our Cow Palace stand must have gotten tongues wagging because, in a big surprise, Graham booked us and the Stooges for three nights at the Fillmore West. They were killer shows, too, even if there wasn't a single bottle of Nehi Orange Soda to share among us.

Playing with the Stooges was always like getting your head smacked. Led by their twisted singer, Iggy Pop (then called Iggy Stooge), they were hellishly loud and brutal. Years later, they'd get recognized as the band that kicked off punk rock.

Our competitive spirit was always stoked high by the Stooges, but how can you compete with Iggy? While his band hammered the crowd into a sweaty panic, Iggy would pour hot candle wax down his bare chest, then dive into the audience and thrash around insanely. Like a traffic accident, you couldn't take your eyes off it.

Besides our sense of rivalry, though, we also felt a close camaraderie with the Stooges. They and the MC5 were the premier bands from Detroit, and whenever we played that town, we always ramped up our performances by several thousand watts. All the Detroit bands had a high-energy style, and that included Bob Seger, Ted Nugent, Savage Grace, Grand Funk Railroad, Brownsville Station, and Cradle, the last, a group of hard-rock chicks featuring Suzy Quatro.

Whatever we were giving, the audiences liked it. Detroit's iron-fisted fans accepted Alice Cooper into the Motor City Bad Boys Club. We began playing more and more gigs out there, and this meant survival for the Coops, even if it was a dingy sort of survival in a cheap motel on the outskirts of town.

Not long after the Fillmore shows, we were in Detroit doing another double bill with the Stooges when we saw just how far Iggy was willing to take it. The crowd was pumping their fists to the gut-pounding beat as Iggy arched his back and flipped off the stage and onto the floor below. He hit hard, but got up and roamed through the hall picking fights.

Backstage, Alice and I sat with the other guys and exchanged war stories.

A groupie barged into the backstage area. She had drippy eyeliner drawn down her face to make it look as if she'd been crying. With great dramatic authority, she carried on with a cosmic explanation of what she thought our band was about. When our interest waned, she asked if anyone would like a blow job.

Playing to the hard-edged Michigan crowds was putting a seriously sharp edge on our skills. Since Joe and Shep were spending more time in New York City, trying to hustle up a new record deal, and we were spending all this time in the Michigan area, it was time we had a real Detroiter as a road manager.

Leo Fenn was a real Detroiter. As a former pro hockey player, he boasted removable front teeth as a badge of honor. He wore panoramic sunglasses and a white fringed jacket with a Vegas Elvis/Beatles hairdo. Like most Detroiters, he loved high-energy rock. Leo spoke fluent Motor City. "Jeet?" (Did you eat?) "Skweet." (Let's go eat.) And like all true Detroiters, he was born to drive a car. He hated road maps. When he got lost, he just drove faster.

Leo knew all the dives and clubs around Detroit. He collected our earnings, budgeted the necessities, told us "Skweet," and nastiest job of all, he woke us up early. Mostly he drove our beer-drenched station wagon all over kingdom come.

We slept two or three to a motel room. The odd man out in the coin toss had to sleep on "the toaster," which was Glen's name for the extra fold-up cot.

This is what a rock-and-roll morning was all about: Leo pounds on the door until I open it. He tosses a bag of donuts on the bed and shouts, "Sko!"

We open the door to another miserable gray Michigan morning. Leo points to the car. We walk toward it like zombies. Michael looks chipper as he parades last night's catch for all to see, before adding her name to his little black book. She sashays back to the sea of lovely groupies.

Glen doesn't show off his groupie, but we all see the trophy: her panties hanging from his belt. Otherwise, Glen is pissed off because Alice is in a cheery mood.

We flip a coin for shotgun. Glen wins and smiles. But before jumping into the front seat, he pours beer on his donut to soften it up.

Double the gigs, double the income, right? That was Leo's reasoning. So we finish one hole-in-the-wall beer joint, load our sweat-soaked equipment into the van, chip the ice off the station wagon windows, and rumble on through the midwestern winter.

Gigs blurred by. For a trip to Toledo from Boston, Leo actually put us on a plane. He chartered an old twin-propeller DC-6. All the seats except the last two rows had been removed to accommodate cargo. After the crew finished stacking our equipment to the ceiling and strapping it in, the band squeezed through. We took our seats in the back.

Our claustrophobic unease was stepped up by the driving rain. The old plane was creaky.

"This makes me think of Buddy Holly," I said.

"Shut up, Dunaway," Glen snapped.

"You can always count on Doctor Dreary," Alice chimed in, "to point out the bright side of life."

It all quickly got less bright. After a white-knuckle hour of flight, the storm grew more intense. Lightning flashed around the fuselage. The plane dropped suddenly. The heavy-duty cases rocked back and forth, and the straps began to loosen. Soon, a mountain of weighty gear began inching its way to the back of the cabin.

We all put our feet up against the sliding gear. Each dip of the plane pushed it into us until it was tight up against our seats. Every arm and leg strained as the plane bounced through the air like a kite. The lightning lit up our faces like ghosts.

The captain's metallic voice rang out from the intercom: "We have a bit of turbulence, but we will be in . . . *[static burst]* . . . Toledo area shortly."

"A *bit* of turbulence?" Glen howled.

After several punishing minutes, the plane did descend. Our muscles were burning from holding off our gear. As the plane taxied down the runway, we slowly unclenched our bodies.

The plane stopped, the doors flew open, and the crew removed enough boxes for us to crawl out. We were actually alive.

"Shit," Glen said.

"I'll see you one shit," Neal said, "and raise you two."

A dark, rolling riff came to me one night in a motel in Buffalo where I sat on the linoleum floor in the glow of the rumbling water heater. I played my bass through a little amp that belched out such a wonderful, growling tone that the riff came out right away. I played it over and over until the wee hours.

Glen staggered in from a party. He liked the riff and agreed it needed some lyrics to match the *Twilight Zone* setting we had by the water heater.

I taught the riff to Glen and decided to hold off writing any lyrics until inspiration hit me. Several hundred miles of bad road later, with us sacked out in a frat house in Cincinnati, the lines did appear. We'd moved into this frat house because some guy said it was going to be empty, so if we wanted to stay there, to go ahead. So there we were, cleaning and settling. I decided to explore the big place.

A long box in a far corner of the attic suggested a coffin. Somehow that thought merged with my tiredness. Then the idea popped into my head that the ultimate resting place was a coffin. I wrote on my pad, "Black Juju." I wasn't sure if I had heard the phrase in an old zombie movie or if I had just made it up. I sang quietly to the imaginary rats, and the lyrics started to flow.

> *Touched by the toil*
> [Weary from working]
> *and plunged into its arms*
> [referring to the arms of mother earth]
> *Cursed through the night through eyes of alarm*
> [the last thing most people see is the fear in their loved one's eyes]
> *a melody black flowed out of my breath.*
> [imagining it as the last song I'll ever sing]
> *searching for death but bodies need rest*
> *Under the soil now waiting for worms*
> [inspired by the classic "The worms crawl in, the worms crawl out"]
> *all that I feel is all that I've learned*
> [we are conditioned to associate fear with death]
> *All that I know is all that I think*
> [we spend our whole lives learning]
> *Dead feelings are cool down lower I sink.*

Drops of sweat ran down the page of lyrics. At that point in the song, I imagined a hypnotic, trancelike segment. I went downstairs to show the lyrics to Alice and waited quietly while he looked them over. He said he liked them. I told him that I had written the song for the dark character he'd done for "Fields of Regret."

We clearly weren't ready for prime time, but that didn't mean we didn't want to stick it to prime time. NBC had a television special called *Midsummer Rock!*, and in June of 1970 somehow we got a place in it. As we drove around Crosley Field looking for the performers' entrance to the Cincinnati Pop Festival, a beer can crashed into the side of our station wagon.

"Are we sure we can do this?" Alice said. "It's going to be on national television."

"This is our chance to do something really different," I said. "Lots of people will see it."

I put a serious tone in my voice as I tried to clarify the new song. We had jammed around with "Black Juju" but never locked in the arrangement. Nevertheless, I wanted to unleash it on an unsuspecting America.

We had snagged five bedsheets from the motel to use on our surprise ending. Alice was to cover each of us with a sheet to emphasize the lyrics "Bodies need rest."

Alice asked, "Does everybody know it?"

"I know it like the back of my ass," Neal said.

Prime time had become smash-mouth time. When we pulled into the backstage area, we looked over the edge and saw chaos. Michael went over to question a shirtless bystander. The astonished fellow sagged woefully. "The pigs are cracking skulls all over the place, man," he said. "They don't want anyone on the baseball diamond. It's roped off, but people can't help it; they just get shoved onto the diamond and the pigs start clubbing them. It's a bad scene, man."

There was no one better at orchestrating this kind of madness than the Stooges, and there they were onstage in full wail. Iggy was in the crowd, defiantly perched on top of a sea of hands. He pointed his finger at the stadium's upper deck and then suddenly disappeared below the surface of the crowd.

If NBC was hoping for a wholesome show, it didn't get it. The police and the fans battled for control. It was like watching a horde of jittery insects swooping and struggling.

"Black Juju" had about as much family appeal as a muddy graveyard. Alice worked out a ghostly, dramatic sketch, which led to his crouching down at the front of the stage and motioning for us all to get quieter. That was our cue to mimic clocks with our instruments. Alice pulled his scarf over his head and held up an oversize pocket watch, which he swung back and forth, chanting, "Sleep, sleep, sleep. Bodies need their rest." Then, softer: "Rest . . . rest . . . rest."

Something hit Alice in the face, and his head veered back. The microphone thud sounded like Muhammad Ali's glove.

He'd been hit by a piece of cake! The spell was now thoroughly shattered, so he paused and thought about how to recover.

We always encouraged spontaneity onstage but did not like having our hypnotic drama spoiled by a cake assassin. Alice grabbed a gooey handful of cake, squished it in his hand, and then held it out as though he were choosing a victim for retaliation. The people in the front laughed nervously and leaned back as he approached.

After a couple of fake swings, Alice paused again, looked around, and smeared the gooey gob in his own face.

We continued our hypnosis. Neal tick-tocked on the rim of his drum. His mirrored aviator goggles made him look loonier than a hatter. Glen slid a silver spoon up his strings, which made an unnerving, high-pitched whine. Finally, Alice screamed, "Wake up! Wake up! Wake up! Wake up!"

"Black Juju" snapped back to a full growl. Neal was pounding his bass drum so hard I felt percussive air hitting my pant leg. An escalating urgency flooded the stadium as Glen's guitar solo soared to the upper-level seats.

Drawing strength from that surge of power, Alice went behind the amplifiers and came out waving a bedsheet. He flipped it up and let it float down over Michael. Another sheet covered Glen, which transformed him into a swaying ghost as his guitar wailed its banshee alarm. I crouched down, and Alice covered me, and then I couldn't see.

Alice flipped open another sheet and let it billow down over Neal and his drums, which looked like a snowcapped mountain. An NBC cameraman hustled underneath and zoomed in on Neal's face. Without missing a beat, Neal raised his goggles, winked one turquoise-shadowed eye and blew kisses to all America.

Before Alice covered himself, he flipped his sheet out over the audience. The sea of arms grabbed it, and Alice braced himself for a tug-of-war, and nearly got yanked off the stage. He let go and dove under Neal's sheet.

If any of the national television audience remained, they had to have been wondering what those gyrating lumps were doing under the sheets.

It occurred to me that our visual cues were not going to happen under there, so I sent out a rolling bass line. The others fell into step. We were laughing as we finished, emerging from the sheets, and Neal's grin was the biggest. We ambled offstage, happy that our concept of pissing off the establishment had apparently been a total success.

We learned later that the television broadcast differed radically from the actual live event. All traces of the violence were omitted. The announcers had called the action play by play as if it were a sporting event.

Nobody had anticipated an eye-shadowed drummer blowing kisses to a national television audience. NBC's phones were ringing off their ever-loving hooks.

That night we slept in beds without sheets.

10.

THE FREAK FARM

LIVING IN CHEAP MOTELS had lost all its charm. So Leo Fenn found us a farmhouse in Pontiac, Michigan, about thirty miles north of Detroit. We perked up. The house would allow each of us to have his own room again. Best of all, it had a barn with a large, heated workshop that would be perfect for rehearsals. Several acres of property meant we could play late without bothering the neighbors.

Michael got busy moving his things into the nicest bedroom in the house, which he would eventually decorate with decent furniture and an upright piano. As in all his rooms, everything would be organized and the place would have a tranquil atmosphere.

Cindy and I claimed a small bedroom with a bathroom. Because she and I were accommodating, people would come through our room to use the bathroom. The newfound privacy allowed me to start drawing and painting again, so I painted a portrait of Cindy and an actual-size drawing of my erection titled *Lower Self Portrait*, which I thought was a humorous extension of myself. Cindy helped the drawing's subject hold interest during the session.

Alice had gotten serious with Cindy Lang, a former model with dark brown hair and big brown eyes. The two of them shared a room on the second floor with Charlie, and Cindy L. decorated it nicely with a few modest antiques and a plush wall tapestry. Their room was very comfortable and welcoming, unless the door was closed, which meant humping might be in progress. Charlie would always leave, of course, so they could have privacy.

Right across the hall was Neal's room—or kingdom, I should say. It was like a clash between a king's parlor and a sleazy bordello. He pasted up flocked red-and-gold wallpaper and painted the trim and the windowpanes black. He hung a glassy-eyed deer's head above his bed, and his standing coat rack was draped with leather belts and topped off with a gold-sequined black sombrero. Several pairs of towering boots stood in one corner, including the boot with the bullet hole in the ankle.

Glen looked around at the occupied rooms. "What am I supposed to do," he moaned, "sleep in the garage?"

"Why don't you use the dining room?" I said. "It's bigger than my room. Plus, it's got a fireplace."

"Then what are we gonna do for a dining room?"

"Who needs a dining room? We don't have any food."

We put quilts over his doors, and Glen taped Reynolds Wrap over the windows, stacked his *TV Guide* collection (in chronological order) on the floor, stuck knives in the wall, set the hands on a broken clock so it would always be midnight, and created Glen's signature mess.

Cindy closed the quilts over the doorways, and the room darkened. Glen smiled broadly and told us that if we ever wanted to hang out in his room, we could. "Just knock before you come in," he said. "But make sure you knock on the quilt, so I won't hear you."

The roadies nailed plywood over the screens on the front porch to create their sleeping quarters, which they decorated with smelly socks and a monstrous stereo. This area became the Stag Lodge, featuring loud decibels and beer served at room temperature, which was plenty cold. You didn't need to be in the room to hear the music. You didn't even need to be in the house. Any volume pansies risked being run out of Detroit by mobs with tire irons.

At times the living room seemed as busy as a bus station. A couple of worn chairs were plopped down in the TV's ever-present glow. In one corner stood a larger-than-life theater standee from *Some Like It Hot*, of Marilyn Monroe playing a ukulele.

"Here's yer per diem," Leo Fenn said one day, handing me a five-dollar bill.

"What's a per diem?" I asked. "Per diem must mean very small amount."

"Ya gotta make it last," Leo said, "'cause yer not gettin' another per diem till next week."

Within two days of any per diem dispersal, pockets were empty. For the other guys, per diem meant Budweiser. When Leo got cornered for an advance on future per diems, he started sawing an air violin in sympathy. He proved to be an air violin virtuoso.

"I looked up *per diem* in the dictionary," I told Leo. "It said day by day, not week by week."

I got an air violin in response. But Neal was much tougher and could wear Leo down with his demanding tone. He also made lots of phone calls to Joe and Shep's office, as did Michael.

The kitchen had a magic refrigerator: Put something inside and it disappeared. The whole kitchen was no-man's-land. The cupboards were the color of gummy varnish. The wallpaper was the color of congealed bacon. Against one wall, surrounded by a giant grease stain, sagged what I called the Death Stove.

Since the fridge had no lock, everybody hid their six-packs. Beer was like prison currency in that house. Bartering, theft, and poker determined who had the beer. Boone's Farm Apple Wine also had a run of popularity in the Cooper household. It kept us inebriated and regular. As Michael said, "A bottle a day keeps the doctor away."

The place became a rocking farmhouse. With all the Cooper bedrooms claimed and girlfriends abounding, there were times when it sounded like all the headboards were simultaneously banging against the walls.

No one could accuse the girls in our lives of liking us for fame and fortune; we had neither. And they were pretty. More important, they were pretty. The group's sexual promiscuity wasn't as decadent as our image suggested. Our relationships were orgyless. In quantity, if anyone kept count, Michael probably tallied the highest number of girls.

Some groupies gained more lasting fame than the fleeting flavor-of-the-week rock stars they admired. They were passionate about the music they liked, and they would travel to the ends of the world to make their favorite musicians feel as good as the music had made them feel. And in many cases, the term *groupie* carried an elite status.

In the volume category, Glen and Neal ran neck and neck for second place. And even though Alice and yours truly were tied for last, we always had big smiles on our faces.

Alice had met Cindy Lang in LA, and they lived together at the Landmark. She dressed like a *Vogue* fashion model and was strikingly beautiful. She and Alice were fun to be around. Her quick wit complemented his like a matched set of throwing knives.

I had the distinct advantage of having a girlfriend who not only designed and maintained the band's stage costumes, but also patched everyone's street clothes. She also patched up tattered egos, and that was another reason the band liked having my Cindy around. Cute and feminine and sometimes naïve to the point of being gullible, Cindy also possessed an uncanny ability to see the truth in people's remarks and actions. Since everyone knew they could get an honest, level-headed opinion from her, folks began to turn to her with their tales of agony, even things she didn't always want to hear. She had more people crying on her shoulder than Ann Landers. ("And it's such a nice shoulder, too," Glen would sigh.)

The truth is, of course, a rare commodity in show business. Out on the road, a band gets showered with so many compliments, it's like walking through a Macy's parade of flattery. Delicate issues get dodged, and tough issues are banished. But Cindy would lay it all out.

Going back to the Arizona days, the guys were protective of Cindy, as if they were all her big brother. She recalls now how the guys would rat me out if I met another girl on the road. The minute we got back, they'd rush right to her with the full, lurid story. Although it wasn't like him to do it, even Alice joined in on the tattling, or he'd tell his Cindy, who'd tell my Cindy. I don't think anyone intended to stir up trouble. It just seemed like our indiscretions were more newsworthy because we came off as a bit old-fashioned. The guys weren't good at keeping secrets, and the other girls relished proving to Cindy that true-blue loyalty was unfounded with any rock musician. But my Cindy was determined to keep the two of us together.

As a nighthawk, Glen attracted other creatures of the night. It was the only way anyone could get to know him well. If a new acquaintance had a regular job with regular hours, Glen had an uncanny knack for converting him or her to his, uh, lifestyle. As his parade of lady friends rolled in, one by one, he gained a reputation for hooking up with the unlikeliest, straitlaced girls: a nurse, a teacher, a librarian.

One day it was a bright-eyed girl with blue shoes that matched her blue purse and the big blue buttons down the front of her tan dress. "I'm sorry, but I've never heard of your band," she said sweetly. "I don't listen to rock music." She might have looked as sweet as a Sunday school teacher when she walked into Glen's lair, but she didn't look quite the same the next day when she shuffled out. Her dress was wrinkled, her hair was ravaged, and she had one blue shoe in her hand. Her woozy expression said that she didn't seem to mind her condition.

In contrast, another of Glen's acquaintances seemed like a perfect match. The household got livelier when Moira showed up. She was a redhead with a cherry bomb personality. Even sharing Glen's late hours, Moira managed to look good day and night. Sometimes we got to hear her screeching as she built toward her climaxes, and it was usually such a long climb. Cindy and I would be muttering, "C'mon, have an orgasm already. Put a sock in it!"

Neal shared his room with Eleana, whom he'd become friendly with when the band lived in Hollywood. She was a pretty girl with golden skin and raven black hair. Both Eleana and Neal had hellfire tempers, so there was lots of fighting and making up. Neal gravitated toward stormy girls. Yelling, screaming, slamming doors, breaking glass, nuclear blasts—anything seemed possible. And Eleana was the stormiest of them all. As his sister Cindy recalls, "Lots of door slamming with Neal's girlfriends in those days."

Michael spent a lot of time behind closed doors. With the number of women in his life, he appeared to be doing a juggling act. Keeping their names straight was tricky—that is, until Kathleen arrived. She had curly golden hair, a square, pretty face, and a restrained, quiet demeanor. She didn't participate in the sarcastic humor that ruled the household. Not that she disapproved; she just didn't have the lightning-quick wit required to survive our particular jousting tournaments.

The ladies were proud to be hot stuff. When we'd go off to a gig, the station wagon would be barely out of the driveway before Cindy Lang, Moira, and Eleana went cruisin' for fresh meat. They were not going to sit around waiting. Cindy Smith was their designated driver, but they had to hear her lecture them about staying out of trouble. They would party until the band returned from partying. Then we would all really have a party.

So much time on the road made a relaxing evening at home *seem* heavenly. But one never happened, because people always showed up to hang out "Motor City Style"—and they rarely left until the party supplies ran out. Then they would drive off to get more shit, and wouldn't return.

Some people crashed on the floor for the night. Things rarely quieted down until the wee hours. That's when the backup beer came out and the relaxing evening really commenced.

11.

SPIDERY EYES

SEPTEMBER 8, 1970, marked our return to Max's Kansas City in New York. The band checked into the Gorham Hotel, and when Alice and I looked out our room's window, we saw the dome of the City Center theater. Staring back at us was a striking poster of a clown's face wearing spidery makeup.

"Alice, take a look at this."

Alice looked out the window and yawned. "That's great, Den."

"You didn't even see what I was talking about. Look at that clown poster down there."

"Oh, yeah. That's really neat." He plopped down in front of the television.

"I've got the feeling that you aren't sharing my enthusiasm."

"I never do."

"I'm going down for a closer look."

Since the clown's spidery eyes had an impact from two stories up, I thought the look would be a great way to get Alice's expressions across to the people in the back row at concerts.

I grabbed a theater program and took it back to the room. Alice now gave the clown's face a closer look while I made my pitch. He agreed that we should go get some of that eyeliner stuff.

When we returned from the drugstore with the eyeliner, we had forty-three cents between us. Seeing Alice's purchase, Neal said, "I *have* eyeliner, you know. You should have asked me."

Alice slapped his forehead and said, "How stupid of me."

"You don't want to use *his* eyeliner," Glen said. "He has cooties."

Alice sat down, propped up his travel mirror, and meticulously applied a couple of lines to his eyes. I watched over his shoulder as the transformation took place.

Alice finished one eye and said, "Hmmmm." Neal and Glen didn't pay any attention until both eyes were done and Alice said, "What do you think?"

"Not bad," Neal said.

"He should know," said Glen, "he's the queen."

Neal grabbed a button on Glen's shirt and asked him if he wanted it. Glen blocked Neal's hand before he could pluck the button off.

Alice looked at his reflection. "I'm not too sure about the stage, but I love it for every day."

Something else happened in New York besides finding Alice his trademark look.

While playing the den of supercool, Max's Kansas City, we didn't see Andy Warhol or any of his painted love children, but the very sound of the band took a pirouetting leap. Facing the withdrawn crowd had gone better than during our earlier visit, although the club manager still gave Alice a hard time after the show for saying "tits" on stage. With his eyes smeared with the new spidery makeup, Alice looked pretty tough defending himself.

"They misunderstood me," Alice said as the manager walked away. "I absolutely did not say 'tits.'" Pause. "Did I?"

Just then, a young guy walked into the dressing room and introduced himself and got right into a hearty pitch. "Hi, I'm Bob Ezrin from Nimbus 9 Productions. I'm a producer who works with Jack Richardson of the Guess Who. That was a great show. I really think you guys have something unique. It's a little rough around the edges, but I can help you capture that energy on a record. I really liked 'I'm Edgy.' That was really great."

Nobody bothered to tell him that the actual song title was "I'm Eighteen."

"We need to get you guys a record deal," he said. "I'll talk to your manager and see what we can come up with." He smiled.

When he left, Glen shrugged. "The twerp's got nuts. I'd offer to buy him a drink, but he ain't old enough."

"Since when did legality ever sway you?" I said.

We went downstairs to the bar. Glen ordered a triple Seven and 7 and tried to figure out how much all those sevens added up to. He soon gave up and asked if I could lend him twenty bucks.

"Was that kid for real?" I wondered. "What has he produced?"

"Do we even like the Guess Who?" Glen asked.

"I like their hits," I said, "but I don't own any of them."

"They make great records," Alice said. "Joe and Shep have been trying to get their producer to come hear us."

"'I'm Edgy'?" Michael said, laughing. "I kinda like that."

"They could use it for a coffee commercial," Glen said.

"This guy sounds like he wants to produce us," Michael said, "so let's see if anything happens."

We weren't aware of the extent to which Joe and Shep had been hounding the Guess Who's producer, Jack Richardson, to hear the band. Richardson didn't see the point and had sent this young associate, Ezrin. He assumed he could then give our band a pass and end all the phone calls. But young Ezrin went back to Toronto with a surprise judgment.

Hearing Ezrin's rave, Richardson said, "If you like them so much, then you can produce them."

This is Ezrin's version, anyway. Richardson himself claims that he was supportive from day one.

Today, Bob Ezrin gets no end of credit for reshaping our music. But let's be clear: He didn't teach us to play our instruments. He wasn't there when we were rocking the VIP Lounge or any of the theaters, clubs, prisons, or festivals where we smoked 'em. But we weren't really writing Top 40 hits, either. Ezrin would change that.

The day Bob Ezrin first appeared at our Pontiac farmhouse, I was wearing green satin pants and a frog mask that Cindy said she got for me "because you look like a frog when you smile." (I vowed to say "Ribbit" till she kissed me.)

"A frog, huh?" Ezrin said, looking at me and smiling thinly. He had come that day to begin preproduction on our first album for the Warner Bros. label. He glanced over to see Glen, who was staring at a gangster movie on TV. The house now had a pet monkey named Otto Fellatio, who had mastered the art of self-gratification. When Ezrin dropped his bag, Otto screeched. "What a cute monkey," Bob said before he realized what the monkey was doing. "Is that monkey doing what I think it's doing?" he said, looking ill. When I responded with, "Ribbit," and he looked even more forlorn and asked where Alice was.

"Upstairs," Glen said, "but I wouldn't go up there if I were you. He's recovering from a sex-change operation."

Having a house full of strangers was the norm. The only way to have any semblance of a private life was to blot things out. At that point, for us, Bob Ezrin was just part of the everlasting parade.

That morning, the girls whipped up some omelets, toast, home fries, and a pot of java. Everybody joked around over breakfast, and then we all headed down to the barn.

Bob kicked off our rehearsal with a chat. "I wouldn't be here if I didn't think you guys were on to something really cool," he said. "But it's raw and unfocused and needs to be refined. That's where I come in. We've got to capture that sick, demented power you projected onstage at Max's and make it happen on a record. Nobody knows what Alice Cooper is, not even me, so we are going to invent Alice Cooper."

The rehearsal room was not just our exclusive territory, it was sacred turf. It's where the band's innermost feelings spilled out and got dissected. Growling amplifiers and loud voices sent out a message to all girlfriends, managers, and visitors to keep their distance. Charlie and our road crew could attend, but they had to leave the music to us.

Suddenly, here's a new guy barging into our inner sanctum, intending to shape our music and our image. These were precious things we had all fought long and hard to develop and maintain, and we held them close to our hearts. Over the years, we had never met anyone outside the band's inner circle (including Frank Zappa) who really understood the true intent of that image. We had watched while the outrageous nature of our vision triggered a constant stream of misinterpretations and press beatings, of which we had grown weary. So, it was with sharpened skepticism that we welcomed Ezrin, who was a year younger than us. He was to be initiated by the fire of our cutting sarcasm. And the only way he would earn his inclusion was by firing right back.

"That's an unusual bass," Bob said that first day.

"It's a Gibson EB-0," I said. "When we were in Phoenix, I took it out in the backyard at my parents' house and spray-painted it metallic green. I used the same paint that I used to paint one of my model cars with. And then I glued these mirrors all over it to symbolize that Alice Cooper reflects society. Onstage, the spotlights bounce rays of light all the way to the back of the room. Cindy calls it the Frog bass."

He laughed. "You really like frogs, don't you?"

We fired up our amps and played a complex string of musical ideas for him.

"You just played enough ideas to make ten different songs," Bob responded. "That's a whole album! Why don't we start with 'I'm Edgy'? I really liked that at Max's."

Michael said, "You mean 'I'm Eighteen'?"

Bob looked surprised.

Michael sat down at the Farfisa organ and began the moody intro. The rest of us came in with the same bluesy embellishments we always played on our sprawling stage version, except this time it was more soulful than edgy.

"Forget the bluesy intro," Bob said. "Let's start with an instrumental chorus."

And so he whittled our epic down, dissecting each little part to make sure everything worked and was tight. The song still had the same message, but now it boasted a more uplifting feel because it was more concise and to the point. The band agreed that we would record that version and play our original version onstage.

The working relationship with our new producer seemed cool, so we began our long, rigorous schedule. Mornings began around ten. After a quick bite to eat and some coffee, the band would migrate to the rehearsal barn and start working. Bob would come and go, but with only a few breaks, the band would barrel through the day and into the night. On average, we worked about ten hours a day.

The most noticeable difference initially was that Bob cut out the fat, and we therefore got a lot more accomplished in less time. The tedious process still consisted of trying out everyone's ideas, but Bob helped us sort through them faster.

I was especially pleased at how indulgent Bob was of my abstract experimentation. I liked unusual patterns, but they ultimately had to be made palatable to the mood of the song. My search-and-refine process took a lot of time. Bob remained patient while I sorted through an infinite number of patterns. But when I hit on something and began to zero in, he'd jump into action, adjusting a note or two, checking the bass drum and guitar chords to make sure everything was compatible—and in a flash, my abstract idea would be harnessed.

I liked to change my rhythm pattern drastically in the middle of a song, for example, switching to a double-time pattern with eight notes instead of four. This sometimes required the others to change their parts. My bandmates had learned many years earlier that I was obsessive about this approach, and Bob recognized the value of it right away. If he hadn't, I may have been forced to follow root notes like most bassists.

There are dozens of great songs I love where the bassist dominantly sticks to playing root notes—if the guitar is playing a C chord, then the bass will play a C note, and then D under a D chord. This method serves songs perfectly, but it wasn't enough for my own personal style. Still, my variety of notes had to serve all the needs of the song. It was a complex puzzle guided by feel.

I might have been influenced in this by Paul McCartney, who liked to write bass parts that were countermelodies—or at least a little bit different from the lead melody. If McCartney's singing hadn't made him so famous, he would have been referred to as one of the greatest bass players of all time.

Neal pounded various beats until new ideas showed up like King Kong from out of the jungle. Neal's powerful ventures sharply contrasted with my ethereal flights. But we understood that once we found our parts, following some give-and-take, we would lock in. I could tell when that happened because it would sound like a locomotive rolling through town.

This chaotic trial-and-error period, during the sensitive early stages of a song's development, usually rendered the rhythm section unstable. Neal and I were distractions. Glen once called us a royal pain in the ass. It most certainly was frustrating to Michael, who would have been content if Neal and I had played the obvious pocket so he could get on with developing the tune the way he imagined it. But that rarely happened, because Neal and I were hell-bent on obliterating obvious pockets. Our spirited determination demanded some toleration. Still, we often hit on things that influenced the direction of the songs.

Flowing over our undercurrent of rumbling turmoil was an ever-changing stream of chord changes, key changes, lyric changes, and arrangement changes. A song could significantly change several times a day, although not always for the better. Yet whenever we painted ourselves into a corner, Glen was always there to remind us to just go for the feel.

Bob wisely recognized the value of our quirky method and allowed us to get our ideas rooted before jumping in and nurturing them to full bloom. His expert knowledge of music served well as a stabilizing factor.

In the time between *Easy Action* and Bob's arrival, our chops had already come together with real strength. Ezrin did, I will say, teach us in a big way how to get a song ready to record. His guidance definitely kicked everything into overdrive.

Ezrin had an uncanny ability to remember most of our parts from the previous day, and this kept a lot of good ideas from drifting away in a cloud of smoke. Without his recall skills, we'd have lost a lot of the music we made in our experimental modes. Bob would say, "That's not what you were playing yesterday. The bass drum went boom boom baboom, boom boom baboom, and Dennis played an E-G-A pattern, and the anklebone's connected to the thighbone . . ."

We would reply, "Huh?" We were like an ever-shifting ocean, and Bob was the navigator.

On my mission to make Alice Cooper as different as possible, I pushed for bigger builds, more unique chord changes, more dissonant notes, and more left turns without signals. I blurted out my inspirations the instant they popped into my head. Most of them were far too abstract to take seriously, but the conceptual approach kept stirring up the creative climate in the practice room.

Michael could be as patient as a saint with my Quixotic quest for the elusive "big build." My vision was clear in my head, but I had trouble verbalizing it. Michael would run through chord after chord until I would say, "That's it," and everybody would sigh in relief.

One day, Alice sat slumped in his chair, beer in hand, staring at a blank page of a yellow legal pad. He looked as if he'd been shot with an elephant tranquilizer. All of a sudden, he leaned forward, set his beer on the floor, and started scribbling away as if trying to catch up with his thoughts. When he finished, he retrieved his beer and stood up.

"Here's the bridge!" He jabbed at the air to emphasize the notes: "Deer, deer, *deeeeer, deeeer*." He loved conducting songs like his hero Burt Bacharach. Musically, Alice's ideas were simple but effective.

Glen leaned across his guitar and said he had one little suggestion. The ash fell off his cigarette as it flipped up and down in his mouth.

Glen's idea had sprung from his guitar part, which he now played. Alice nodded. "Yeah, that'll work." Glen's guitar part thus affected the bridge in a fairly significant way. The discussions about song credits would come later.

So when he arrived, Bob Ezrin didn't come upon an indecisive band floundering for guidance. He walked into a hive of killer bees stingingly protective of their honey.

Michael stepped up to the microphone and sang:

What have I got that makes you want to love me?
Is it my body or something inside me?

As Glen and I watched his left hand to pick out the chords, and Neal joined in, Michael went on about a girl who couldn't see the real person behind the "rock star" image.

I told him it could be a monster hit if Tom Jones did it. But a sinister character, I said, wearing mascara and shoddy tights, would give the song an entirely different meaning.

Alice picked up Michael's lyric sheet and put on a bawdy twist: *Have you got the time to find out who I really am?*

Now it was provocative. In in my opinion, rousing curiosity was the Alice Cooper group's calling card.

Michael's cutting guitar tone pierced through everything in its path as he launched into an uplifting song called "Caught in a Dream." As we worked out our parts, Bob began to fine-tune the arrangement. It didn't need much. Michael took the leads while Glen handled the rhythm. Alice sang exactly what Michael did, but by now his maturing voice added strength. Michael's song proved to be pure, effortless fun.

"Second Coming" came from Alice's strong lyrical imagery, which seemed to reflect his religious upbringing. The words felt right for the album, especially after Bob Ezrin enhanced the melody with a sophisticated piano part.

I only know that Hell is getting hotter
The devil's getting smarter all the time

    I watched Ezrin's left hand and let it influence my bass lines. Glen and Michael quickly adapted these configurations, and soon enough the complex classical patterns became effortless and a strong unified feel took hold. It was unlike anything we had ever done.

    Michael, however, felt that the treatment was too classical for the band's edgy image. I kind of liked it, but didn't argue. Glen recoiled completely from the argument. Learning lines like that seemed like high school all over again, and Bob was an authority figure and therefore an object of mistrust. Glen shuffled off and cracked, "Next he'll want us to sing like choirboys."

    Despite Bob's first taste of friction, we felt we had put in a good day's work, even though, back at the house, Michael continued his anticlassical argument into the wee hours, rekindled it over breakfast, and then dogged us with it back down to the rehearsal room.

    Once the subject had been beaten into the ground, we ran down "Second Coming" again. This time, Michael and Glen came up with some nice countermelodies, and the song gained more strength.

    The sense of fun returned with another song, "Sun Arise." In 1961, it had been a hit for singer and cowriter Rolf Harris, who'd had an earlier hit with "Tie Me Kangaroo Down, Sport." Alice had bought it back in our high school days, and we'd liked it ever since. Alice hummed the droning sound to present the song to the rest of the band. He sang "sunnnnnnnriiiiiiizzzze" and pointed to the guitars to answer him. He sang again, pointed, and was answered again. He decided to have the guitars play a droning melody.

    I suggested a "big build," and with Neal's percussive attack, the song came to life. Bob, Michael, and Alice developed the elaborate "row-row-row-your-boat" overlapping vocal section that built through to the ending. In the studio, the round would reach even greater heights with the addition of a female vocalist.

    Everything felt like it was in high gear. Neal got an endorsement deal from Slingerland drums, and soon a shipment of eighteen silvery, sparkly drums arrived. When he got them all set up and tuned to the guitars, he looked as happy as the first lark of the morning.

The combination of having better equipment, our own house, our own secluded practice room, and this new Boy Wonder from Canada gave us the underlying feeling that something big was about to happen.

To add to that feeling, Bob Ezrin sat in with us onstage for two concerts in Detroit. Bob's impeccable piano and organ playing rounded out the sound, and as a surprise, we played the songs from our yet-to-be-recorded *Love It to Death* album.

Something needed to happen soon. With Joe and Shep in New York, we felt out of touch and under pressure. We weren't sure how much longer we could hold out.

When we listened to cassette recordings of our live shows, one thing stuck out clearly: The dilly-dallying between songs had to go. So we decreed that the guitar tuning had to be fast, and all the knob-fiddling, beer-drinking, crotch-adjusting procrastination was out.

I thought we could heighten the mystery by not talking between songs. Alice liked the concept, so he spoke only occasionally. And when he did, he avoided clichés like "Come on, put your hands together!" or "Hello, Denver! How's everybody doin' tonight?" Instead, he invented his own comments: "Some people say we're crazy, but I think you're all crazier than we are." Or "What's the dirtiest word you can think of?"

The latter line was Alice's way of rebelling against promoters who threatened to withhold a portion of our pay to discourage us from uttering lewd words or making obscene gestures. Ever since Jim Morrison exposed himself onstage during a Doors show in Miami in 1969, all the rock promoters were on edge. So Alice encouraged the crowd to say the dirty words for him.

Michael convinced us that it was only fair to the paying audiences that we develop a more concrete show. After a lot of bull sessions, we concluded that the band had to combine spontaneous abstract improvisations with tight arrangements. So, while maintaining the illusion of total chaos, we began a balancing act.

We had no trouble imagining elaborate stage concepts. In one idea, we'd have a scientific laboratory complete with buzzing Jacob's ladders. Alice would lead an anteater around on a leash—and pour a jar of ants on his crotch. That concept, like most of the others, was financially out of reach. We could barely afford the ants.

Some of our better spontaneous moments couldn't be recreated—such as the night Alice flicked his sword on the strap of a girl's blouse and caused her top to fall down. Other things, such as his twirling a bare lightbulb at the end of an extension cord, could be improved with repetition.

To add more mystery to the show, Charlie killed all the lights between songs. Early on, Pink Floyd had dynamic experimental lighting featuring tricolored electronic strobes. In San Francisco's psychedelic halls, rear-projected blobs of light had become legendary. But Charlie's method of using lights to accentuate the mood within each song set a new standard. Ethereal or explosive, his interpretive lighting magnified the musical moods dramatically. We didn't know of any other lighting designer who could match him.

Alice Cooper had found direction. We planned to replace pot and beads with beer and shredded leotards. Mock peace with mock decadence. Free love, however, could stick around. We didn't want to change everything.

I figured the world would want to find out what made Alice Cooper tick, especially with such a demented lead singer. And I believed that a lack of explanation on our part was key to building that curiosity. That strategy served us well.

I felt strongly that mystery was a powerful tool. The band capitalized on its effectiveness for about a year. Then, to my frustration, little by little, through interviews with our garrulous singer and Alice's sudden interest in golf and schmoozing with the old-timers, it eroded. Years later, I viewed Alice's appearance on the *Hollywood Squares* as the final blow.

12.

LOVE IT TO DEATH

IF BOB EZRIN'S SMILE had been any broader he would have needed a bigger face. "Hi, guys," he said, "come in and meet Jack."

In December of 1970, we walked into the control room of the RCA Studios in Chicago and saw a bearded guy wearing a flowery dress. He was slapping a baseball bat in the palm of his hand. He stood up and introduced himself as Jack Richardson.

This was Ezrin's boss, the big-time record producer we'd been so eager to get.

"That color really suits you," Alice said. "Where do you shop?"

Richardson swiveled his hips back and forth and said, "Oh, this ol' thing?"

"It's just fabulous," Michael said.

Richardson laughed and said the dress looked a lot better on his wife.

The winter of 1970 had us shivering. Back at the farm, it was sometimes so cold that the shampoo froze in the bottle. We'd been on the run as a band for three years and needed a serious progress upgrade. Warner Bros. had been skeptical about our ability to get a hit, so this recording session was do-or-die. Warner had demanded we have a seasoned pro like Richardson on hand.

Richardson pointed his bat at a rough-looking guy sitting at the control board. "This is my Chicago thug, Brian Christian. He's our engineer." The brawny guy looked like he would have been more at home at a Sinatra session.

"Hi, Al," Brian said in a gruff voice. "Hi, guys."

Beaming with confidence, Bob said, "Let's get started." He rubbed his hands together and took his place behind the recording console.

Jack quickly disposed of the dress and took a position on the side. The dress stunt was clearly his way of telling us what he thought of guys who went by the name Alice. But by this time we'd heard every crack there was from men who felt the need to show off their manly bona fides. Did Richardson hate our guts? We weren't sure.

Whatever the producing dynamic, the situation was clear: We needed a hit. Our two previous albums had been rush jobs, but this time we had a more reasonable budget. We weren't showing it yet, but we were stressed.

"Let's start with 'I'm Eighteen,'" Bob said. Neal set the tempo, and we ran it down.

Bob's voice rang over the monitor: "Glen, you're playing a major scale against a minor chord."

Glen scratched his head and said, "Whatsa matter, don't you like jazz?"

When we listened to the playback through our headphones, it sounded a lot looser than any of us had expected.

"I think we can play it better when we're warmed up," I said.

We ran it down until the fourth take, which Bob liked.

"I still think we can do it better," I said. I thought it felt sterile compared to our live version.

"It's great," he said. "Let's move on. Let's do 'Is It My Body.'"

We went for a take. Jack Richardson pushed the talk-back button and said, "The timing's all over the place." A silent discussion took place behind the control room glass. Jack said he would pull the timing together by beating on an aluminum ashtray in the control room and feeding it to us in our headphones. When they were ready, Brian

Christian pressed the talk-back button and said, "Take off the hockey gloves and try it again, you carps."

After nailing the song, we decided to go for "Caught in a Dream."

And that's how fast the album progressed, which wasn't unusual in that era. I'm not saying we were at the level of the Beatles recording their first album in just one day, but we had rolled through hundreds of shows by this point and we were a fast-moving outfit that synchronized quickly.

Our only issue was our guitars. We probably spent half of our first day getting the two guitars tuned up against each other. At one point Jack suggested that my Gibson EB-0 was the culprit, and they sent out to the music store to rent me a Fender Jazz Bass. It didn't solve our problems, and the longer neck forced me to change my grip. But everyone agreed that it sure sounded good.

Despite looking as if he'd lost patience, Jack sprang to life for each take. He would stand in the center of the studio conducting, and when he moved with the beat, the whole room moved right along with him. His enthusiasm was inspirational. He was like the Jolly Old St. Nick of rock. We got a number of good takes and packed up for the night.

The next day, we decided to record "Black Juju" with live vocals. We nailed the very first take. Michael was worried about a dissonant note, so we did a second take that was perfect. But we liked the version with the dissonant note more and made that our keeper.

"What should we do next?" Bob said.

Alice said, "How about 'The Ballad of Dwight Fry'?"

Brian asked, "Who the heck is Dwight Fry?"

"He was the juicy-spider-eating guy in *Dracula*," Alice said, speaking of the 1931 movie starring Bela Lugosi. Dwight Frye is the creepy actor who plays Renfield. "And he was the abnormal-brain thief in *Frankenstein*," Alice continued, ever the maestro of showbiz minutiae. And just to be different, we'd changed the spelling of Frye's surname.

I went in the studio, picked up my bass, and sat down next to Glen. I stared at him until he said, "What?"

I said, "Play the most demented guitar break you've ever played."

He slid his hand through the air. "It's a breeze, man."

The red light flashed on, and Michael started the song with an acoustic guitar. When the song came to the lead guitar break, Glen's head slumped forward in deep thought as his notes melted like one of Salvador Dalí's clocks. As I played along, I stretched my bass strings slightly out of tune to accentuate his disturbing sound.

It was an exceptional guitar break. The demented interpretation of an asylum inmate was, for Glen, an effortless task. That was his talent. You could ask him to play sunny sky, or mud, or a big moon, and he would do it. It might be a very strange big moon, but he would do it. He didn't worry about sticking to the proper scales—he followed his emotions. He often joked that he never let the right notes get in the way of the feel. This gave him tremendous freedom.

Everyone agreed that it was definitely the take.

Afterward, Michael overdubbed a doubled track of the acoustic guitar to get a chiming effect. Then Bob showed that he was no amateur: He recorded an Alka-Seltzer plopping into a glass of water, then slowed the tape way down to simulate the sound of an explosion.

"Have you ever heard a recording of a real explosion?" he asked. "It sounds like shit."

But we weren't done for the night. We slammed through Michael's song "Long Way to Go," and got a keeper. Then we walked out of the studio.

It took us five days to get the bed tracks before we were ready to add the overdubs. Brian Christian showered us with his typical encouragement: "Take off the hockey gloves," he'd grunt, "and try it again."

Michael double-tracked all his guitar parts (i.e., duplicated his guitar recordings for a fatter sound), and Glen doubled some of his. Our tuning issues were all over the map. Some songs we had tuned to the Steinway piano, some were tuned to the organ, and still others to a tuning fork. It all had to match, and of course it didn't.

After two days of piano and guitar overdubs, the tracks were ready for the lead vocals. In the darkened studio, Alice sat on a tall stool flipping through the lyric sheets clipped to a music stand. Mike Roswell handed him a can of Budweiser. Alice popped the top, and it hissed loudly through the studio monitors. Leaning into the mic, he said, "Beer makes you smart. It made Bud wiser."

"What are you in the mood for, Alice?" Bob asked.

"A milk bath with Julie Christie?" He took a loud sip of beer. "Let's do 'Eighteen.'"

Alice appeared to be relaxed, but he snapped into character as soon as the recording light flashed on. I sat in the control room and listened. We had grown used to hearing his voice through beat-up stage mics that smelled like stale beer. So the quality of this studio's microphone and the clarity of the studio monitors made him sound like a million bucks. I suspected that the expensive studio microphone would soon smell like stale beer as well.

I had a few phrasing suggestions, but didn't want to disrupt the intimate flow that Ezrin had established. The looming deadline had added enough pressure. So I tried to season my suggestions with humor.

"The line 'I've got a baby's brain,'" I said through the talk-back, "is the opposite of Brigitte Bardot's chest. It's flat."

Bob laughed and called for another take. When Alice sang the line again, he cupped his hands in front of him like he was copping a feel from Brigitte Bardot.

When he had every verse and every chorus, we went back to check for any lines we thought could be stronger. Alice made vocal recording look easy.

When we were done, Bob cranked the studio monitors and we smiled through the playback. Nobody was popping any champagne corks, though. Having two failed albums under your belt will calm your fever.

Mixing the album was a mad dash to the finish. Neal would reach over Bob's shoulder and push a slider up. Ezrin liked the guitars *under* in the mix, but the band liked the guitars hot, so he was outnumbered.

Wanting to take full advantage of the latest technology, by 1970 standards, Bob instructed Brian to "compress the shit out of everything." His eloquent technical terminology referred to a device that squashed the loud parts, which in turn magnified the quiet parts so everything was in your face.

We recorded only nine songs, but that was all right with Bob. He said we needed big grooves in the record so we could master it hot—i.e., make a loud record. A longer running time would have meant more, and thus thinner, grooves. Trying to fit too much sound into a thin groove could actually cause the needle on a long-play record to jump and skip.

So the record was loud, and was the best-sounding product we'd ever made.

It should be obvious by now that we worked as a unit. Then a little business discussion occurred that made me stroke my chin and wonder.

"I wrote most of the songs," Michael Bruce said, "and I don't think it's fair to split the writing credits equally anymore."

"I think everything should be split like we originally agreed," I argued. "We all work really hard on every song."

"Songwriting consists of two things," Michael said, "lyrics and melody."

"The group works as a unit," I insisted. "It's impossible to separate who did what. All of us come up with ideas all the time. How can you separate all of that into two things?"

"Easy," Michael said, holding up two fingers. "Who wrote the lyrics and who wrote the melody?"

"Divvying up inspirations is a bad idea," I said. "It'll pull the creative unity apart."

Michael stuck to his guns. Alice voted for individualizing. Neal thought that Michael, to be fair, deserved more credit. Glen just shrugged his shoulders and lit a cigarette. There had been occasions when Michael grumbled that Glen's great guitar break didn't mean Glen should get a writing credit. Glen's personality wasn't wired for business confrontations like this. If things had been settled with fistfights, he'd have been in there swinging. But he was no match for Michael's aggressive tactics on the song credits.

So even though our first two albums had credited music and lyrics to "Alice Cooper," which meant the five of us, now the majority voted for a change. I said I'd support the decision.

Michael got a pad and pencil and we began going through each song, assigning credit. My lack of participation wasn't out of bad sportsmanship but rather because I knew I had suggested a million ideas but wasn't clear on whether they added up to a writing credit. Plus, while I was still mulling over my contributions to one song, Michael would already be on to the next. So credits got claimed, although deservedly, for lyrics and melodies that I felt my dream poems and ideas had inspired.

When the dust settled, I felt overlooked on some songs but generously credited on others. I figured that was fair enough and drew an easy breath that the feeding frenzy I'd anticipated had not happened.

While we could divvy up the songwriter credits, we were certainly not dividing the group. Alice Cooper was the five of us.

From day one, the band had agreed to use the name with the mutual understanding of equal ownership. I clearly remember the night in Phoenix at Lorena Weed's house when we took on the name because it was followed by a stupendously melodramatic session with the Ouija board. At that moment, the five of us agreed that we would only accept the name Alice Cooper as a group name. Our later decision to allow Vince to also use Alice Cooper as an individual name didn't change the fact that we five were the Alice Cooper band.

And I was confident that no matter what changes the future would bring, our original agreement was cemented by the good faith of our friendship. The fact that we had recorded two albums under this group name, and even shared writers' royalties under that one name, well reflected that approach. And Neal made sure that every contract we ever signed specified Alice Cooper as five guys sharing equally. We were the Five Musketeers; all for one and one for all.

One evening in February 1971, all the guys gathered in the cold room back at the Pontiac farmhouse. Our roadies Ronnie Volz and Marty Preece had put together a tremendous sound system out of misfit parts they'd gathered in our travels, and now they were playing the hot-off-the-press acetate of *Love It to Death* at skull-pounding volume.

Way across the field was a big prison farm. We were sure the inmates could hear our Frankenstein sound system pretty clearly. Usually when they liked something, they would send up a cheer that we could hear across the field.

All this noise was a setup for our brainstorming.

To do this fine thinking, we didn't get strafed. Anyway, decent pot was scarce in Detroit. By the time it had filtered through every town from Mexico to Motown, it had been reduced to stems and seeds. ("No class," Glen would opine, gazing in disgust at the dismal stuff.) With no reasonable high at hand, the Detroit drug culture was fueled by chemicals such as crystal mescaline and PCP, which would later get the innocent name Angel Dust. I joked about its being concocted in some unknown basement by a guy with three eyes. To say these drugs inspired mood swings would be to call a tornado a change in the weather.

But that night, the roadies had scored some killer weed. Alice and Neal didn't smoke pot, but the rest of us abstained only during recording sessions, live performances, radio interviews, and other occasions that required a natural level of stupidity. As a rule, our favorite bud was Budweiser; that was king with the Coops. We did notice, though, that Seagram's whisky was growing excessively popular with Alice and Glen.

Celebrating with cold beer and a joint, yelling to be heard over the music, and patting ourselves on the back for the new record, we looked toward our next act.

"Come on," Alice yelled. "Let's get serious."

"How about an execution?" I yelled.

"The Cage of Fire?" Neal yelled. Everyone laughed.

"Hey, according to the Ouija board, you're a witch, right?" Michael yelled, "So how about burning you at the stake?"

"And we could roast marshmallows," Glen yelled.

"A gallows," I yelled.

"How would we fit that in the station wagon?" Michael said, laughing.

I yelled, "An electric chair!"

"Yeah, let's fry him," Glen yelled.

Michael yelled, "We'll tie you to a stake and light a fire under your feet."

"Wait a minute," I yelled. "An electric chair. We'll electrocute him."

Alice yelled, "Where are we going to get an electric chair?"

"I'll build one," I yelled.

"I'll help you," Marty yelled. "What do you want it to look like?"

"Well, let's see," Alice yelled, "how about making it look like an electric chair?"

This is just how it was with us. Who's going to walk out of that meeting claiming full credit for an idea? It was a group of so-called minds leaking on the floor.

It took another late-night discussion to find a reason to execute Alice. During "The Ballad of Dwight Fry," a sadistic nurse was to get strangled by her tormented inmate when he escaped from his straitjacket. The mock murder would be punished by a mock execution, followed, ultimately, by a mock resurrection. As with Quasimodo, King Kong, and Frankenstein's creation, the audience would feel pity for the monster, and Alice would emerge heroic. So we imagined.

Our morality play concept was the culmination of years of random theatrical ideas, the notions we'd considered, molded, argued over, mocked, nurtured, or booted. Now we had this simple concept, elements of which dated all the way back to our Halloween dance at Cortez High School. The music, the character, the crime and punishment—it all fell into place. It was if we'd been striving for this one drama all along.

The band had no resistance to the idea of pushing our villainous character out front and making him the focal point of the show. It was a natural progression. Our hands were busy playing the music; Alice's hands were free. His job as the lead singer was to deliver our collaborative message. Everyone understood this perfectly and felt comfortable being the driving force behind it.

Putting an electric chair into your act—well, it's all a matter of execution.

We were close friends and creative equals. The sum of our energy was the chemistry that made everything work. Alice Cooper was a *group*.

The telephone rang. Leo Fenn hollered in my ear, "Den, turn your radio on!" His high-pitched voice cracked like a whip. "Hurry, they're playing 'Eighteen' on CKLW." I hung up, ran to the living room, and switched the radio to the Canadian AM station. There it was: "I'm Eighteen" blasting from the little speaker.

The phone rang again. I bellowed the news up the staircase, and Alice came sprinting down. He grabbed the ringing phone and stretched its curly cord into the living room.

"It's Leo!" he said. "He says to keep calling the request line as many times as we can!"

He hung up and joined Michael, Glen, and me in front of the radio. When the song ended, Michael said, "It sounds better than I thought it would."

"It sounds pretty damn *gooood*," Glen said.

Neal stuck his head out his door and said, "They're playing it?"

"We're on the radio, man," Glen told him.

Michael went to the phone and dialed the request line.

Alice said wonderingly, "It really did sound good, didn't it?"

"I guess that's why Ezrin kept checking the mix through the little speakers in the studio," I said. "The bass sounds good."

"The bass sucks," Glen said. "My lead carries the whole song."

"Your lead sounds like a fucking kazoo, Buxton," Neal sneered.

"Oh, yeah! Your drums sound like you're poundin' your pud."

"Kiss me, sailor," Neal said, twitching his eyes in a goofy way.

For the rest of the afternoon, Michael, Neal, Alice, Mike Roswell, the road crew, and the girlfriends all took turns phoning the CKLW request line. Finally, Alice suggested it would be a lot easier just to get our friends to avalanche the station with calls.

Within three days, "I'm Eighteen" became the most requested song in the history of CKLW. The station played it every fifth song—it was the heaviest rotation outside of the Beatles. Our personal phone campaign didn't account for the overwhelming volume of calls the station received, though. Apparently, lots of people liked the song enough to request it. For several weeks, if you tuned in to CKLW, "I'm Eighteen" had just played, was in play, or was coming right up.

Although the station was Canadian, its signal reached all over the midwestern United States. We suddenly had a real national reputation.

Having a hit record changes everything, but the funny thing is, we had adapted to stardom long ago. In our overheated imaginations, we had been stars since Cortez High School. Having had an oh-so-minor hit in Phoenix, being taken on by Zappa, having that chicken outrage in Toronto—we always knew we were famous. We were just glad to know the world had caught on to our way of thinking.

After so many years of hard work, hearing "I'm Eighteen" blast out of the radio that day was an expected event, if only a trifle belated.

Our first New York City show of the *Love It to Death* tour was at the prestigious Town Hall. In our eyes, this confirmed that good things were really happening now, and it fueled our confidence and momentum for the tour.

But something else was happening. Besides having a hit, we also possessed new infamy. Even from an audience of swells in Washington, DC, for instance, we would hear shouts of "Where's the chicken?!" This would be followed by a chant: "Chicken. Chicken. Chicken."

Ever since the chicken incident in Toronto, audience reaction had changed. Rumors and wild elaborations flew like feathers in the wind, and no one was more pleased than Alice. He'd hear that a fan was going around saying, "Alice bit the head off a chicken, sucked its blood out, and spit it on a girl's tits," and he'd laugh and laugh and repeat it for anyone who'd listen.

We were kind of used to it. The previous year, a rumor had spread about Alice and Frank Zappa engaging in a gross-out contest onstage. Supposedly a farting duel escalated to the point where Zappa pooped on the stage, and Alice seized the victory by scooping up a handful and eating it. For a long time after that, fans would lick their hands and give Alice a thumbs-up.

Sometime in 1971, Joe Greenberg took the band to lunch with the writer Lester Bangs. (Years later, Bangs would be memorably portrayed by Philip Seymour Hoffman in the Cameron Crowe movie *Almost Famous*.) Bangs recorded our conversation for an article, then came out to the farm and fired guns at beer cans with us. His story ran in *Creem* magazine, with Alice on the cover without his makeup.

Creem was great, but *Circus* was the first rock magazine to treat us like stars on a regular basis. Its teenybopper format featured bombshells like "Dennis's favorite color is green," which contrasted sharply with the band's outlandish photos. For many teens, these articles were their first introduction to Alice Cooper, and for a couple of years *Circus* subscribers accounted for a substantial portion of our growing following.

But even though some writers were willing to introduce us in a very positive way, negative press still seemed to be Alice Cooper's fate. Much to the band's increasing frustration, the majority of newspaper articles focused on our name, image, and theatrics and rarely mentioned our most passionate asset, our music. We were humbled when some great musicians—even Bob Dylan!—voiced their appreciation for us. But we were usually frustrated when we read our press.

A squirming snake came dangling down in front of my face. I was backstage at the fairgrounds in Tampa, Florida, in January 1971, catching my breath after a nice encore. I drew back from the snake and looked up. There was Neal, holding the snake and grinning.

"It's a boa," he said. "Some idiot threw it onstage."

The snake clung to his arm, its forked tongue flicking in and out.

"I'm not giving it back. If some dumb fuck treats it like that, he doesn't deserve to have it."

So he adopted the boa and named her Kachina, after spirits revered by the Pueblo back in Arizona. Neal took his cuddly new pet everywhere, and when he got back to the Pontiac farm, he draped her across the antlers of the glassy-eyed deer head mounted on the wall above his bed. Whenever you heard a scream, it meant that a girl had entered Neal's room.

"It's creepy to have a snake hanging above your head when you sleep," Cindy yelled at her brother. Then she cautiously reached out to pet the snake.

So Neal went to the local pet shop and returned with an aquarium, a heat lamp, a book about boa constrictors, and a live rat. Suddenly he was an expert on snakes, saying things like *She likes to eat blah-blah-blah,* and *She likes temperatures between blah-blah and blah-blah,* and *You can tell she's a female by looking at her blah-blah-blah.*

Everyone crowded into Neal's room to witness the first feeding. Kachina moved anxiously inside her glass aquarium with its screened cover, which Neal had secured with a brick. Neal slid the cover to one side and dangled the rat down by its tail. Kachina became alert. Neal dropped the rat into the cage, slid the screen back, and replaced the brick. The rat didn't seem to have a clue that it was in bad company.

"What's for supper, ya dirty rat?" Glen snarled.

Kachina remained still until the right moment, and then struck like lightning. She wound her body around the squirming rat and didn't let up on the big squeeze until her victim hung limp. Kachina's jaw disengaged, and in went the rat's head, then the body, then its black, leathery tail. The lump inside Kachina resembled a rat.

"That was theatrical," I said.

"But you feel bad because the rat didn't do anything to deserve it," Alice said.

"We've used chickens onstage," Neal said. "Why the fuck don't we use Kachina?"

Incorporating the boa into the show didn't require any great stretch of the imagination. The snake projected powerful erotic significance.

"You have to handle her very gently after she's eaten," Neal said, stroking the snake as she glided toward Alice's hand one day. "We'll have to plan her feedings. She can't be onstage right after she eats, and she might bite if we try to use her when she's hungry."

Alice listened and contemplated his new partner. Kachina nudged her head inside his sleeve and glided up his arm. Alice's eyes grew big. He laughed nervously and said it tickled. Neal told him to be careful because Kachina might mistake his nose for a rat.

After talking about what song we would use Kachina on, we chose "Is It My Body," which had a slow bump-and-grind section suitable for snake handling. We even wondered about getting an exotic stripper to waltz with Kachina.

To enhance Neal's new theme, Cindy made him a jacket with rats sewn all over it—not rubber rats, but furry dead ones that had crossed paths with a taxidermist.

Kachina was about to become a star.

The tour dates were coming faster, and aside from the occasional roller rink, we weren't playing dives anymore. We were getting good billings, at civic auditoriums, theaters, and festivals. At night we were still returning to motels, but at least we knew the towels had been laundered.

When we went back to LA in July of 1971 we were booked into the Continental Hyatt House on the Sunset Strip. Other visiting rock bands had partied so hard there that it was now known as the Riot House.

We walked into the crowded lobby and were hit up by fans looking for autographs. One guy, though, said my signature wouldn't be necessary and handed me an envelope. It turned out to be a legal summons from Zappa's manager, Herbie Cohen. I handed it off to Joe Greenberg.

Herbie's record company, Bizarre, had lost us to Warner Bros. Herbie, a tough, brawling character who used litigation like some people use a knife and fork, was ready to cause some grief.

But this wasn't the night to think about that—not with the swarming bacchanalia of the Riot House in view. We went up to our rooms, changed into tuxedos, came back down, and climbed into some black limousines.

The Ambassador Hotel was a grand old Los Angeles establishment that had become world famous for its Cocoanut Grove. It had also been the scene, three years earlier, of Senator Robert F. Kennedy's assassination. But on this night, Alice Cooper was about to shake the hotel's dignity with an event that even Fellini might have raised an eyebrow at. Warner Bros. had secured the Venetian Room for a no-holds-barred coming-out party.

Since the Alice Cooper group was to be the main attraction, we had to shine above a list of invited guests that promised an outrageous array of outrageousness.

Throughout the afternoon, a long line of limousines dropped beautiful people off to stroll the red carpet under the hotel's white overhang. The hotel's façade looked like a cross between a flying saucer and a giant wedding cake.

Our limousine arrived fashionably late. With the exception of Neal's red velvet bow tie, Alice's spidery eye makeup, and our long hair, the band had dressed to kill in traditional black tie. The red-carpet crowd cheered.

We entered the Venetian Room. A sizable ice sculpture of Porky Pig stood in the center of a table laden with an elaborate display of food. My monkey suit felt a notch more uncomfortable when I saw the hordes of Hollywood freaks who had ignored "black tie" and gone berserk with their attire. Several girls wore see-through blouses—and there was a lot to see. As I walked around the room, some of the celebrity faces that registered were of actors Richard Chamberlain and Jean Stapleton; the writer Rod McKuen; musical talents Neil Diamond, Randy Newman, and Bruce Johnston; and Ahmet Ertegun, the president of Atlantic Records. They hobnobbed and rubbed shoulders with the GTOs and their brazen counterparts, the Cockettes, flamboyant dudes in drag.

We stopped to watch TV Mama, a singer who seemed to weigh at least three hundred pounds, all of it packed into nothing more than an enormous pair of shocking pink panties. With massive bare breasts swaying back and forth, she belted out some gritty blues. When her song ended, her guitar player announced lasciviously, "She may be TV Mama to you, but she's TV dinner to me."

The Cockettes swished around the room with cigarette trays. One fellow, who wore an enormous red wig with a white flower behind one ear, offered teeny weenies on toothpicks as hors d'oeuvres. Alice accepted a cigarette and said, "A prop is a prop."

Cindy and I made it a point to go over to thank the Warner Bros. honchos Joe Smith and Mo Ostin, who'd thrown the spectacular bash. We chatted with Joe's family a bit. It was his daughter's birthday. God knows what she thought. It had been just a couple years since Joe and Mo came to see us at the Whisky and walked out wondering how they'd explain to the board about signing up a bunch of cross-dressers. Now here they were, getting jostled by the likes of the Cockettes, the Plaster Casters (a duo of groupies who made plaster casts of rock stars' erect penises), the GTOs, TV Mama, and every other variety of pagan flesh. Hey, a hit record will put anyone in solid with the boss.

At the end of the cocktail hour the band was herded into an elevator to go upstairs to get ready for our performance. The elevator doors opened at every floor, allowing glimpses of wild factions of the party. On one floor, the doors opened to reveal a girl flashing her breasts. Alice laughed and turned to us. "At this point," he said, grinning, "that's not even surprising."

A circle of recognizable faces was formed in the hall just outside our dressing room. As I passed through, someone held a tiny spoon under my nose. I snorted. As I tried to focus, the guy asked if I could play on crystal mescaline.

Oh, *no*. I had just made a big mistake, and the news hit me like a fighter jet blasting through my nostrils. I hurried into the dressing room and told Glen.

"It'll be cool," he said. "It ain't like they're going to fire us or anything."

The show began with Alice reaching up and swinging a crystal chandelier to and fro with his sword. Hands waved in our faces as we delivered a short set in this exquisitely unlikely setting. Halfway through the set, I entered deep space. Based on the froggy expression on my face, Cindy could tell I was tripping my brains out.

Michael, Glen, Neal, and Alice held the show together.

After the set, my body entered an elevator, and as the doors opened on each floor and we beheld various pilgrims in deteriorated frames of minds, I suddenly needed a peaceful environment. I ended up in a roomy coat closet with Cindy and her best friend, Linda, and Linda's husband, Bill. They all thought it was a good idea to bring me back to earth with a gin gimlet.

When we emerged from the coatroom later, we saw Miss Mercy standing on a sofa with a small crowd around her. She pointed at the floor and growled out words that she apparently thought would conjure up the ghost of Brian Jones. Cindy tried to talk her back to reality, but it was useless, so we gave up and headed down to the Venetian Room.

There we had a hellish view of stoned-out guests in pathetic shape. The celebrities had all vanished. Our friend Monica Lauer, who performed the "Mommy, where's Daddy?" voice on "The Ballad of Dwight Fry," buttonholed us.

"Where were you?" she said. "You missed everything." She told us that they had wheeled out an enormous cake with the words "Happy Bastille Day, Alice Cooper" written on it. Miss Mercy had popped out of it and thrown gobs of gooey frosting at the guests. Monica pointed out a newly married couple rolling around on the floor. He wore the gown, and she wore the tuxedo. Both were smeared with pink frosting. Meanwhile, hotel staffers chased a Dalmatian around the room. The dog had enough speed to stop and lick random gobs of frosting and still outrun the waiters.

I felt grateful that our record company would throw a party of this magnitude just for us. Of course, I had no clue that it would all be paid for out of our future earnings.

13.

KILLER ON THE LOOSE

SUCCESS SHOULD BE A BIG APHRODISIAC for creativity, right? Knowing that people love you should make it easier to produce more wonderfulness. But it doesn't necessarily work out like that.

Call it the big conundrum of rock-'n'-roll prosperity. Hitting the big time means having a lot more to do and less time to do it. Deadlines come crashing down on you like a Kansas hailstorm. You hurry and write some songs so you can do a string of gigs and race back into the studio. And, hey, make it snappy, because you've got a radio interview, a photo session, and, oh yes, the groupie with the fluorescent pink sequins on her dimples wants your body.

At least with the success of *Love It to Death*, we knew for the first time that our songs would actually be listened to. Riding high on confidence, we found our abilities at their sharpest.

Michael had proven himself to be a prolific songwriter with a knack for catchy hooks. Alice's vocal spirit had gained a strong edge. Together we had fine-tuned our ability to write lyrics for the Alice Cooper character—sometimes with chilling clarity. Alice could recognize good lyrics when he saw them, and smartly avoided changing them, but whenever there was room for improvement, he was masterful at taking someone else's lyric concept to a higher level.

That had always been the unspoken rule: Any song on the table was open for improvement by the whole band. It was a simple understanding that served us well.

Alice's stage confidence kicked open new doors, too. Never again would he address the crowd with the faintest hint of uncertainty. Instead, he challenged, commanded, and even insulted audiences. He brought that new confidence to the sessions for our next album, *Killer*.

Glen was happy just being able to buy new strings whenever he needed them. That went a long way toward making him feel like a star. He didn't care much about owning brand-new equipment, but he loved being able to say, "I'll take it," especially in pawnshops.

Neal and I knew each other's playing styles so well that it seemed as if we had fused into a single machine. Ironing out particular parts required some arguments, but as far as rhythmic invention, we saw eye to eye. When our playing agitated people, we were pleased. I liked artistic agitation, and he was okay with bigger-than-life agitation.

Michael, Neal, Glen, Alice, and I all shared in the creation of our monster—the character called Alice Cooper—but from a theatrical standpoint, we knew that our monster needed to have the spotlight. So downplaying the collaborative effort that had gone into the Alice Cooper character brilliantly portrayed by Vince/Alice was the group's choice. And the occasions when Alice presented himself as the entirety of that character, he did so with our support.

So Alice stepped into the shoes of this creation, and with astounding confidence, too. He brought power to the character and fed off its power, as himself and as the creation. In our eyes, as our creation strengthened, the duality of the name as a band and as a character seemed well within the public's comprehension. Most people didn't have much of a problem figuring it out.

In reality, however, the band, without fully realizing it, had become a two-headed snake with one head destined for amputation. Alice Cooper (the group) had done things that no one had ever done. But in the eyes of the media, Alice Cooper (our creation as portrayed by our singer) was a singular entity. People began to assume that the entirety of this lead character was one man's brainchild.

We had always known that our buddy Vince, portraying Alice Cooper, was a natural for the headlines. We were comfortable with that—it was part of the plan. So we were secure that everything would stay on track because we were all the best of friends.

As we looked toward 1971, we had a house, a rehearsal room, decent equipment, a record label, two great producers, and our share of good-looking girls. *Killer* was going to be one hell of an album.

I opened my lyric book and said, "The song is about a guy who gets a phone call from a girl."

"This ain't a mushy girl song, is it?"

"Hold on. She asks him if he would like to go to a movie, so he jumps in his car and hurries over to pick her up. So the guy doesn't see her waiting at the curb and he accidentally flattens her. It ain't mushy. She gets squashed."

"Not exactly another *Romeo and Juliet*," Glen said, "but it'll do."

We checked our tuning until it was, in Glen's words, "Close enough for rock 'n' roll." Then I ran through the chords, A, C, D, F, A, and Glen fell into the pocket. When the song was cooking, I quit playing, picked up the lyric book, and began to sing, *The telephone is ringing, you got me on the run* . . .

I knew "Under My Wheels" would have a better chance if I presented it to the band with strong guitar backup. I had practiced singing the song while strolling through the grassy fields surrounding the farm with Michael's pet raccoon tagging along behind. When I actually sang out loud in front of Glen, though, I couldn't hit the notes that I had imagined. Yet when Glen started sorting out the chords, he didn't mind my hashed-up song keys. On the contrary, he almost preferred the flaws. This made me feel more confident.

Before I could submit the song, I had to get Michael's input. One night in a motel in Buffalo, I tipped the couches forward and we crawled into this makeshift fort with our guitars.

"What the hell are you nimrods doing under there?" Neal asked us.

"I'm showing Michael my song, but I don't think your drums will fit under here."

"That's okay. I can handle rejection. My heart's been broken a thousand times before."

I was delighted at how easily Michael fell into the same basic rock feel that Glen had mustered up. We played the song over and over, and when we finally crawled out, we were confronted by Neal, who had gone to eat and returned. "You guys were under there for two fucking hours."

"Did you miss us?" Michael said.

"So, what do you think?" I asked. "It's called 'Under My Wheels.'"

Neal grinned. "Leave it to you to write a song about running over a chick."

When we got back to Pontiac, Michael kicked off the band's rehearsal with "Under My Wheels." I scrambled out my scribbled lyrics, moved over to Alice's mic, and jumped in singing. Michael sang along in the spots where he could remember the words. And when Neal and Glen joined in, chills shot up my spine because I knew the song had found its way home.

Alice sat on his stool listening until I motioned for him to take over. I handed him my notebook with my handwritten lyrics and manned my bass. The song rolled out smoothly, and when we finished, nobody made a big deal out of it, which, in our band, was a sign of approval. I didn't expect any pats on the back. Silence meant the song had reached an acceptable level.

Michael and Glen were working out a screaming guitar intro when Bob Ezrin came in. He suggested that Neal and I embellish each chord with a bass and drum crash. We loved the idea. I suggested a build into a Presley-sounding bridge, and Bob had an idea for the guitars to leave a hole leading back into the second verse. I added a bass slide down in that hole. We didn't worry about an ending because we were sure the song would fade out on the record.

KILLER ON THE LOOSE / 197

How fast were we moving now? The following day, Michael introduced "Be My Lover." He kicked it off with some big, strong power chords that rang out with such crystal-clear authority that I decided to delay bringing in the bass part. Michael's basic arrangement was good, but we added a build, a stop, and a slow, chorus ending. Glen's part added rhythmic variation, which the bass pattern broke away from and rejoined intermittently. Alice sang what Michael was singing, but stronger.

Feeling we'd had a productive rehearsal, about eleven hours, everyone packed up and went up to the house to watch TV.

I hurried to catch Michael before he put his guitar away. I told him I had an idea for a song and asked if he felt like sticking around to work it out. He put his guitar away and sat down at the Farfisa organ. "What have you got?"

"It's about a killer on death row who is walking to his execution, and the lyrics are his thoughts."

I began playing my somber bass line, and Michael joined in with low organ notes. As the mood gained momentum, I became apprehensive. I was afraid the organ would soften the edge.

But Michael had learned Ezrin's technique: He took my musical novel and boiled it down to a concise story. Each time the organ feel strayed from my intended mood, Michael brought it back before I had to say anything. After about a half hour, Michael said, "I think we've done enough for the night."

"Should we write all this down or something?"

Michael smiled and said, "I'll remember it." I patted him on the back and we headed up to the house to tell everyone.

"A death row song," Alice said with his eyes fixed on the glowing tube. "That's great! I can't wait to hear it." What he really meant was *I'm watching television right now.*

"Sounds cool," Glen said. What he really meant was *Do you have any beer?*

Cindy, who had been sewing costumes in the basement, said, "That's great, Captain. They should do a whole album of your songs." But what she really meant was *Let's get naked!*

The next day, Michael and I kicked the rehearsal off with "Killer." Bob Ezrin took over the organ while Michael and Glen invented some extraordinary guitar parts. Another song done!

Alice thumbed through my book of dream poems. When he found something he liked, he sat with his chin propped on his fist, staring at the page as he got caught up in the music's mood.

Suddenly, Alice belted out a melody that flowed as naturally as if he already knew what Michael's song should be.

Desert Night Storm I feel you near me
Wrestling through the dark half asleep
Hot and dusty the lightning thundering
Desert Night Storm comes crashing by

Tell me where in the world I'm going
I've been waiting much too long
Do I hear a Tornado Warning?
As I gaze into my palm

Trees are blowing and softly calling
Silken winds blow upon my face
Dreaming in them I'm listening deeply
Wild Coyote starts to pace

Flashing crashing headlights beaming
Shotgun explosion blasting loud
Tell me where is this madness ending
Desert Night Storm tell me now

My poem inspired the meter and the melody of the lyrics, and the mood of the song, but by the time we recorded the final track, the lyrics became "Desperado," which Alice thought was more fitting. I agreed, and didn't mind going uncredited—well, not completely, anyway.

Throughout the creation of the *Killer* album, the Alice Cooper group continued playing flurries of live shows. As Shep put it, "Boom, boom, boom."

In August of 1971, we returned to RCA Studios in Chicago to record *Killer*.

It went fast, even though we were interrupted by the broadcast signal coming from a new radio station next door. There we were, deep in the concluding section of "Dead Babies," when out of no place, strains from "Light My Fire" came leaking all over our tracks.

Brian Christian said they were going to line the walls with lead foil to stop this. Meanwhile, they didn't like the sound of my bass and, again, rented a guitar, this time a Fender Jazz Bass, from a store down the block.

The band took off, and I was alone with Jack and Bob, rerecording my bass lines. Unbeknownst to me, a writer for the *Chicago Tribune* named Bob Greene had arrived looking for material for his column. He sat in the darkened control room taking note of my dirty pink corduroy pants and waist-length hair.

He wrote a pleasant column about what he saw. We'd see Bob Greene again down the line, and his reporting would have an important impact on us.

The following day, the studio phone rang and Ezrin answered. "Hey, Rick Derringer!" After scoring with the McCoys ("Hang on, Sloopy"), Derringer was now touring with Johnny Winter and getting a name as big guitarist. He was in Chicago, so Ezrin invited him to the session and told him to bring his guitar.

Glen had just recorded a blistering-hot rhythm guitar part on "Under My Wheels," and I really liked the lead guitar break he had played during rehearsals, but Ezrin had asked Derringer to do a guest spot. We had once jammed with the McCoys, at Steve Paul's The Scene, and Glen liked Rick, so it wasn't an issue.

When Rick arrived, Glen and Bob showed him what amps were available. "Under My Wheels" was coming over the playback. Rick tuned up a bit, adjusted the tone on the amp, and faster than a speeding bullet, knocked out a scorching lead break. He was a seasoned pro and a cool guy, but I knew Glen would have preferred laying down his own lead break.

Finally the album was ready to mix. I packed up the rented Fender Jazz Bass for its return, but then got the pleasant news that the rental fee outweighed the sales value, so the bass was mine. I imagined mirrors and Austrian rhinestones all over its curvy surface. That broken-in bass became my lifelong friend. I still have it. This is the guitar that the Fender Custom Shop would one day borrow and replicate for sale as the Billion Dollar Jazz Bass.

Killer was the title of the album because we'd smelled a theme: The girlfriend gets squashed under the wheels of a car; the spy in "Halo of Flies" has a license to kill; the "Desperado" is a gunfighter; little Betty dies because of neglectful parents; and the murderer on death row is a killer facing execution. Then there was our new stage guest, the boa constrictor, a cold-blooded killer by instinct. We decided it was fitting to put a mug shot of Kachina on the album cover. *Voilà,* we had a loose but effective theme album.

I thought a hit single meant you had it made, but the list of haters only seemed to get longer and longer.

Many people in the business couldn't see past our image, and thus didn't give our music a fair listen. While we were getting the frisky attention of girls backstage, there were an awful lot of women who said we looked weird. Then there was the Humane Society, which thought we were murdering chickens. The promoters were afraid we might be hauled off to jail in the middle of a show. Television stations were afraid of sponsors pulling their advertising dollars if we got even one precious minute of airtime.

While other bands were doing plenty of television appearances and films, most of those doors remained shut for us, even though we had the visual goods.

Radio airplay meant more parties. Cindy Lang was always up for a party, but coaxing Alice out of our house for that wasn't easy. He didn't bother to seek out parties because they came to him.

Unlike the blowout binge drinking that many Detroit party animals indulged in, Alice maintained a personal, ongoing sipping marathon. Whether he was alone or in the midst of some party orbiting around him, he seemed happiest when staring at the television with a beer clutched in his hand.

Alice maintained that he didn't drink to get his courage up to go onstage; the shows were the easy part. He claimed he drank to pass the boring time between shows. Television also provided an escape. He found shows like *The Beverly Hillbillies* to be mesmerizing. He was rarely alone, but with TV he could shut out the world.

Glen was a compulsive TV bug, too, but he also did other things, such as showing people his vintage *TV Guide*s, flipping cards into a hat, or throwing knives at a wall. He kept the party going long after Alice or any of us had packed it in.

Like any other up-and-coming rock band, we became a magnet for people in warp-speed party mode. As one group of party people went home to "re-Cooper-ate," others showed up in full anticipation mode.

People came and people went, but the band lived in the thick of the soup. It became difficult to view life as anything *but* a party. We partied at home, we partied on the road, and sometimes we partied until we thought our heads would explode. After overdoing it a couple of times, I thankfully learned to exercise moderation, but there never was any shortage of temptation.

Our shows were now rising in intensity. We could feel it. We had the power to shake the crowds, and we did. The electric chair we'd built fit on top of our station wagon, but now it was time to up the ante to a big hanging scene, complete with gallows and thunder. We could afford a bigger truck now, so it was time to put that scene in our show.

The Warner Bros. prop department built the gallows to our specifications. It had to be collapsible and yet sturdy enough to sustain the punishment of the road. Then we had to rehearse the illusion until we were convinced it was safe beyond question.

"The Ballad of Dwight Fry" featured the Alice character in a straitjacket in an insane asylum. The evil nurse abuses him, so he strangles her. I wrote "Killer" to accommodate this scenario. Neal had a marching drum cadence, while Michael carried a torch as if he were leading an angry mob. In a dramatic scene, Glen would muscle Alice up the stairs and put the noose around his neck while securing the cable to the safety harness, while I wore a priest's robe and hat and followed them up the gallows stairs reading from the Bible.

Obviously we had prerecorded music take over in the middle of this scene. After a tense moment's silence, Glen would pull the lever. Alice would drop with a clunk and appear to be swinging from the noose. Then there'd be darkness and we'd put a skeleton (named Emery Bored) into the noose. With the skeleton swinging, we'd slip away through the fog, rip off our breakaway outfits, and come out playing "Still Got a Long Way to Go." It's okay, fans. Your hero is resurrected.

Ambitious? Yeah. Fun? Aw, we didn't need to read the critics on this scenario. We felt the fans' reaction. They were having crazy fun, and they let us know it.

A big factor in the sharp intensity of our shows was that Joe and Shep kept booking us in theaters. The acoustics were just the best in those old grand movie houses. When playing the occasional festival, we could tell how the sound and visuals were lost on half the crowd. But in a theater, Charlie had total control over the lighting, so every person in the audience got the full impact of the show. We were right in their laps, shaking them by the lapels.

To eliminate our feeling of isolation, and cut down on costly long-distance phone calls, the band decided to move closer to our managers' offices in New York City. Joe and Shep had leased a place for us that was an hour away, in southern Connecticut. So in 1971 we packed up everything we owned and hit the road.

What a change. "A world apart" doesn't begin to describe how different Connecticut was. To us, it seemed like another solar system.

Greenwich is just over the line from New York, in leafy old Connecticut. For a long time it was a tax-free state, so all these Wall Street tycoons came over from the city and built huge baronial manor houses in this lush, garden-like setting. The cozy downtown streets gave off the aroma of rich gentility.

Since we'd just left the rough precincts of Michigan's industrial sector, we felt as if we'd walked out of a slaughterhouse and onto the set of some tasteful Edwardian play.

Our limousine driver followed the directions up a winding road lined with opulent homes. We turned onto a driveway guarded by stone walls and iron gates. The grounds had a variety of trees, including juniper and cedar. Placed among them were statues of gargoyles, elves, and nude ladies.

The house, called the Galesi Estate, had been built in the 1920s by an early screen star, Warner Baxter, who starred in the 1933 Busby Berkeley film *42nd Street*.

"Fancy schmancy," said Glen as we rolled up the driveway.

"Oh! This little shack?" Alice said.

"It's about time we got a house you can fart in without everybody smellin' it," Glen said.

Cindy and the roadies and girlfriends came out to meet our limo. No stranger to fairy tales, Cindy looked up at the huge house with me. "I cried when I saw it," she said, happy and sunny.

I hugged her tight. Then Neal hugged her. There was lots of hugging and handshaking all around. This magnificent place was our new home.

"I can't even begin to describe this house," Cindy said. "And wait till you see Mr. Galesi. He's very handsome."

"And single," Cindy Lang added.

"I bet Mr. Galesi doesn't have one of these," Alice said, flashing his amber ring with a prehistoric spider fossil inside. Our St. Bernard, Gretchen, came out of the mansion with her tail wagging. While I hugged the dog, Cindy told me that the neighbors had already put us on alert that their German shepherd was in heat and driving all the neighbors' dogs crazy.

It wasn't the last time the neighbors had something to say about animal rutting.

We followed the girls into the mansion, and they showed us the solarium to the right and the enormous ballroom on the left, where our crew had stacked up all our equipment. The fireplace was big enough for all of us to stand in, so we did. The cathedral-like ceiling was aflutter with paintings of angels. At the far end of the room was a massive window with no glass.

"That's where the orchestra plays," said an immaculately dressed man who walked in trailed by another man. "I'm Francesco Galesi," he said, "and this is my chef. If you like great Chinese food, he's the best. Chinese food isn't any good unless you eat it right after it's prepared."

He gestured around. "The low wall hides the orchestra, but their music floats through the big window above," he explained. "That's so guests don't see the musicians."

"That would never work for us," Alice said.

"We could toss our chickens through the window," Neal said.

Galesi gave us the whirlwind tour, pointing out the fine oil paintings, the carved wooden panels, the mirrored doors throughout, and the terra-cotta ceiling tiles, which he said he had imported from Italy. We were in awe.

After he left, Cindy took me up the staircase to our new bedroom, which had a polished white marble fireplace with black granite inlays. The room had a balcony. I looked down and saw our limousine.

"Shep wrote me a check for designing the clothes for the band," Cindy said. "He wrote a note on the check that said, 'Statement: fifteen thousand hours' work at point zero one cents per hour.' I'm sure he thought that was cute.

"I mailed some of the money to Mom, and then I went shopping and bought some green Astroturf for the bathroom and a white fuzzy rug for our bedroom, which will be all white. I also got a white quilt and this lace for the ceiling around our bed."

I grabbed her and said, "Let's try it out."

Stage one of touring too much is when you wake up and it takes a minute to remember what town you're in. Stage two is when you have to ask someone what town you're in. Stage three is when you don't give a damn where you are.

Soon we were out of our mansion and into the motels again. We had been road rats for years, but now our schedule kicked into overdrive. The band was living in a never-ending whirlwind where we'd start the day in Columbus, Ohio, have some lunch in Michigan, and by afternoon be on a flight for Newfoundland.

We got to know the Holiday Inn menu by heart, and the lady who worked in the cafeteria at O'Hare International Airport got to know us well enough to scold us whenever we didn't eat our vegetables. At times it seemed like we'd fall asleep in one town and wake up in another—with girls whose names were interchangeable, not because the girls didn't have unique personalities, but because our exhausted brains couldn't keep their names straight.

With success pulling on our sleeves, we didn't feel hardships diminish, as we assumed they would—on the contrary, the struggles began to consume every aspect of our lives. Now we had food, but we had to eat it while people asked us to sign our napkins.

Were we complaining? Nah. Do you complain about banged elbows after a roller-coaster ride?

On December 1, 1971, a rousing performance at the Academy of Music in New York City officially kicked off the *Killer* tour, which featured Cindy Smith portraying the Nurse in our stage show, Charlie Carnal's lighting, two roadies, a sound mixer, a road manager, our two managers, and the five of us.

The press was coming around in droves now, and we never knew what kind of reviewer we were going to get. It might be someone from the underground press who secretly despised us, or it might be a mainstream reporter who'd turn out to just love our depravity.

When Lester Bangs reviewed our first album, he called it a "tragic waste of plastic." That hurt. But his lengthy review of *Killer* in *Rolling Stone* was astonishing. Noting our "ICBM-like ascent from semi-obscure weirdo band to the glamour and unreality of stardom," he compared "Under My Wheels" with the best of the Stones and alleged that the album ranked with the best of anything released in 1971.

We were all over that review, so we didn't mind when *Rolling Stone* sent a reporter named Chris Hodenfield out on the road with us on the *Killer* tour. He wasn't loud and intrusive like some people who came through—those people never lasted long before getting driven out by verbal abuse—nor was he awestruck. He just seemed to be having a good time, asking a question now and then, never writing anything down.

But, boy, he sure heard what we were saying. He captured our hall-of-mirrors lives and shock-value sarcasm. When the issue containing his piece hit the stands, we all snagged copies. We had made the cover of *Rolling Stone*. Annie Leibovitz, pretty new on the job herself, had photographed Alice with Kachina wrapped around his contorted face. The cover image was as raunchy as the article. In fact, people thought it was repulsive, which only thrilled us more.

More and more people were hanging around the Galesi Estate, and that only made it tougher for the band to create music. With our hectic tour schedule, our brains now often felt as useful as bowls of dog kibble, but still we brainstormed. At least we had a place to write and rehearse the next album. Only, instead of a drafty old farmhouse, it was a gilded ballroom. In the midst of a major tour, we wrote and recorded *School's Out*.

Recording a conceptual album with any semblance of continuity while executing a major tour went smoother than we had imagined. Fighting through a battlefield of distractions, *School's Out* got put together like a five-thousand-piece puzzle on the dining room table.

Since "Under My Wheels" hadn't struck the chord with teens that "I'm Eighteen" had, we were determined to come up with something that would. And once again that special kind of song was guided by Michael's songwriting savvy.

"Okay, what are the lyrics going to be?" Ezrin said, taking a seat on the carpet. He wrote the title "School's Out" at the top of a blank page.

Alice rolled off a beanbag chair, jumped up, and hollered, "Nothing goes overlooked by Inspector Clouseau!"

This was the first time we all felt certain that a particular song would be the single. We had worked out the music, but we wanted to perfect the lyrics.

The first verse and the pre-chorus fell easily into place. So did the first chorus, but we hit a snag on the final line of verse two. True, the theme of the song called for sophomoric lyrics, but even so, our five brains started spewing out some pretty dumb stuff. The harder we thought, the dumber the stuff was. Finally, it struck me.

"What is this like?" I asked. "It's like school!"

"Can we go to recess then?" Glen whined.

"We're the kids at the back of the class that this song is about. Why are we stuck?"

"'Cause we're stupid?" Neal said.

"Right. Well, *you* are . . . No, we're stuck because we can't even think of a rhyme."

"You're losin' it, Dunaway," Neal said.

"That's the line! We can't even think of a word that rhymes!"

Now Bob smiled. He scribbled this in.

Glen had a tremendous, rowdy riff to start the song. He'd been doing a lot of late-night jams with a character named Rockin' Reggie Vinson, a guy we liked so much that he became a regular part of our revels. That riff, I must say, is great enough to march through time with the best rock riffs ever created.

The thing about Glen's guitar playing was that almost nobody could duplicate his visceral punch. I've heard lots of accomplished musicians play this barnstormin' opener, even the guy who presently plays with Alice, but none of them have had Glen's unique scream. The reason the riff works is because of Glen's rebellious attitude. You heard that thing and you knew it was coming from the surly kid who'd been told to sit in the back of class.

Neal and I let Glen establish his riff, and then we came in with the same kind of shots the bass and drums did on "Under My Wheels," followed by a lengthy driving fill before falling into the verse pattern where Alice sang our new lyrics. The idea was to kick the song off as big as we possibly could.

The Record Plant in New York City had a definite feeling. You could sense the air of music celebrity hanging on the walls. John Lennon, Aretha Franklin, Stevie Wonder, and many other great artists had recorded there. Roy Cicala ran the studio, and he had a crack staff that included Paul Prestopino, who was a master technician, and two hotshot engineer/producers named Shelly Yakus and Jimmy Iovine. Those guys, with Bob Ezrin at the helm of the production, were all important ingredients in making "School's Out" a hit.

We had learned a lot about the recording process, so now we knew how to set up our equipment. I had moved my bass amp away from the drums and surrounded it with sound-deadening baffles. Michael and Glen did the same with their guitar amps.

We had some late nights ahead. Still, we were finding time now and then to run out and do some gigs. Having played "School's Out" to the live crowds, we found the feel of it really energized.

We dedicated one night in the studio to getting down the guitars on "School's Out." Michael and Glen already knew what they wanted. But when Glen was going for the lead break, the track was cluttered by the sound of rattling, clanking, and scraping noises. Finally, Bob ordered him to remove all his chains, jewelry, and chicken claws. With his voodoo accessories piled on a stool beside him, Glen was suddenly so quiet that it seemed as if he'd left the studio. He nailed the break.

Now it was time for the vocal sessions.

"Can someone bring me another beer?" Alice's voice echoed loudly through the studio monitors. "Wow." He laughed. "My voice should sound like this every time I ask for a beer."

Neal got him a beer. And with echoing loudness, Alice popped the tab and took a sip.

"Are you ready?" Bob asked. "Let's roll the tape."

With confidence in Alice's vocal abilities, and with a few words of humor and encouragement, we watched Ezrin and Alice put the icing on our cake.

Well, we got no choice
All the girls and boys

We had planned to bring in some kids to sing the "No more pencils" section, and suddenly there was Bob's son and his friends. They fit the bill perfectly and added the right touch of cynicism. We added a school bell on the ending, and the song was ready to mix.

This would be the first time Bob didn't have Jack Richardson watching his back in the mix. Bob spent a lot of time on it. Shep was present, and although he glanced up at the clock a few times, he respected Bob's expertise and was careful not to rush him. Nevertheless, when we heard Ezrin's final mix, we all thought, Why not try for a better one? So Roy Cicala gave it a shot. His mix was also very good, but we still thought we might be able to get a better one.

So Shelly Yakus and Jimmy Iovine took over the controls. Following the same standard procedure that the other guys had used, they pulled all the volume sliders down to zero. They began from the ground up with the bass drum. They fine-tuned every nuance of each instrument with a variety of specialized outboard equipment and carefully moved the sliders with the concentration of an archer before releasing his arrow. Despite the loud volume of the music, their focus demanded a dead hush from everyone in the room.

Result? They hit the bull's-eye.

Now we had a hit song that could lift a dead man out of his seat and get him bouncing.

As for Jimmy and Shelly, in due time they would take over Herb Alpert's Record Plant West and be godfathers to a monumental string of hits.

We now had enough pull with Warner Bros. to get them to do a snazzy album cover. The *School's Out* jacket had perforations so that it could fold out into a standing school desk. A.C., MICHAEL B., G.B., N. SMITH, and D.D. were carved in the wood. You lifted the desktop flap to find a poor report card, marbles, gum, a slingshot, and a switchblade. Rather than a paper dust jacket to protect it, the vinyl record came wrapped in pastel-colored paper panties.

The panties made the news when they came into port and were rejected entry because they weren't flame retardant. They had to be shipped back to Spain to be treated. The news media picked up on the story.

The delay didn't matter to us. We had a magic panty-dropper of a hit song.

Working in one of the best recording studios in the world was a revelation. But a different kind of revelation smacked me in the face one day while walking with Michael down a hallway toward the studio.

I noticed a sticker on a locker door. It appeared to be an image of us that I didn't recognize.

"Have you seen this one?"

"No," he said as we went for a closer look.

"Hey!" I said. "That's not us."

The sticker announced the band as Kiss.

"One guy is a cat," Michael said. "They should be called the Copycats."

"That's not even subtle," I said. "I really thought it was us."

So it began. Just as we had borrowed elements from our hero bands, now it was happening to us—the makeup, the glitter, the theatrics.

Still, we weren't going to let any tears ruin our mascara. We were headed to Europe in June.

Besides becoming a shrewd negotiator, Shep Gordon had also become a masterful promoter. True, even the Earwigs had known how to milk the press for all it was worth. We created new opportunities and fed off those opportunities and never stopped thinking in those terms. But Joe and Shep were equally cunning, and they worked hard to pull the strings to publicize us in big ways.

At times our combined efforts resembled the sensational gimmickry of a circus coming to town. No longer did they have to call the LA cops to alert them of a band playing in—"Gasp!"—clear plastic pants. Now that we had become newsworthy, they grabbed every opportunity to take us to the moon.

In June we were in London, getting used to the time change and the beer change, when the telephone chirped. Michael answered it and immediately spun around and told me to change the TV channel.

News helicopters were circling above Piccadilly Circus, the busiest intersection in London. Rush-hour traffic had come to a standstill in a massive gridlock. Turns out a flatbed truck had broken down at such an angle that it blocked traffic in all four directions. The driver had the hood open and was checking the engine as news cameras and the bobbies in blue swarmed in.

Rising up from the truck's bed was an upright billboard with an enormous Richard Avedon photograph of Alice. He was reclining with nothing covering his privates but Kachina. Suddenly not only every person in London knew about the concert, but people around the world did, too.

The driver finally "figured out" why the truck wouldn't start, and got it going. He got hell from the authorities, but we got our photo all over the front pages.

Back during our first European tour, in 1971, we'd been worried about having to start all over with the European audiences, but we learned right away not to sweat: Our early connection to Frank Zappa was the magic key. The same applied for this tour. Although Frank's American audience was small but devoted, in Europe—especially Germany and Holland—he was considered a musical giant who rubbed shoulders with Beethoven. Just for having once drunk coffee in his kitchen, we were now accorded all courtesies and respect.

Besides, we ran into much bigger things to worry about.

The bloody scene in Holland was simply not our fault. The first time we walked through the entrance of the Amsterdam Hilton, we noted its sheer size. We weren't thinking of its danger.

"This is the biggest revolving door I've ever seen," I said as we circled through the giant doors two at a time. "It must be thirty feet high."

"It's smaaallllllllllllllllll," Glen said.

"Tiny," Alice corrected.

We were scheduled to play the renowned Concertgebouw, a legendary, century-old concert hall with the best acoustics we had ever heard in our lives. Our show was scheduled for 4:00 a.m. It was explained to us that the normal hours belonged to the old gaffers and the wee hours belonged to youth.

I was sleeping in my room when the phone rang.

"It's Shep. It's time to go, man."

Sleepy-headed, the band gathered in the enormous lobby with guitars in hand. At the signal from the roadies, Glen followed Michael into the giant revolving doors.

Tilting my bass case upward, I prepared to go next.

CRASH!

Shards of glass crashed down inside the revolving doors.

The door between Michael and Glen had burst. They ducked their heads while the rest of us watched in horror. *CRASH! CRASH!* Each falling piece allowed the one above it to break loose. We looked up to see a six-foot sheet of glass with a terrifying point like a guillotine blade slowly come loose from the top of the frame. Sickeningly, we watched it come crashing down and land between Michael and Glen.

When the shattering racket stopped, Michael and Glen stood motionless, trapped between the unbroken outer doors. Broken glass was piled up to their knees. More dangerous hunks of glass still hung precariously above their heads.

The hotel management swarmed in and tried to slide the doors open, but the glass was heavy, and with more glass threatening to fall, it was too dangerous to try to move anything.

After Michael and Glen's muffled voices assured us that they thought they were okay, an excruciatingly slow procedure began. Piece by piece, inch by inch, the hotel guys removed hunks of glass until the opening was wide enough to get Michael out. An awestruck Glen followed.

Blood oozed from a small gash in Glen's right elbow, but other than that, miraculously, he and Michael appeared to be unscathed.

Michael blamed Glen for jamming the door with his guitar case, and Glen blamed Michael.

"We'll take Glen to the hospital and meet you at the concert hall," said an assistant to the show's promoter.

"You can do that?" I asked. "Don't you have to fill out paperwork and everything?"

"No." He laughed.

Michael shook his head to get the glass particles out of his hair and climbed into the back of the limo. "I hope the show is this exciting," he said. By the time the limo pulled away, hotel maintenance guys had already begun nailing sheets of plywood around the entrance.

The magnificent Concertgebouw resonated with history. But on that particular night, the classical composers peering down from their massive gold picture frames were witnesses to the Alice Cooper group trudging across the thick crimson carpet.

"Is it just me or are their eyes following us?" I said, looking up at the portraits.

"They look like they're mad at us," Alice said. He paused and said quietly, "I hope Glen's all right."

"Did you see that big pointed sheet of glass?" I said. "I can't believe it landed right between them and they weren't hurt."

"It could have cut somebody in half."

"It seems like a dream."

"Yeah," Alice said, "but I was wide awake as soon as it happened."

The dressing room buzzed with mingling gentlemen and exquisitely bejeweled women with glorious cleavage.

Carolyn Pfeiffer, our PR woman, introduced Alice and me to an actor with an angelic face. She told us that he had been in Fellini's *Satyricon*. Alice told him how much he liked that film, as well as Fellini's *8 1/2*. I told him my favorite was *Nights of Cabiria*.

Shep walked in and announced, "Glen's on his way."

"The show must go on!" the show's organizer said, inciting polite laughter.

"It would take more than a truckload of jagged glass to stop Glen," Alice said. "It would take a math test."

"Hey!" Glen shouted as he walked in. Cheers filled the room.

"Hey G.B.," Alice yelled. "How are ya?"

"They saved the arm, but they had to amputate my sleeve," Glen said, pointing to the missing sleeve of his skull-and-crossbones costume.

"Cindy can fix it," I said. "How's the wound?"

"They gave me a couple of stitches," he said, "and some pain killers that aren't half bad."

Ronnie Volz and Charlie Carnal came in laughing. "You should see the guy who's performing now," Ronnie said. "He's sticking spikes through his tongue and rolling around on a bed of nails and walking on glass."

"And our guitar player gets hurt walking through a fucking door," Neal said.

"Den, can ya pass the ketchup?" Glen asked, pointing to the food table. I did, and he shook the bottle until a glob landed on his bandage. Everyone laughed.

"What can I say?" he said. "We're a theatrical group."

The stage had thick, lush carpeting. The majestic crystal chandeliers sparkled like prisms. The ornate ceiling can only be described as heavenly. Above all, acoustically, every tonal nuance of music rang warm and true. The mind-boggling history of the place mixed with our relief that Glen and Michael hadn't been sliced to ribbons gave us an immense inspiration.

We had performed in a myriad of dive bars, theaters, and outdoor festivals, with varying degrees of accomplishment, but that night, we were honored to be in the midst of stunning perfection. And we felt that we rose to the occasion.

After the cloud of feathers had reached the upper balconies, Glen highlighted our encore with a burning solo on "Under My Wheels," and then we walked back to the dressing room as Beethoven's eyes followed us.

"I'm not sure he liked our show," I said, pointing up at Ludwig's portrait.

"Oh, him?" Alice said. "He always looks mad about something."

At the end of June in 1972, we played the Empire Pool, as the Wembley Arena used to be known. Big place—at least twelve thousand seats. The Beatles played there three times.

We were backstage while Roxy Music opened for us, and who do we see walk into our dressing room with an open-faced grin but Iggy Pop. (This was the name he now preferred over Iggy Stooge.) We welcomed him, and although we had known each other only about a year or two, we chatted about what seemed like old times.

He hung out while we played "School's Out" to warm up our voices. He said he'd liked our Alice billboard thing on the news, wished us luck with the show, and said he would be lurking out front somewhere. His visit was a reminder that the Detroit energy was an influential ingredient that had carried us all the way to this show.

That night's tremendous audience marked the conclusion of the *Killer* tour. By now, Alice's trademark can of beer had been replaced by Seagram's VO and Coca-Cola. Glen was drinking a lot of VO as well. As their consumption increased, so would the negative edge to their humor. The shows stayed tight, but the hard work and the hard drinking continued without a break.

As time and a few casual relationships came and went, my heart could no longer deny my attraction to the blonde angel Cindy. So, despite deep loneliness when she wasn't with me on the road, and amid temptations galore, I became faithful.

Even though neither of us had ever been entirely exclusive to each other before, she was the first to recognize our love. I was slower to read the signs, but it was definitely a two-way street. Days were empty when we were apart. From where I was standing, she was the most beautiful girl I'd ever seen. She was *everything*. This mysterious force kept drawing me back until I knew I would be lost without her.

Talk about hot nights. Or afternoons. Or early mornings. Anywhere, anytime, really. When it came to hot, hot sex, we gave our pet rabbits a billion-dollar run for their money. Being out on the road so much, sometimes we had to be creative about it. The way backseat of the station wagon faced backward, so Cindy would disappear under my blanket for a while.

The band spent so many years in shared hotel rooms that everybody and their girlfriends could be watching a gangster movie with the enthusiasm of a Super Bowl party and somebody might be in one of the beds getting it on under the sheets. No big deal. It was the free love era, and we were a rock band.

Still, when it came to sex, you had to be resourceful. There were a few very creative places for BJs, like the back room at the Dancing Domes club in Detroit, where, once, one of Cindy's powerful kisses inspired me to pull her behind the furnace. It was reasonably clean back there, and we thought it was funny, so Cindy went down. When we were past the point of turning back, though, the rest of the band came clomping into the small room. Cindy and I were in the shadows, with only a few vertical pipes between us and them. They could have spotted us easily.

Michael said, "Where is Dennis? He should be here to hear this."

I could hear fine, but whatever he had to say couldn't possibly have been as interesting as Cindy taking me to the stars.

The concepts for our theatrical shows began to form during the early songwriting stages for each album. Cindy was part of our idea brainstorming. She'd take us all aside and get our ideas, and her pen would be flying.

Then she took measurements, which always got comments like "Oooh, that feels good. Can you measure a little higher?" But she could dish it out as well as take it. Once, when Michael teasingly said, "Why don't you come into my boudoir and measure me?" Cindy just shot back, "I've heard there's not much to measure."

Michael confidently replied, "Well, I am the stud of the group."

Cindy: "I've heard that you're the *stub* of the group."

The truth, of course, was very different. Michael had a long trail of panting groupies to vouch for his prowess. But Cindy wasn't going to miss a beat. Fast lines and sarcasm were our daily bread, and all the girlfriends learned to master them.

Occasionally, a guest would wander into this daily feast of fast, poppin' scorn, and his or her face would blanch. People naturally interpreted our friendly conversations as scorching nastiness. So we'd smile and shrug and explain, "He's just joking."

When the costume designs and fabrics were agreed upon, Cindy would go off to a fabric store. The sewing machine would be whirring away into the wee hours of the morning. Hard deadlines were her rocket fuel. Her ability to make costumes appear overnight seemed like magic.

It's worth saying all this because some quick thinkers get the idea that "chicks with the band" are no more than sweet-smelling bedspreads. That's not fair to the women who really burn with creative force.

Cindy's psychological ministrations were also valuable. Glen, for instance, listened to her. I do believe his train might have derailed years earlier if it hadn't been for Cindy. With his extreme touchiness—wherein a mild comment would be seen as the imposition of a rule—Cindy could get away with remarking about his leaving beer bottles everywhere. Or how about thinking with your brain instead of your penis? She was just trying to instill some scruples into the advanced craziness of a rock band.

The Alice Cooper group redefined the image of a rock star. We weren't the only band breaking the mold, but we set a new direction. Cindy was an essential part of that—a creator of our stage presence and soother of souls offstage. For me, there was also the cosmic-carnal side.

For her, more than anyone I have ever met, reality included the forever kind of love. After living together for a few years, Cindy and I got married in 1974.

14.

BOWLING THEM OVER IN HOLLYWOOD

JULY 23, 1972. The Hollywood Bowl is a beautiful outdoor amphitheater cut into the hills right above town. You can walk to it from Hollywood Boulevard. About seventeen thousand people can take seats there. Since 1922 it had been a major venue for orchestras and evangelists and whoever else could pack them in under the stars. Then, in 1964, the Beatles played the Bowl and changed everything. Supposedly they were taken there in a Brinks truck. Then the Doors and Hendrix had historic shows there. No question, it was a primo venue, and if you could play the Bowl, you were big time.

We'd really been rocking in the month leading up to our return to Hollywood. We had killed them in Europe. And best of all, we had a bona fide hit with "School's Out." While our *Killer* album had produced some respectable singles with "Under My Wheels" and "Be My Lover," songs that got the audiences lathered up and motivated, they weren't hits on par with "I'm Eighteen." But now you could turn on the radio anywhere in the country and hear "School's Out."

We'd played to enough big crowds that we didn't feel nervous about the Bowl. But we were still on our toes. This wasn't just Warner Bros.' press department telling Hollywood we had arrived. This was *Hollywood* announcing to us that we had made it.

Still, anxiety was creeping into the picture—over Alice's and Glen's drinking. Nothing could be said to either of them, though, without a real backlash. And this was the town where their ongoing affair with the bottle had begun.

We were staying at the Riot House on Sunset. We had about an hour before leaving for the sound check, so I told Cindy I needed to look in on Glen.

I made sure no fans were around when I knocked on his door. He was awake and let me in.

I noticed someone was sleeping in his bed. "It's great to get back to Hollywood pussy," he said. His saucer rattled as he tried to steady a cup of coffee, but he assured me he was fine.

I said I'd come back later if he wanted some privacy. He absently responded that he had already fucked her twice. The girl didn't move or make a sound.

He looked at me with dazed eyes. "We're playin' the Hollywood Bowl, Den."

"Yeah." I laughed. "We're gonna show all those backstabbing jerks a thing or two."

"They all hated us, but now they'll be suckin' up big time." He grinned as he accidentally spilled some coffee on the carpet. I tossed a napkin down, and he stepped on it with his bare foot and instantly recoiled. "Hey, that's hot."

The phone rang. It was time to head down to the lobby. Glen waved me off and said, "Don't stay so long next time."

As our limousines pulled up to the Bowl, we saw early fans holding up diplomas that read, "I Saw Alice at the Hollywood Bowl." The Hollywood groupies were already circling. Alice and I had our Cindys, but Michael, Neal, and Glen were like kids in a candy store.

Our limo's windows were rolled up, so the groupies couldn't hear Neal and Glen talking dirty about them. "Look at those tits! You can see right through her blouse!" Neal barked in his pirate's voice, "She's got nipples the size of doubloons." Glen responded: "She didn't get those lips from sucking on trailer hitches."

Alice observed airily, "I'm sure they still remember you guys down at the free clinic."

As we pulled into the backstage area behind the Bowl, we were very excited, even though we kept our cool. Our roadies had everything in its proper place, with an exact measurement from the front of the stage to the amp line, so we would know exactly where the front edge was. I took note that the front of this stage had a slight curve to it. The "exact measurement" thing dated back to the danger of injuries during our blinding feather storms, and though we had replaced the feathers with bubble machines, à la Lawrence Welk, the measurement kept things consistent. The stage was like our living room, and we didn't want to have to look to see where the furniture was.

In those days, the Bowl had a big reflecting pool going across the stage front. This put the audience at a distance, which, sadly, was also one of the effects of the big festivals and the monster arenas. There was now a barrier between band and audience, and you really missed that close connection.

What we didn't expect was the sound restrictions. Orchestras and evangelists were one thing, but hard rock was another. Folks in the affluent neighborhoods surrounding the Bowl had put in complaints. Thus, word came down that we were limited to a certain number of decibels out of each amplifier. The volume was extremely low. All we could hear were Neal's cymbals and drums.

To compensate, the Bowl had had little low-volume speakers hung at the end of each row of seats. That might have worked for an orchestra, but we were rock and roll. At the volume they wanted, you just didn't get the sustain on the guitar notes. And it was hard to hear musical cues, so now we had to double up on visual cues.

We had lots of things up our sleeves that evening, such as hiring a helicopter to drop paper panties onto the crowd—panties like the ones we used for the dust cover on our *School's Out* album. Of course, we also had our snake, our gallows, bubble machines, and giant weather balloons filled with smoke and confetti.

A lot of tour gimmickry originated in the band's rehearsal rooms.

By now our management was on board with our coming up with these ideas. For the Bowl, the guys had pulled out all the stops. I had this idea of filling the Bowl with corn flakes and wondered if Kellogg's would sponsor us. But our image was so controversial in those days that not even Budweiser would give us a tumble.

That night for the show, there was enough electricity in the air to set the hills on fire. It was nice and warm. LA always had smog hanging overhead, but it was still a beautiful night.

To introduce us, Joe and Shep had hired Wolfman Jack, the LA deejay. The Wolfman was a crowd favorite on his own, having gotten famous in the 1960s at a pirate station called XERF-AM, which operated across the Mexican border. Tonight he was to wear a sheik's outfit with a turban and ride onstage on a camel.

A camel? This led to some problems backstage. We had union guys and officials barking up our legs. We were used to the Humane Society, the ASPCA, and everybody in the world showing up at our concerts, all of them operating under the mistaken belief that we were subhuman cretins who shouldn't perform. But now we were faced with a union grievance. They claimed we couldn't use the camel because we hadn't hired a guy with a shovel to clean up after the beast.

Shep immediately swung into action and said we didn't *want* anything cleaned up because we were *hoping* the camel would poop onstage. In his calm, soothing voice, Shep told the union guys that the steam off the camel's poop would be a visual effect. That's what we were going for.

This was total bullshit, of course. Camel shit, too. The union guys stood their ground, and Shep wouldn't back down. He got louder and louder until he finally convinced them that was the real reason we weren't paying for a clean-up guy.

Of course, we were all trying hard not to smile. This was just another of Shep's brilliant displays of his ability to turn anything around in our favor. Shep never forgot a negotiation. If a guy refused to be persuaded, he'd better not need anything from us in the future, because Shep never forgot. But I will say he also remembered the guys who did us favors.

Union guys appeased, Cassius the Camel had to be encouraged to go up a set of steps and onto the stage. In his sheik's regalia, Wolfman Jack gave us a long introduction in his signature gruff voice. "And this place can light up, right now . . . we gonna blow you out this evening, aw, aw, my, ha ha . . . ha ha. I told you, light up tonight."

When he finally bellowed, "Do you feel it? Then let's hear it for Alice Cooper!" Glen got close to his amp and played one note he managed to sustain. Then the rest of us joined in little by little, and built it up ever so slightly, consistently, building, building, building. The lights started to flicker a bit, and you heard cheers from the crowd. They knew the show was under way. Our intro built to this giant crescendo. Then Alice came out, and we broke into the opening number, "Public Animal #9."

Alice swaggered out to his microphone and sang, *Hey, hey, hey ya*. Michael, Glen, and I sang along in unison. The attitude was defiant, and the look was glitzy yet threatening, especially under Charlie's expertly dramatic lighting.

Me and G.B. we ain't never gonna confess/We carved some dirty words in our desk . . . And so the theme of the show was established.

As soon as that song ended, Michael launched us right into "Be My Lover." Alice snarled, *We had a beer or two, or maybe three, four, five, six, seven* . . .

Even though Alice and Glen had been drinking all day, they were in top form. Our third song began with a moody organ but soon became recognizable as "I'm Eighteen"—but it was our original, sprawling version. Now that our energy level had compensated for the low volume, we were all cooking, and Glen's solo was on fire. The ending was big enough to be a show closer, and the crowd bounced up and down as if their seats were electrified.

Glen checked his tuning in the dark, while Michael grabbed his guitar and started the raunchy intro to "Is It My Body." Alice pulled his leotard down to expose one shoulder. Ironically, the Hollywood crowd ate this up—the same crowd that used to yell insults and leave early. We added a middle section that dropped down to a very sensual bump-and-grind feel, while Alice brought out our snake and the two were framed in a stark spotlight. He sensually sang to the snake, *I'm goin' to the graveyard to pick up some bones, they might be yours and they just might be my own.* Kachina slinked up his arm as he pointed her out toward the crowd. Alice's sinister sexuality seethed from that spotlight and slapped conventional thinking smack dab in the face.

Only three years earlier, the 1960s had mounted a revolution, but this was a revolution of a previously unimaginable proportion. Faster and faster, our tempo raged before hitting a screaming frenzy and then an abrupt halt. Then Neal's accelerating drum roll returned the song to its original ending. Glen tossed his pick toward the crowd, and it landed in the reflecting pool.

The show had just begun and we were just getting warmed up, but we could have walked out right then and there and left everyone with a very vivid impression. Yes, it was heavy and dead serious, but it was also a bunch of teenage friends having the time of their lives.

The energy was outrageous, onstage and out in the audience. It was a stellar night.

After the show, we got back to the dressing room to find everybody in there, including the GTOs and all our friends from Los Angeles. Elton John was there, and he was *raving* about how we dressed and how cool our duds were. We had the glitter outfits that Cindy had designed, with the feather boas and everything else.

During the show, I didn't see any of the panties drop out of the sky. Shep was going to refuse to pay the helicopter pilots, who claimed that they had dropped them.

The next day there was a picture in the morning paper of panties lying on the roofs of houses in the surrounding neighborhood. It turns out that there had been enough of a breeze blowing, from the helicopter blades or whatever, to blow most of the panties all over the place. So that got us as much publicity as the show itself. We couldn't have planned it better. Then we heard that the pilot had been slammed into jail. After seeing the press, Shep bailed him out, but even so, the pilot got into a mess of trouble.

Still, it was an incredible night for us. We had finally conquered Hollywood. Once and for all, we had put nails in the coffins of the people who'd made fun of us, and there were a heck of a lot of them in Hollywood.

After the show, we hauled back to the Riot House and caroused like it was the fall of Rome. So many parties were going on in the hallways that you could barely walk down them. There were dozens of groupies and people who had come to the concert and dressed up accordingly. It was like a wild Halloween orgy.

The final reward of the evening was when Shep gave us each a check for a thousand dollars. It was way more than we had ever gotten.

That was the night I finally let myself believe we'd made it.

Daytime brought a different light. Glen and I meandered down Sunset to a reliable old coffee shop called Ben Frank's. It had an odd, angular roofline, as if it were a big wooden cabinet that had fallen off a hillside. We'd had many a night there in the starving days.

I had to have a talk with Glen. I was getting worried about him. Even though "School's Out" was on its way to becoming the biggest-selling single in the history of Warner Bros., the nonstop grind showed no signs of letup and the feeling of being a tightly knit group had begun to wear thin. Mentally and physically, we had been driven to the brink of exhaustion. At the same time, Michael, Neal, Glen, and I were feeling resistance from management about having an equal say in our own band.

Despite that friction, the band had remained reasonably close. Even in his most drunken state, Alice never faltered in his friendship with us. When he wasn't too drunk, he continued to be fun to be around. All this obscured the severity of our problems.

It appeared to be happening without Alice's knowledge, but the dynamics were shifting away from the original sense of collaboration—the group energy that had gotten us this far. It was enough to stir up any underlying resentment and rebellion.

As Glen mused on all this, he compared our situation to a scene in *Abbott and Costello Meet Frankenstein*, where Lou keeps seeing a candle move, and Bud thinks he's crazy. I knew exactly what Glen meant. Things were changing dramatically, but not everyone noticed. We were on the verge of reaping the rewards of years of hard work, but it was sliding out from under us, and it seemed that others in our organization barely noticed the candle moving.

Even in the depth of those rough times, dealing with a lot of suspicions, it didn't keep Michael, Neal, or me from giving every show our best effort. Meanwhile, heavy drinking was causing some of Alice's and Glen's performances to falter.

The hammer was coming down, but it was on Glen's head.

Now, in the coffee shop, Glen opened up. "They're out to get me," he said of the people who didn't like his drinking. "Forgetting the words is worse than messing up a note in a riff, isn't it? But my head's on the chopping block while they're all trippin' over each other to get Vince another drink."

I knew Glen was right, but I didn't know what to do about his situation. Rather than doing anything to correct the problem, he was just using it as an excuse to drink more, which only brought the hammer down harder. Alice had immunity; Glen didn't.

Glen finished his BLT and smoked a cigarette while he drank another cup of coffee. I knew that he didn't care that his smoke annoyed me, so I didn't bother to say anything. But I reached across and snagged his pickle.

"Didn't want it anyway," he cackled.

15.

HELLO, DALÍ

AS MORE AND MORE PEOPLE began pressing their faces into ours on a regular basis, we had to know who they were. We had a great ally in Carolyn Pfeiffer, who handled our public relations. She and Derek Taylor had done great stuff for us in Europe, and we looked to Carolyn to sort out whether the new guy in the room was a disc jockey or maybe Omar Sharif. A contest winner or possibly Bianca Jagger? We had to know what to say to these people! Carolyn went on to become a famous film producer, but at the moment she was steering us through the surging tides of humanity.

Then Salvador Dalí entered our lives. When Joe Greenberg told me that he had arranged for me to meet the great Surrealist at the St. Regis hotel in New York to discuss an art project, I ran to Carolyn for advice.

"Oh, he's easy," she said. "Just call him Maestro. That's all you need to know. Trust me."

Dalí had an idea about doing a 360-degree hologram of Alice. He said that Alice and he were "the world's two greatest artists." As we nervously waited for Dalí at the hotel bar, Cindy laughed and nudged me. "Why are you so nervous? You're as crazy as he is."

The wait wasn't long. I saw a reflection of light and turned to see

Dalí and his wife, Gala, walk through the door with another man. Dalí looked straight at me and walked right up. I extended my hand and said, "Maestro."

His face lit up like I was his best friend in the universe. He politely introduced Gala and the young scientist who would be handling the hologram. After Dalí got drinks for everyone, he escorted Cindy to a table and swept her up in gaudy conversation.

Dalí made our heads spin with a multilanguage explanation of his vision. When he did land on English, it would be in fragmented sentences involving flaming giraffes and such. He seemed exuberantly sincere. With the tips of his mustache curled behind his spectacles, his giraffe-hide vest, some pungent odor that had to be intentional, and a fancy cane topped with a gargoyle's head, he was every bit as Surrealistic as his paintings.

As the bar filled up with people, Dalí greeted them and ordered drinks as if he were the host in his own home. He did live, I guess, in the hotel.

Dalí clapped his hands to get everyone's attention and ordered Vichy water and honey. The bartenders looked like they had seen all this before. Dalí set the glass of bubbly water on a pedestal and began pouring the honey from the jar he dramatically raised higher. As it hit the cold water, the honey turned into globules. Dalí summoned applause, and got it.

Cindy and I went back to the Galesi Estate that night with high hopes. For our second meeting, Charlie Carnal and Joe Greenberg came along. This time we met in Dalí's apartment. It was all friendly until Charlie made a move to sit down in a wheelchair with an open umbrella attached to it.

"No! No!" Gala shouted, "You can't sit down there." While Charlie apologized, she explained, "If you sit there, rain will come pouring out of the umbrella, and it makes a big mess."

Dalí, cloaked in the same outfit and the same foul odor, continued talking as if he hadn't been interrupted since our last meeting. With a flourish, he showed us a plastic model of a brain and announced that this was Alice's. In its center was a chocolate éclair crawling with ants that had been painted, he declared, by the great Dalí!

When we lined up to say goodbye, Dalí kissed each person on both cheeks. When I got to him, I produced a lithograph of his *Don Quixote* that I'd brought with me and asked if he'd sign it. Dalí clapped his hands, and everyone gathered around as I held the print steady. Dalí started with a tiny dot. He drew and drew, but it was still just a dot. Then he got a maniacal expression on his face and wildly signed "Dalí." He repeatedly hit the picture with the pen while everyone applauded.

I didn't walk out of there. I floated.

When the photo shoot finally happened, Alice was draped in a couple million bucks' worth of borrowed diamonds. They had a revolving stage just large enough for Alice to sit on cross-legged. The stage would turn slowly for the 360-degree shot. Dalí was there to orchestrate, but he looked completely exhausted. Afterward, rock-'n'-roll photographer Bob Gruen took photos of everyone with Dalí, but I passed because my hero looked so weary. I told him to go get some rest, and he shook his head in appreciation.

The project took a disappointing turn when the big, official unveiling of the hologram happened and I wasn't invited. While Alice went, the rest of the band was left behind in the Midwest, between tour stops. That hit me hard.

Years later, in the late '80s, the Guggenheim museum staged a major Dalí exhibition, which Cindy and I naturally had to see. As we were about to leave, who should appear but Dalí himself. People quickly encircled him, but he spotted me and started walking toward me with a grand smile. Alas, even more people surrounded him, and his bodyguards swept him away. The hubbub looked like swarming ants.

Ever since the early days, starting with that article about the Earwigs in the Cortez High *Tip Sheet,* we invented reasons to warrant write-ups. It became second nature for us to spread rumors about our shows. Then, when we started traveling, it was way easy for us to gleefully reinvent our stories in different towns. As we moved into our era of reinvention, our press interviews grew more and more "interesting."

Alice's natural talent for interesting gab blossomed in interviews. Whenever a wiseass writer thought he could out-fence Alice, he found himself in a blizzard of matter-of-fact abstractions that were elusive to challenge, and therefore Alice won. Even if Alice couldn't hornswoggle writers into believing him, they still walked out with plenty of interesting stuff to write about. If a reporter asked me why we wore sequins, I would say we were artists and liked visual effects. But Alice would say that we were merely *reflecting society*.

Hey! I'd think, that's what the band was talking about last night!

The sad part was when our managers also began to think it was all Alice. They weren't in the rehearsal room hearing Michael's songs for the first time or my conceptual ideas. All they knew was that I was a generally quiet guy and therefore didn't have anything critical to offer. I was still the keeper of the flame, the Crusader, the Gipper, and the drill sergeant. But since I preferred the Wizard of Oz position, behind the curtain, it was Alice who took center stage.

True, Alice was in the hot seat more than the rest of us. That was just the nature of the beast. He was the guy whom people hovered around while he spun his tales. But then it became his comfort zone, and he wouldn't have had it any other way.

As new crew members came into the picture, they were thrown into our own version of boot camp. They had no choice but to learn our language and agree with our artistic direction and pursue it wholeheartedly with us.

Talking with rock writers was one thing. But when the media got more mainstream, the discrepancies in our stories began to be compared and challenged. Alice was good at dancing around that stuff, but it became harder for him to remember what he had said from one interview to the next. And the band's participation in interviews—that is, our tendency to answer questions with what had actually happened—caused a few clashes. Thus requests to interview the rest of the band began to dwindle, and the pressures on Alice only mounted.

The brotherly nature of the band helped Alice handle the volume of attention from outside the group. He knew we were behind him all the way. Even when we were apart, even in this new climate of concern, we were still together like one unshakable spirit. Still, the time came when our support wasn't enough to bolster Alice's courage. The "occasional" beverage turned into a bottomless can of beer, the Budweiser in his hand morning till night. Every day. He was a sipper, and even after a full day of sipping he was in reasonable control—a functioning drunk, as they say. Then he started on hard liquor, which began to affect the functioning. During some interviews, he appeared to be pretty drunk—though, truth be told, some of that was a bit of an act, an endearing part of the Alice character.

His tipsy ol' character was quite a departure in a music world occupied by potheads. In the first rush of hippiedom, where mellowness ruled and acid trips were discussed with great solemnity, it was a screaming novelty to see a hard-rock guy in leather and chains drag himself around like Dean Martin just coming off a bender. A lot of hippies still thought of booze as "Dad's" weakness. Now Led Zeppelin, Alice Cooper, Keith Richards, and the writer Hunter S. Thompson were making booze look like great raffish fun again.

So we had two guys who drank a lot, Glen and Alice. Neal drank, too, but other than in his earlier psychedelic excursions, he paced himself. He chose the proper occasions to get wasted, and he was always reliable when needed.

Everybody knows what rock stars do. What else is new? Well, living with it is a lot different from what people imagine. The humor got edgier, even egotistical at times. This was new. It was something that seemed to happen when Glen shared his VO with Alice. That's when the sloppy drunks surfaced. And then that stream of clever wit that had always made our endless travels bearable could slide into nastiness that made me turn up the volume on my cassette player.

This made a major difference in the band's discussions. Instead of hitting on ideas for our shows, we'd hear about what an asshole somebody was. Exceptionally funny negativity became exceptionally *unfunny* negativity.

Working on new material? Not anymore. It's hard to talk to a cross-eyed, slurring drunk, and what would he remember, anyway? It was like talking to a blur. None of it made any sense.

After all these years, the Alice Cooper group was on top.

With all the fame, however, it seemed that the band couldn't find time alone. When finally we did get a moment of solitude, it was such a welcome relief that nobody wanted to spoil it with a heavy discussion of these issues. And emotions ran so deep that nobody knew where to begin, not even Michael, who was usually fearless.

Still, I thought it was high time for all of us to spend an hour, just one hour, alone, talking. I believed that by ourselves, we could solve anything. We just needed to know we were going to stick together as a band. It was my twenty-seventh birthday request.

We were in Glenville, North Carolina, on my birthday, December 9, 1973. Mike Roswell was supposed to round everybody up for me. A room was rented specifically for the occasion. But when I got to the room, I saw it was empty. There was a box with a cake in it. I waited alone, thinking the guys must be drumming up some surprise.

After a half hour of silence, I called Roswell. No answer.

Then Ronnie Volz showed up. He sat on the bed and asked where everybody was. He made calls but got no answers. After an hour, we both decided to bail. I told him to take the cake.

I didn't take the no-shows all that hard. On the road, I usually couldn't keep track of what day it was, let alone anyone's birthday. I had just wanted that meeting to happen.

Later that day, Neal gave me a bottle of champagne and explained that at the time slated for the party, he'd been talking his girl, Babette, down from a huge drama. Michael apologized for having missed my party. Glen said he'd never liked birthdays, anyway—the idea of conforming to social expectations bugged him. He loved to give gifts, but never when it was expected. And Alice had had to do an interview.

I never found out if Alice even knew about the party. I just knew I couldn't take it personally.

At the height of the band's popularity, and the bottom of our spirits, Alice was clearly being promoted by management as an individual artist. You could see the band's shift in importance on our promotional posters, which now featured Alice as the star. And then there was the incident with the limo.

Neal saw things in black and white. His solid-as-the-Rock-of-Gibraltar demeanor got him through anything. Then one day we saw how deeply he was feeling things. One night after a brilliant show, he was sitting in a limo waiting to get going when somebody leaned in and told him to get out because that was Alice's car. Neal's composure disappeared in a flash. He *exploded*.

A corner had been turned. Moments before, he was getting cheered by fans on the sidewalk. Now he was getting treated like a backup musician.

16.

CONCEIVING BILLION DOLLAR BABIES

IN 1972 OUR TOURS didn't have us on the billion-dollar train. Not when folks were paying $3.50 a ticket. We had a billion-dollar presentation, but our Dom Pérignon magnum was full of Bud. Still, the success of the *School's Out* album meant that we were selling out arenas. Now that we had escaped the farm to live in a Greenwich mansion, we came up with the idea of the *Billion Dollar Babies* album. We wrote the songs around the concept of wealthy brats who could do anything they wanted.

We decided that we were going to get a mobile recording truck and park it in the driveway and wire the house as our recording studio. That way we could come right down from our rooms and get to work.

Although we all had rooms at the mansion, Alice had also taken an apartment in New York City and was spending more time there. He was doing the reverse commute for his workday. This went against the notion we had had of working from home.

He always showed up on time. But he was also missing. If your best friend has a problem, you sit him down for a serious heart-to-heart. I had done that several times with Glen, and I did it with Alice.

Cindy Lang was on her way out to go shopping, so I went to Alice's room in our big house. We chatted about this and that, and finally I said, "You know, the last few shows didn't sound too good."

"We all have off nights," he replied with a smile, then noted that we had to make sure our sound mixer Artie King pulled G.B. out of the mix on those nights.

I said, "I'm not talking about G.B. You've been forgetting the lyrics and singing off-key, and that's not like you."

"We all have off nights," he said again, "but we bounce back. You know?"

"I'm worried about Glen's drinking," I said, "and I'm worried about you, too."

"Oh, this?" He held up his whiskey and Coke. "This isn't a problem." He took a sip and said not to worry; he'd be fine at the next show.

I wasn't the only one making encouraging visits like this. Neal and Michael also dropped by. Shep had some words, and the roadies showed their concern. But our concern only made the drinkers uncomfortable, and soon Alice and Glen began avoiding these conversations as if they were a public execution.

You could see that quick little glance when they took a drink, as if they were thinking, I don't care what they say.

So you try to compensate by turning a blind eye. And you deal with the kind of ache that happens only when someone you love is in trouble.

The whole house was our studio. Our rehearsal room was a big room where we stacked the amps and drums. Sometimes we'd record in the ballroom, which was too gigantic for normal recording. We'd also record in the solarium, the billiards room, the den, even the tiny bathrooms. Guests had no idea that the microphones in the bathrooms were live. More than once some bit of loose talk or decadence got amplified and blasted through the monitors.

At our first session for *Billion Dollar Babies* we started out with a song of mine titled "Coal Black Model T." I thought it should be an old rockabilly thing, where an old Model T is speeding down the highway, like Robert Mitchum in *Thunder Road,* and the car smashes into a tree and Alice dies. So the song in my mind would be this kind of outdated song, and when he died, the music would go into this ethereal, futuristic Karlheinz Stockhausen thing.

Alice rightfully changed the lyrics to "Slick Black Limousine" so that it would fit the album's theme, and I went right along with that. The song didn't make it on the album, but we had a blast recording the Stockhausen part in the solarium.

We sifted through our other songs. All we knew was that we wanted, somewhere, to be singing a chorus of "Billion Dollar Babies." Our initial attempts to make those heartfelt lyrics edgier only got silly.

The next day, Glen and Rockin' Reggie came down after working on a song all night. It was a beautiful, strummy kind of a song. Rockin' Reggie wrote amazing songs very much in the style of Roy Orbison. That's what this song was, a beautiful ballad about a "billion-dollar baby."

Because Glen so rarely brought songs to the table, we stuck with this one, spending hours going over it and trying to come up with a way to make it seem like the outstanding track of the album. But it wasn't quite working. The song just kept staying in this beautiful ballad area.

I jumped up and said, "We gotta light some dynamite under this song if it's going to be the title song!" Everybody looked at me like "Well, whaddaya got?" All I knew was the feel, so I turned my amp up—as if it weren't already loud enough to shake the shingles—and played an aggressive bass run. "*That's* what 'Billion Dollar Babies' has to be!"

And that was it. Then Michael showed me the next chord, and I made my riff follow down to there and go through it, and then I had the riff pretty much locked in.

There were now new musicians to add to the mix. Guitarist Mick Mashbir and keyboardist Bob Dolin were on hand to jump in with some fast, professional additions. Their presence did not help Glen's sagging confidence. They were there because Glen was not showing up when he was supposed to.

Glen was not free from blame. You can't handle the stress when you've been up all night, whether the reason is a bottle or a naked girl. You can't show up frazzled, with your eyes all red, and go in and play your best. And playing your best was all we had time for. We didn't have digital capabilities back then, where we could go back and manipulate notes. It was all on the tape—every cough, gargle, and plinked note.

When people insisted on trying to help, Glen would rear back like a cornered bronco. Soon his troubles only doubled. We would be finishing a song and he would walk in, plug in with a burst of feedback, light a cigarette, and say, "Why's everyone so early?"

The ferocious confidence he had onstage was not there during recording sessions. There is a lot of pressure when that red light goes on in the studio and those dollars are ticking away on the clock. In the earlier days, he'd managed to pull it out, but those days were behind him.

Mick was a talented guitarist. We'd known him since Phoenix, and we'd jammed and partied with him plenty of times. We were always happy to put him up when he was passing through. But now we had to call on him for some serious guitar playing. *Nobody* had Glen's torch-this-joint energy, but Mick was punctual, always in tune, in control of his feedback, diligent, and cooperative. Same for Bob Dolin on keyboards.

Getting the "Billion Dollar Babies" track down meant showing the guitar players my new riff until we all had it tight. Meanwhile, the other guys took a break at the pool table in the solarium. Neal came up with this amazing drum part, and the song took on an aggressive feel. It was no longer a ballad. Rockin' Reggie had been around us long enough to know how we could rough up a pretty song.

Once the music was set, Alice was inspired to tweak the lyrics and take them to a whole different place.

This was before anybody had a clue that Donovan would be invited to sing on the song. (That happened later, when we were doing some extra recording in London and he happened to be recording in the next studio.)

I'm not sure what Glen's input was on the final take, but I do know that he had a lot to do with the feel of all the songs. Some days he was up to the task; some days he wasn't. But just trying to figure out if it was a good day or a bad one wasted a lot of time we didn't have.

It became easier to let Glen sleep through our early morning recording sessions than to wake him up and end up having to tell him that he wasn't cutting it and he should stop. These kinds of confrontations were very awkward and emotional, and he didn't take them well. But they happened more than we would have liked, and soon, Glen wasn't getting any chance at all to record his parts.

He wasn't aggressive about it; he would just walk out saying things like "Oh, I was under the impression that this was a band." All this was a heavy undercurrent to what, on the surface, was still a long-term friendship with a guy we still had a lot of fun with. And he still had a lot of fun being around us.

"Raped and Freezin'"—that was one of Michael's great guitar riffs, a rhythmic rock kind of a thing, and we decided at the end of it to go into kind of a traditional Mexican dance feel, and then at the *very* end of it, while mixing, it occurred to Ezrin to add a bunch of people shouting, "Olé!" The Spanish feel was a throwback to the *Easy Action* album, where we did a similar thing on the song "Below Your Means."

Besides Mick, we called on Steve Hunter and Dick Wagner, too. There was no denying that those two guys were strong guitarists. They had come together in a Detroit band called Frost and had then played for Lou Reed. They brought a slick feel to the album, which worked because of our theme about rich rock stars, but it couldn't match Glen's distinctive spit-in-your-face attitude.

All our songs were written with stage presentation in mind. We wanted the album to have a big introductory song to kick it off; then we wanted to build up to a big ending. In those days of two-sided vinyl recordings, we wanted to build the first side up, and then build the second side up even further.

Ezrin brought in the song "Hello Hooray." We didn't know it had been on a Judy Collins record. We sat and listened to this friendly tune sung by a guy on an acoustic guitar, and said, "Yeah, well, that's good, but a little more mellow than we were thinking." We knew we had to make it our own. So we listened to it again, guitars in hand, improvising chords, following it but not staying too close. Alice began jotting some ideas on lyrics. It evolved into a big production.

We decided that the *Billion Dollar Babies* show would begin with everything white, and we would flood the stage with a billowing white cloud of fog, and then "Hello Hooray" would begin as we walked out of the cloud. During the recording session, this visual image helped us imagine the grand feel of the song.

By the time we were doing a full-blast rehearsal, Bob weighed in with some ideas for the important crescendos. Now the band's unmistakable momentum was building, and we had an Alice Cooper extravaganza.

Having a song like "School's Out" on the charts really had us thinking of having some other seasonal hit. Then it came to us. "Hey, wait a minute. What about the upcoming election? Let's write a song called 'Elected.'" We leaned on a song we had done on the *Pretties for You* album, called "Reflected." We thought, Let's modernize it, bring it up to date, and make it exciting enough to be a hit. Neal and I set up a driving rhythm that showed our love of the Who. I came up with a riff for the ending, which somebody later called a "cascading bass line." (I don't know the name of the person who coined that term, but whoever it was, thanks! I like it.) Bob Ezrin approved of the riff, so again, just as on "Billion Dollar Babies," I showed it to Michael and Glen, and we all learned the riff.

Dolin came up with a lot of stuff, even on "Raped and Freezin'," where the guitar riff lay there in the verses. He came in with a persistent Little Richard–esque piano note and tied it all together.

"Unfinished Sweet" was very whimsical, and it became a signature tune in our stage act. We had this idea of Alice in the dentist's chair getting laughing gas, which caused him to go into a big dream sequence. When we recorded it, we had all those visuals in mind.

Everybody had a cold, or what somebody referred to as "the London flu." We had just toured Europe and were totally hollow-eyed and spent. We also needed one more song for the album. Somebody came up with the bright idea of flying to the Canary Islands, a Spanish archipelago just off the North African coast.

We landed at night and drove up to a towering, isolated hotel on the beach. All the lights were on, and these bellhops in red suits with round caps were standing at attention like they expected the royal family or something.

I asked the desk clerk, "Which room do I have?" And he responded, "Any room!" Cindy and I looked at each other.

We asked for our room key and he said, "Well, you don't need a room key. You can pick any room!"

Something seemed weird. Cindy and I chose a room overlooking the ocean, and watched while an army of people brought in big bowls of flowers and fruit. They cheerfully explained that the hotel had just opened and we were the very first guests to stay there. Fireworks started going off. Customers!

The roadies hauled in our amps and set them up on the top floor, with the drums and all the trimmings. We had one more song to write, and it was time to get to it.

And there we were, just a band again. Happy to have only ourselves, the old gang, writing together. We went at it with some old-time efficiency and had a lot of fun. We poured on the tricky, Yardbirds-esque things we'd done when we were the Nazz. By afternoon we had a song called "Generation Landslide." I thought it was the best song on the album, and that Alice's lyrics were the best ever. Later on, Bob Dylan cited them in an interview.

"Generation Landslide" was also the perfect example of Glen playing tight during the writing process. Without the glowing red light of the studio, and without the glowering gaze of a producer breathing down his neck, he played like a marvel.

When we recorded it later in the studio, he ended up not playing on it, save for rhythm guitar. Glen played by feel, and in the studio the only feel he could muster was of a hangover and resentment.

Still, the creation of the song was a revelation. Alice was really into it. It felt as if the band were really going to come together again and make it through this storm of separation that had been threatening. In one day in the Canary Islands, without all the extraneous input and rigmarole, we had proved that we could write just as well as ever. So it kind of looked to me like this was this big breakthrough: The band finally was back.

The island was something else. Walking down the dark sand beach, we saw how popular the place was for Scandinavians, who liked to lie out nude in the rolling, hilly dunes. When Cindy and I went hiking out beyond the beach, we saw a bunch of naked people sprawling there. As prudish Americans, we did a quick U-turn, which was pretty ironic, considering we were such licentious fire-eaters.

As rock-'n'-roll people, we thought we could do a photo shoot in the dunes. We got on some funky clothes and went crawling around in the sand. Cindy and Ronnie Volz took a lot of photos, and Glen was in top form. We did a picture in which he was crawling down a sand dune to the dried-up watering hole and was doing this melodramatic shtick about seeing a mirage. Fun day.

The Canary Islands experiment proved that if we were left alone, the magic would come back. If we had just stayed in that hotel for a spell, worked on that hotel roof, in that environment, with that dynamic, I think the band would have pulled out of its funk. We'd have produced *albums* of material. But the days of our getting a break like that were long gone. Something else was always more important.

The goal of the *Billion Dollar Babies* tour must have been to make a few million dollars; we read about this intention, although we weren't millionaires. The tour sure wasn't designed to promote our health. In ninety days, we hit fifty-nine cities and performed sixty-four demanding shows. We didn't just stand there and play. We did a physically active two-hour show.

At least we had the plane.

The *Starship 1* is mostly associated with Led Zeppelin, because of rock photographer Bob Gruen's iconic picture of them standing in front of the plane with their name splashed all over it. The plane was gold and burgundy. Bobby Sherman and his manager owned it and started renting it out to other bands. Before we got it for the *Billion Dollar Babies* tour the Allman Brothers had it.

At the last minute, just before we were to use *Starship 1*, there was a lot of chaotic freaking out on the part of Shep and our road manager, David Libert, and the crew. Because the Allmans had gotten rained out in Florida, they'd kept the plane an extra day. So now we were freaking out about possibly having to fly commercial. Yeah, that's right. Only a couple of years after riding with the freight, we were now private-jet people.

When the plane finally arrived, the side of it read, ALICE COOPER. It looked really good.

In those days, you would walk across the tarmac and go up the steep stairs to get on the plane. Lots of groupies tagged along, and roadies wearing T-shirts that read, "No Head, No Backstage Pass." That's what rock-'n'-rollers were getting reputations for, and some of our people were diving in headfirst. There was a lot of that kind of attitude going on, even though it was just a wild bunch of musicians, roadies, and everybody else having fun on the road.

Cindy and I walked up the stairs and into the plane, and the first thing we saw was this lush, tacky carpeting. Then there was this long bar with a Hammond organ at the end. So you're going, "Oh, wow. Well, this is something!"

There was a television above the bar, and in those days you just didn't see that anywhere. The television, of course, had porn movies playing on it, and that meant you'd get something like *Deep Throat* followed by cartoons. Cindy would be groaning, and I would groan, too, because I always felt uncomfortable sitting with a bunch of strange girls with a porn movie showing images that were as intense as thoracic surgery.

I saw the whole thing as a kind of black hole of distractions for the band, keeping us from focusing on what we needed to do. In the old days, instead of canoodling with girls, we would have been talking about what we were going to do in the show. So all this glitzy luxury went against my driven obsession with the band and what the band should have been doing.

Cindy and I had always shared the opinion "You're a grown-up. You can make your own choices." Still, she might have had something to say to the others about these distractions. I never did. Not about the girls, anyway.

When you walked back farther into the plane, there were a couple little rooms. And way in the back was the all-white room, with shag carpeting and a faux fireplace. This was the room where you took the groupies to get it on. It was used quite a bit during our flights. I think Cindy and I might even have used it once, but we always felt like it was covered in germs or something. It sure wasn't as spotlessly clean as, say, behind the furnace at the Dancing Domes.

As extravagant as the *Starship 1* was, it didn't have a table suitable for blackjack, as our previous chartered planes had, so a makeshift arrangement had to be rigged. It was critical to get a betting game going.

That first flight, I just wanted to lie down and try to sleep a little bit, but it was hard because there was so much going on. Dave Libert was giving a little show as he recounted the day's dramas, and he'd play all the voices. He always got laughs when he impersonated Shep. Michael noodled on the organ; people were drinking.

Having a bar on the plane did not make it easy to keep tabs on Glen's and Alice's drinking. With the bar right there, of course they were going to start soaking up a bunch of alcohol. And we had to ask ourselves, *Did this mean another bad show was coming?* Even though the roadies had their way of watering down Alice's drinks, he'd always start way too early in the day.

By this point we were not able to critique our own shows. We were now playing big arenas, with gigantic stages and all that lighting and the incredible volume and half the room couldn't see us anyway. So a lot of the alcoholic looseness was forgiven—we hoped—even though, from the stage, we could see that things were not on the level. There were nights when the concert would degenerate into Alice engaging in a long, drunken conversation with the audience, and our keeping a pulse of music, but thinking, Come on, Alice! Let's move it along in the song here!

Michael began to make snarky remarks during these holdups, and to my regret, I did, too. Alice would be trying to act like a tough guy, and Michael would say into the microphone, "Oh you're really tough" or something like that. And that was *not* professional. We shouldn't have done it. Our overextended moods were getting a little deep.

There was no denying that we were filling arenas. Our success had moved way past any daydream we might have once had while sharing a sack of tacos in the back of a station wagon. The arenas would be packed—every seat. Even if Joe and Shep had to slip the remaining unsold tickets to a radio station, or if the roadies just handed out tickets, there was not going to be one empty chair. The roadies loved giving out tickets for BJs.

We were playing this gigantic machine—or getting played by it. Still, you can enjoy a merry-go-round even when everything is a blur. The only thing I could focus on was Cindy, so I hung on real tight.

We loved the fans even though their return love was sometimes suffocating. For a couple of years now the fan mail had been flooding into our manager's office, and Gail Rodgers, the invaluable office manager, had been sorting it out. Most of the letters were heartwarming, and showed that we'd inspired authentic devotion. But some—we could almost hear Gail screaming—were sensationally gross, such as the voodoo dolls or the infamous used condom that a fan said was a tribute of his love.

From the beginning we had always talked about what we might do in a movie. We imagined the usual dark and sinister stuff, the same as in our music and shows. We sure weren't thinking in terms of canned corn and schmaltz, but somehow that was what got inflicted on us.

Our managers arranged for us to star in a "film" to be titled *Good to See You Again, Alice Cooper*. Financing came from *Penthouse*, the skin magazine. Shep brought in Joe Gannon to direct. Now, Gannon was a likable guy, and he had some showbiz history. He'd been a road manager for Bill Cosby and had done some staging for Neil Diamond.

Whenever Alice and I used to sit around dreaming up movie ideas, we thought we could take things to the next level and do a film that had never been done before. The other fellows hungered for that, too. We wanted more than just a filmed performance. We wanted Surrealist dream sequences; we wanted to get Salvador Dalí involved; we wanted menacing, evil stuff drawn from the Land of Shades, something to shock the world.

Then Joe Gannon comes in and he's going *outside* the group for advice. We were totally blocked out of the creative process. For some reason it was considered "outside our line of expertise." The next thing we knew, we were on a plane to California with instructions to do what we were told.

What they wanted was some Monkees-style shtick. *Let's turn Alice Cooper into something comical and kicky!* Glen and I thought it was galling beyond belief.

The first scene was shot on the Warner Bros. lot. A large white set had been built to look like some old Busby Berkeley movie musical. There was a big staircase and a white piano. We were introduced to an actor named Fred Smoot, who was to play a part in the film. He seemed funny and charming enough, but we got the feeling they hadn't searched among Hollywood's top-shelf talent to cast the role.

Then they told us we were going to have to wear wigs and play an old Broadway chestnut, "The Lady Is a Tramp." Hey, great song for Sinatra. But for us?

Gannon explained the concept: We'd play the song, get mad, break up the set, and storm out. We kind of liked the idea of our destroying the set. And maybe if we stalked out the door we'd march into something better.

The next day we went out into the country to an isolated, mountainous area. They brought out a minimal film crew, along with an elephant and a camel. It was shaping up to be even more degrading than the studio scene.

In one scene, we were all supposed to get on the elephant, with Alice sitting in front. The elephant was supposed to walk toward the camera and we'd be waving our arms. By now we were almost ill. This was *totally* Monkees-type drivel.

A helicopter was to fly over and film us on the elephant, but the sound of the chopper frightened the poor animal. It instantly took off in a frantic rush, with us on its back. The trainer ran alongside, barking orders. The guys in the helicopter decided to follow us so they could keep filming, and that scared the elephant even more.

We were trying to hold on to this rampaging beast, but, you know, it wasn't a horse. As it ran faster and faster, we could feel it tremble with insane fear. What else could we all say but "Whooooah!"

Just the word to stop a stampeding elephant.

Finally, someone wised up and got the helicopter out of there. The elephant was brought to heel, looking like a big, sad wreck.

The finished film was also a big, sad wreck. The one positive aspect of it was that the live stage show, filmed over two nights of concerts in Houston, was pretty good. It's one of the few decently filmed recordings of our band at its peak.

Since we were then heavily into the *Billion Dollar Babies* tour, we felt that at least we would be able to capture the tour in all its glory. But even that hope was dashed. Charlie Carnal created this amazing theatrical lighting that bounced off layers of Plexiglas built up for the stage. But the filmmakers decided to put one spotlight on Alice, and everybody else was in the shadows. I was upset, and demanded some answers, but was told that the film crew preferred less lighting so the scene would be "more dramatic." I argued that I'd never heard of a camera crew asking for *less* lighting. And cutting down on our dramatic lighting to *add* drama? Come on.

That was our movie. When I saw it in a theater in Greenwich, I squirmed in my seat like an eel on a hot plate. Whoever it was who finished the production, they knew it was cheesy, too, and tried to save it by grafting even more cheese on it in the form of clips from old W. C. Fields movies and whatnot. It made my skin crawl.

Getting thrust into a crappy project like that threw buckets of water on our fire as a band. What was happening? Up until then, Shep had known how to capitalize on our threatening image and how it could outrage parents. Around 1973, though, it seemed as if he'd decided it was time to throw all that out and go for making Alice a household name. In the earlier days, he never would have allowed people to see Alice on *Hollywood Squares*, *The Muppets*, or *The Snoop Sisters*. Now he was encouraging this showbiz side. Things were fine when the band supplied the concepts, but now we no longer held the reins.

Alice had his own conflicts about the struggle between the Vince and Alice personalities. He'd claimed ownership of the Alice Cooper character, and he was fully adept at nurturing the stage version, but his true nature was Vince.

Our fans saw the *Billion Dollar Babies* tour as this big, gigantic, wonderful success, but from the inside, it was one of my least fun tours ever, and I don't think I'm the only one who felt that way. We were now hauling some extra emotional baggage, and our friend Vince was isolating himself from the band.

For some reason Alice always had people around who would gladly do things for him. He was very comfortable with this, and actually kind of helpless without it. He's so likable, too, that you didn't feel like a chump for coming to his assistance. Once in a while the guys in the band would rib him, but by and large we accepted it. Everybody knew that was his nature.

On tour, we had this high-speed-acrobatics team of people. If we came up with an idea, all Alice had to do was tell the nearest person, and the wheels would be in motion.

Example: Once, we needed some straitjackets as props. We weren't going to go cheap as we'd done in the early days and just turn a white dress shirt backward. So word gets filtered down to Gail Rodgers in the New York office. She gets on the phone to Bellevue Hospital and announces herself as from "the Cooper Clinic" and says, "We need straitjackets!" They calmly informed her that they no longer used them and that drugs were now preferred. But Gail talked them into finding some.

While the band "seemed" to be the center of attention, on the road it was actually Dave Libert—the fast-talking, high-speed, streetwise New York guy who was the tour manager for the *Billion Dollar Babies* tour—who commanded center stage. Dave had thin features and a hefty amount of dark curly hair. He was always in the hot seat.

By 1973, we'd lost our old roadies. Les Braden had decided he wanted to slow down and live in Vancouver. Road manager Leo Fenn had gone to work with his sister-in-law, Suzi Quatro. So now it was the skinny, curly-haired Libert who'd always be *coming through*, going one way or another or talking to somebody or other, his briefcase always at his side. Inside it were his maps to determine how far it would be to the next city, airline tickets for the whole entourage, names of hotels, the itinerary listing all the gigs and all the hotels. Libert was always in a hurry to get to a phone, which in those days required pockets full of quarters.

Before Libert came to us, he sang in a band called the Happenings, which had a few chart toppers, including "See You in September," so he was a natural showman. I was once in his apartment in New York City and noticed he had a gold record on his wall. I said, "Hey, I know that song!" He just said, "Oh, yeah."

Libert was always telling me, "Hey, let's get a bunch of girls and have a freak scene!" He did manage to have a roomful of naked people once in a while out on the road. A lot of times this determined whether we would stay in one town after the show or hurry on to the next town. It depended on where he could find the most girls. Everybody would be exhausted, but instead of going back to the hotel and getting sleep, we'd all head to the airport. Later, when he managed tours for Suzi Quatro, even she was surprised by his yen for parties.

The other big factor that shaped the itinerary was that Alice was now really into playing golf. So which town had the best golf course?

Libert also had this great ability to decide, on the spot, instantaneously, whether a problem needed to be dealt with. He'd be walking by and somebody would call out a request, and he might say, "Oh, okay, I'll send the roadie to get that to you," or maybe "I suppose you want a blow job, too?" And just keep walking.

Libert had to deal with everybody: the limousine drivers, the roadies, the truck drivers. He was also kind of a bank, so if someone had to run to a music shop, he'd have the whip out. A guy with that many duties—how could you begrudge him a party or two?

The first time we met the Amazing Randi, we were speechless. And we were *never* in that condition, especially when we were all in a hotel room watching television in New York City. We were sitting like that one day, engaged in our usual high-toned repartee, when out of nowhere we see a bearded guy standing in back of the room, doing magic tricks, making things disappear, yakking away like an old burlesque comedian. We all turned into goggle-eyed gawkers.

This was our introduction to the Amazing Randi, and he became part of our lives. He was nominally in charge of the guillotine, but being a magician, he put himself in charge also of entertaining the world.

Our stage guillotine was no amateur affair. Built by the Warner Bros. prop department, it was twelve feet tall, and that blade came down heavy. It was supposed to be safe, but I stood by while they tested it many times, and that blade could easily have cut off someone's head, or at least given them a haircut they'd never forget. Randi became the guardian of the blade. No matter how exhausted we were when we hit town, Randi would be examining that guillotine.

The other waking hours of Randi's life were devoted to getting all the attention he could. At dinner, he'd ask the waiter for salt—and then, right before the waiter's eyes, make it disappear and ask for more. You'd pity any policeman who gave Randi a hard time. He'd dare a cop to put handcuffs on him behind his back, and in minutes he'd be dangling the cuffs in front of the surprised cop's face.

Every band needs its own magician, really. Randi loved the life. He'd go to towns in advance and get all kinds of publicity for us by going to the local banks and breaking himself out of their safes. He'd get put in a straitjacket and then a coffin and get dumped in a river. He had an endless supply of stunts.

We enjoyed having Randi around, and so cast him as the Executioner in our show. He also played the Mad Dentist in a song called "Unfinished Sweet." He'd pretend to drill Alice's tooth with a giant drill, and then Cindy would come out in a giant tooth costume and do a cute tap dance. Alice would go at her with a huge toothbrush prop, while Michael made erotic noises into a microphone. Good fun. Randi always played his part with great gusto.

Even for the best magicians, though, there is that one little thing you don't count on. During our *Billion Dollar Babies* tour, Randi did a promotional stunt where he hung upside down from a crane over Niagara Falls. It was winter and very cold. Above him on the line was a camera that showed him struggling his way out of a straitjacket. But he really *was* struggling. One thing he didn't anticipate was that the mist from the falls would freeze his beard to the straitjacket. He managed to get out of it, but he had to leave bits of frozen beard behind.

In December of 1973, we were sent out on the road for the *Billion Dollar Babies* Holiday Tour. The popular *Chicago Sun-Times* columnist Bob Greene joined the tour to research a book. We had positive feelings about Bob, so we gave him a role, playing Santa Claus—who, in our show, was to get beaten up.

I wasn't crazy about this vaudeville claptrap, but it worked in the show. So Greene was writing this book about us, and running around taking notes. We were showing Bob the time of his life. Boy, talk about giving your executioner a tip for his troubles.

There was a girl named Rebecca working with us. As hard as she tried, we didn't think she was doing her job very well. But Bob liked her. And in his book *Billion Dollar Baby*, he makes it sound like she was the only person holding anything together!

When he wasn't with Rebecca, Bob pretty much hung out with Alice and Shep. For all his time on tour, Greene came to my room for about half an hour and talked to me and Cindy. His questions were disturbingly loaded. He focused on negative things, and I tried to turn it around and focus on positive things. Sure, there *were* negative things, but he just hammered on them. Cindy and I began getting a bad feeling about all this.

Shep did, too. After the tour, Shep said he had flown to Chicago expressly to talk Bob out of doing a negative book. It didn't work.

Oh, I liked Bob's writing, and it's an exceptional rock book, but he missed a very human element in the band. When he sat there listening to the guys in the band make fun of the guy who wasn't in the room, he didn't notice that it was just our way of talking. *Any* guy who left the room to take a piss just knew the other guys would be brutally mocking him behind his back. We'd been doing that since high school! Yet in Greene's book, there isn't any differentiation between the sarcastic humor and the genuine candid concerns. It all sounds like malice. When Alice saw the book, and specifically the things we'd said about him when he'd leave the room, he felt he'd been stabbed in the back. And so the book became just one more lever separating Alice from his partners.

17.

MUSCLE OF LOVE

THE BIGGEST CHALLENGE to making the *Muscle of Love* album was trying to get the band working as a unit again. The rare magical chemistry was now diluted. Not only was Alice nursing a sense of betrayal, but Glen was growing a chip on his shoulder the size of a sequoia. His bad habits had grown, too.

The first time I realized that Glen had dipped into seriously heavy drugs was just before the release of *Love It to Death*. He made a little slip of the tongue one day, and my worries stoked up fast. This was a guy whose idea of sharing a six-pack was drinking four to your two.

But my worries were generally calmed by Glen's behavior. Whatever drug he was doing, he kept it well masked behind his drinking. I wasn't completely naïve, but denial and Glen's solid playing pushed the anxieties out of my mind.

When his playing abilities did finally start to slip, it was easy to blame his insomnia issues. Few could stay up as late as Glen did. Nobody, except maybe Rockin' Reggie and their lady friends, knew what went on during those all-nighters.

During the *School's Out* sessions, Glen's overdubs took longer and longer to nail. One time, when he couldn't get it together, we jumped all over him. It was our last hope that he'd sober up and get back into gear.

Every day, however, he had to hear reminders of the tons of money that depended on our output. He wasn't responsible just for helping the band do a good job; he was responsible for this vast machine.

After we finally ganged up on him, everything was different. In his mind, it was no longer the band against the world; it was the band against *him*. He assumed a distant attitude.

Our decision to record *Billion Dollar Babies* at home at the Galesi Estate had proved horrible for him. Glen's room was taboo during the day because that's when he slept. He wouldn't answer his door till late afternoon. The onerous task of knocking on his door and yelling usually fell to Dave Libert, who knew that even if Glen answered, he'd be wrecked and furious. One time, Glen answered the door with a knife in his hand.

Glen's habitual insomnia began when he was a teenager. I think that's because the night allowed him to do as he pleased, while parents and all other authority figures slept. And whether it was playing his guitar, looking at *Playboy*, or drinking beer and smoking, he enjoyed being sneaky about things.

When Glen did appear at our sessions, he still brought the guitar-playing fire. But he always had a gadget to adjust or squealing feedback to get under control. He knew he was being thought of as the problem child.

It tore my heart out to see Steve Hunter and Dick Wagner brought in to record Glen's parts on songs he had influenced, and right under Glen's own roof.

Glen's growing disappearing act left a seething vacuum. Since we all liked Mick Mashbir, we asked him to join us on the *Billion Dollar Babies* tour. Finally the pot boiled over. Glen blamed Michael for bringing in Mick, and now he openly detested Michael.

Michael, for his part, was getting restless. He had been going at it like a songwriting machine, but not everything he wrote fit with the band's character. He began to grumble that he had enough "non-Cooper" songs to fill a solo album. (It would take all four of us jumping on his very stubborn head to get any changes to a song. After he pulled Mashbir into our circle, he had another ally for his kind of music.) But Michael could surprise you. "Hard Hearted Alice" turned out to be one of my favorite ballads he ever wrote. The mood of the lyrics by Michael and Alice nailed what the band was going through—sad, sophisticated, and forlorn. It just needed a slashing dose of Glen.

Who's to say Michael's love songs weren't the right thing? An album of entirely relatable love songs might have tripled our record sales and gathered in new fans. It's possible.

I began to see a new logic. Maybe Michael *should* do a solo album. During the one-year break that we had all discussed, we could get Alice and Glen cleaned up and come back as a real band, stronger than ever.

Then there was Alice. Now he was making remarks about how tired he was of doing the same old Alice Cooper thing. He wanted to try acting. Maybe this was to be expected—he was now hanging out with major showbiz talents like Soupy Sales and the Muppets. He had also befriended John Lennon, who, besides the Beatles movies, had ventured into acting in *How I Won the War*.

I thought Alice was a great dramatic actor in our show, but outside of that he seemed more of a comedian. For all his wit, I strongly believed he shouldn't be doing things that would kill the Alice mystique for good. He felt differently. He seemed to think that the idea of being this ghoulish character mixing it up with old-time showbiz shtick was funny.

These new dynamics made it very difficult for me to get my songs considered. I had to settle into a traditional role as a bassist, the background guy locking into more obvious grooves.

And now Bob Ezrin was gone, too. Some devoted fans think we shot ourselves in the lizard-skin boot when we let him go, but Michael, Neal, Glen, and I had gotten frustrated at his high-handedness during the *Billion Dollar Babies* recording.

One day, during the *Babies* rehearsals, the four of us were working out a song when Bob and Alice appeared with a song they had written called "Sick Things." Bob sat right down at the piano and began to bang it out. We exchanged glances. So we were all supposed to drop what we were doing and learn their song? That seemed a little ironfisted to us. I liked their song, but this new imperious manner in our rehearsal room was like a shot of acid in the face.

These mixed emotions led to a confrontation when we were preparing the *Muscle of Love* songs at Nimbus 9 Studios in Toronto. We were all excited about a new arrangement for the song "Woman Machine." Everybody was in a great mood. We charged into the song but didn't even make it through the first verse before Bob stopped us. He wanted to make changes on a song he hadn't even heard yet.

Michael challenged him. Bob was affronted, and took the challenge as a lack of appreciation for his role. This was not what Michael had intended, but Bob was insulted and walked out. We were caught off guard, but it sure wasn't the first time tempers had flared. We didn't see the need to quit playing and run out into the street and coax him back.

But Bob stayed gone. Really gone. And now his old boss, Jack Richardson, was in the producer's chair, with Jack Douglas as the engineer. Richardson had a big heart, but he was out to get the job done. He had a reputation for delivering a strong product on budget and before the deadline. He had made a lot of great-sounding records, too. Those classic singles by Bob Seger and the Guess Who really jumped right out of the speakers.

There was a certain amount of joy in the sessions now, because Jack allowed us to feel more like a band that was playing together. Things didn't seem as regimented as the *Billion Dollar Babies* sessions.

Michael really wanted this to work with Jack because he was the one who'd initiated Ezrin's departure, even though that may not have been his intention.

Mick Mashbir and Bob Dolin were fun to have around. Both are excellent musicians who bring lots of great suggestions. Alice and

Michael liked being able to say, "Give us some strings here," and have Dolin swiftly deliver the violin arrangement on a platter. And Mick and Michael did plenty of sweet-sounding double leads in unison.

We were on a never-ending tour schedule, with limited breaks to create this album. We had pulled off that job before, but only because all the band members stuck together.

Still, we were overworked. We just couldn't handle that volume of work without any real break. And two weeks off to write an album didn't count as a break!

Plus, the overwhelming popularity we had achieved had brought too many people into our world. We couldn't discuss anything without buttinskis. And Alice was in New York all the time, continually getting pulled away for a million interviews.

We decided to come up with a common theme that we could all think about no matter where we were. The theme was "the band in the early days."

We were floundering until Michael's song "Muscle of Love" triggered one of Alice's promo-savvy ideas. What if the *Muscle of Love* album were packaged in a plain brown wrapper like an "adult magazine," and with a stain on it? The idea came late in the game, but we loved it. The band had always thought of ideas for our album covers. Now, how could the rest of the songs apply to that concept?

Cindy drew up ideas for the new show. Our costumes would have stains all over them. Alice would be the street whore. We would be the seedy guys pushing the *Muscle of Love* in the plain brown wrapper. These were the kinds of threatening characters on which we'd built our name.

In September 1973 we went out to Hollywood to record at the famous Sunset Sound studios. Down the street from the studio was the graphics outfit Pacific Eye and Ear, which was in charge of our album cover art. They decided that we would all wear sailor suits for the cover shot.

What did sailor suits have to do with the group's image? Who knew? We were summoned to do photos for "our" album cover. On the first shot, we're sailors on leave in front of the "Institute of Nude Wrestling." I'm on the left side, paying off a dwarf pimp who stands in front of a hooker.

We were in a great mood, but folks from the neighborhood were really pissed off. Pacific Eye and Ear had decorated the front of its studio so convincingly that people thought an actual Institute of Nude Wrestling had moved into the neighborhood. So out come the neighbors, all up in arms, one woman even carrying a sign: "Clean Up Hollywood."

Glen just said, "Lady, don't get your crotchless panties in an uproar."

He was in a great mood. We all were. You can see it in the album photos. And that is just one sign of our brotherliness. For all his problems, we were always happy to have Glen there as a sidekick.

The jokes were flying, but I still thought this whole sailor thing compromised the band's image. Next to our music, our image was critical. So why toss it out the window for a cute scenario? Why were we paying people to come up with ideas that weren't as good as ours?

We had lost control of our art, and our magical formula had been disrupted, so artistically, we were crippled. The one drug that kept working was the huge hit of adrenaline that zorched us every time we got up in front of a massive audience.

Most of the songs came to life in the rehearsal studio at the Galesi Estate but at Sunset Sound, we whipped them into shape. We'd wanted to record there because the Doors and the Paul Butterfield Blues Band had gotten such great sounds there.

At the first session, Jack Richardson stood in the middle of the room and we had all of our instruments set up in a circle rehearsal style. We started running down the tunes while he said things like "Get rid of that pre-chorus and let's go straight to the chorus. Neal, I want you to give me a roll there and then we'll kick right into the chorus." He'd start directing, and because he was this big guy, he would energize everything and you'd feel the whole room move with him.

Neal and I played "Big Apple Dreamin' (Hippo)" the way Michael wanted us to. He finally got his way: We played the obvious pocket. It was a good song, so it carried well that way. It just didn't have any of the bass and drum flash that we usually incorporated into songs. We weren't striving to make unusual things happen. This might have been standard practice for a lot of great rhythm sections, who were told just to provide a foundation for "the creators," but it was a radical departure for us.

Jack was himself a great traditional bass player. He had started on upright bass before he became a producer. So I'd encourage him to play, and I'd watch him or play along with him. That led to my tapping his style, which was more traditional. I admired traditional bass playing, but I'd never really played it, so I did some on "Crazy Little Child." The song required a kind of barroom style of playing. It would come natural to a guy who played in a downtown bar every weekend, but I just didn't have those patterns down. So I learned. Even Neal's usual apeshit abandon was in check. There was among us in those sessions a lack of enthusiasm for pushing the Alice Cooper character as we always had. You couldn't hear it in the music. And you didn't sense it in our camaraderie, but it was lurking in our collective gut.

Our notion of "getting back" really came to life on one song. Going back to our high school days at the Northern Drive-In, Alice and I had always devoured the latest James Bond movie. Now we wanted nothing more than to write one of those huge theme songs. When we found out that Ian Fleming's *The Man with the Golden Gun* was up next to be filmed, we were on it like salt on chips. Glen was hot for it. Alice jumped in with some great lyrics, and Jack Richardson hauled in a horn section.

James Bond! It certainly felt like a band returning to its roots. We were like excited kids again. Now we're cooking. I could already taste the popcorn. I could see some nude silhouette dancing across the big screen as our song thumped on the soundtrack.

Our song might actually have had a chance, but our *Muscle of Love* sessions clashed with the deadline for the submission of songs for the movie.

The Bond soundtrack job went to Lulu.

Based on "Hard Hearted Alice" and "The Man with the Golden Gun" alone, I thought this album was a winner, even though it didn't have the edge and overall consistency that Glen could have brought to it.

We all wrote "Never Been Sold Before," but Michael led the charge with some complex chord changes. Every time the song got rolling, he'd throw in these changes again. I thought this broke up the beat too much, and I'd say, "Stop, Michael! What are you changing it for? What you just played is good. It's great!" But he'd keep changing it. We were used to this. I mean, he had always pounded out his ideas until we were ready to strangle him, but we knew he wouldn't walk away without a great song.

Jack pulled the song up to another level by luring in an amazing cast of background singers: Liza Minnelli, Ronnie Spector, and the Pointer Sisters. That was one gorgeous choir.

Neal had a Spanish guitar with nylon strings. That guitar was always sitting around the various band houses. I think more of our songs were written on that guitar than any other guitar we ever had. Neal played barre chords and also had great feeling in his voice. One day, he played his song about a teenager—a theme we favored. "Teenage Lament '74" would be the first single of the album. Michael came up with some tasty signature guitar lines for it.

That was *Muscle of Love*. If you lifted the four best songs off it you'd say, "Wow, what an amazing album!" And back then, how many albums came out that you could say that about? But the album had to follow the smash success of *Billion Dollar Babies*, so of course the critics were extra hard on *Muscle of Love*.

The fans seemed to love the album, but it struggled along until Warner Bros. put out *Alice Cooper's Greatest Hits*, which of course sold out faster than any of our other albums.

I thought the packaging of *Muscle of Love* was going to make it the greatest thing to hit the record bins—this brown cardboard box with a stain that says, in shocking pink letters, "Attention: This Carton Contains One (1) Alice Cooper Muscle of Love Fragile." But what happens? The record stores think the stain is real and they return the albums as damaged goods. That alone killed the momentum for our sales.

And we paid extra for that stain! Come on, people, the stain was genius!

The record companies, we found out later, had a secret mandate for artists: Each successive album had to do better than the last. You might think the execs would have appreciated steady sales. But, no, they had increased orders from the outlets to deal with, and if they saw a high number of returns, the artist got the blame. So instead of getting a pat on the back for selling hundreds of thousands of albums, we got an invisible hex sign on our posteriors.

18.

BREAKUP

WHEN ANY TERRIBLE THING HAPPENS, you try to pinpoint the precise moment when everything went wrong. Over and over you look for that one thing that could've changed everything. Our breakup was like the accident with our van so long ago—one moment we were dreaming, the next we were tumbling.

When we played the massive concert in São Paulo, it was just us cooking hard like your basic rock-'n'-roll band. No worries about falling on the slippery Plexiglas surface or running into steel posts covered with sharp glitter. There was no flight of stairs between us and our singer. We felt like we'd just gotten out of prison and were free. And gauging by the way we rocked 'em, we had no shortage of power.

Before that concert, there were times when we wondered if we might try dropping the theatrics for a while. It would have fit my criteria for always giving audiences the unexpected. And the skeptics could no longer have put us down for "hiding behind theatrics." Our music was strong enough to shine on its own.

Our stage shows had become kind of risky, no question. We'd seen an increase in serious threats. Dangerous incidents were happening—hammers, broken bottles, darts, beer cans, and M-80s were being thrown at the stage. Two bodyguards were hired for the group, but they ended up spending all their time with Alice, where they enjoyed partying and asserting their sense of importance. This obviously didn't help relations among us. We didn't go for being treated like outsiders. Whenever we confronted them about their attitudes, they'd just say that Alice and Shep were the bosses.

Glen instantly saw the bodyguards as a wedge intended to split the band apart. When we lost our tempers over the guards' behavior, we were painted as being unreasonable. This only made us madder.

As any given evening wore on, Alice would get more sloshed, and the guards would become more annoying. Alice's room became their party room. *Outsiders, get lost!*

So we took a break. Michael had accumulated a whole pile of songs that didn't fit our group, so he told us he was going to do a solo album. This prompted Neal to announce *his* intention to do a solo album. Nowhere did either of them say anything about leaving the band. That was just never considered. Having been pushed to the margins, though, Neal and Michael might well have been thinking of their long-term survival. But leave? Unthinkable.

I had some songs, too, but they were all intended for the Alice Cooper group. I guess if loyalty is a weakness, then I'm a wet noodle. Still, I fought tooth and nail against the idea of solo projects. I fully intended to spend more time with Alice, without the bodyguards around, but he moved to Malibu, and the phone proved to be useless.

You may be wondering how recording solo albums could be viewed as "taking a break." But music was in our blood. It's what we did. Getting off the road and out of that stressful environment was all we needed. We certainly weren't planning to take up knitting poodle sweaters.

Neal naturally asked me to play on his album, *Platinum God*. Cindy helped considerably, too. We got in touch with a hot-rod guitar slinger named Michael Marconi, who we had once seen level a club crowd in Buffalo, to play lead guitar.

For his album, *In My Own Way*, Michael Bruce brought in two great players from the Young Rascals, Dino Danelli and Gene Cornish. He also tapped Mashbir and Dolin. For all that talent, though, Michael may not have brought his completely undivided attention. Maybe he should have gotten rested and sobered up before tackling such a project. His is a solid album, but I had higher expectations.

During all this, as we would find out later, Shep and Alice sure weren't resting.

After three years of beating it to a frazzle, the time had come to depart the Galesi Estate. No longer was it in *House Beautiful* condition. Glen had fired guns at the statues like it was a desert target range. To my shocked disapproval, he also threw knives at the oil paintings. These were gestures directed at what he felt had gone down in that house. In the fall of 1973, we packed our socks and skivvies, carted off our amps, and departed the Galesi's rock star bedrooms forever.

Neal got married to Babette Remmes, and Cindy and I decided to share a house with them for a while in Old Greenwich. One day, Neal and I were loading our stuff into a van at the Galesi Estate, when we stopped in the garage and saw stacks of Alice Cooper posters on pallets going all the way to the ceiling.

"Hey," I said. "These might be valuable."

"Nah," Neal snapped. "Leave 'em. We've got to get out of here."

Neal and Babette liked to throw big, splashy parties with her fashion model friends like Bebe Buell and music biz folk like Todd Rundgren, Johnny Thunders, and Mick Rock. But as wild as those swingin' soirees got—and they did—we were all careful about inviting Glen.

Glen had moved into a house about a mile from ours, but it was enveloped by a heavy, shady vibe. While he did have some cool friends, the chiselers and dealers were beginning to muscle them all out. By this time, Neal and I were exhausted with the hordes of hangers-on who had turned our last year at the Galesi Estate into nightmare alley. But at Glen's house, it was open season for hanging out—as long as you didn't bring any rules. So we were forced into making it as clear as possible that while Glen and his girlfriend, Susan, were welcome at our house, we did *not* want the other people there.

As for Michael, he moved to a house in Hartsdale, New York, a half hour away from Old Greenwich.

While Michael and Neal were still at work on their solo albums, we finally learned the scope of Alice's solo project. It was in the form of a soundtrack he created for a television special, *Welcome to My Nightmare*, which aired in March 1975. The accompanying album was released on Atlantic Records. Ezrin produced the recording and played keyboards, Steve Hunter and Dick Wagner did the guitars, and the album had two bass players, Prakash John and Tony Levin.

Alice actually got a hit out of it, too, "Only Women Bleed." Curiously, it is the sort of song with soft edges that we'd have never let Michael Bruce bring to the group. It tapped those middle-of-the-road radio stations in a big way, ironically proving Michael's point. But, in my view, the co-designers of that dark Alice character were no longer around to enforce his critical edginess. Where once there was outrage, there was now a character with much wider appeal. It was like Elvis all over again.

The TV version of *Welcome to My Nightmare* was a big production with dancers and props, and Vincent Price lending his voice. Looking at it from afar, I could only reflect on the concepts that I thought were ours.

More than that, I felt blindsided, and it tore me apart.

When we got wind of Alice's venture, Michael had just completed *In My Own Way* and Neal was nearly finished with *Platinum God*. The news hit all of us pretty hard. What the hell had just happened? The band had been cut out of the picture. Alice's show was getting all kinds of attention, and we became the guys who didn't want to do spectacle anymore, so Alice was going to continue on his own. To us, it was totally baffling. Neal, Michael, Glen, and I were hardly staging any kind of rebellion.

I'm not sure where anyone got the idea we didn't want to do a big show. We sure had no issue with stagecraft. I had initiated the concept of theatrics and had crusaded nonstop for it. Otherwise it's unlikely the band would ever have done theatrics in the first place. Once we found that we could have fun with it, plus draw crowds, we all came up with ideas for theatrical spectacle.

No, the real issue was that we wanted to continue creating our own theatrical ideas and not someone else's. I believed strongly that our power was in the dark side of the Alice character. Dance routines and fluffy monsters would have upset the critical seriousness.

My sour grapes aside, his show was spectacular, with amazing dancers and a great concept. The songs were good, too. But I wouldn't be alone in thinking that it was also the best solo show Alice would produce for decades.

Other people were stepping into our shoes. It should have been a grand slam for the team. Instead, most of the team watched while the show went on without us.

Up to that time, it was always a group of five. This unity was just understood. If the band *was* going to properly break up, it would need to have been put into motion by five guys sitting in a room and taking a vote. But five people certainly did not come together to decide this fate.

When *Welcome to My Nightmare* came to Madison Square Garden, the venue security wouldn't allow me to go backstage. They opened a side door and made me leave the building. I think I invented some new cuss words while standing outside.

In the days that followed, it seemed like everybody in the world was congratulating me on my Nightmare tour and asking for free tickets.

I was starved for some kind of explanation, but I guess I'll forever be haunted by it. Friends in the music business have suggested that reducing the size of the band also reduced the number of profit splits.

When I talked to Joe Greenberg about it not long ago, though, he said that cutting the band out was never the intention. It was just easier for promotion, he said, to go with Alice alone. But Joe had departed during the *Billion Dollar Babies* tour. He said he could see it was falling apart and wasn't fun anymore.

To my surprise and thorough disappointment, a vast number of fans believed that we refused to do theatrics. Magazine writers went to cover Alice's next big thing, and somehow forgot to call the rest of us for our thoughts. And once the story was written, it became part of "the clippings" that other writers referred to, and the next thing you knew, decades have gone by in which the same bizarre stories have been retold and perfected like some drunk's old alibis.

When we learned of Alice's defection, Michael, Neal, and I had already been developing the next Alice Cooper tour, what we called the "Battle Axe Show." The guys who supposedly wanted to drop theatrics were sinking our own money into the next big theatrical production. I think it would have been our best ever. But now it was nearly impossible to believe the group's agreement to continue after a "recuperation break" would still somehow be honored.

Around this time I developed a dread for looking in my mailbox due to the legal nature of my mail. Communications were very limited. We were never officially notified that we were out, so I kept waiting for an outcry. If the public or the label honchos didn't accept Alice Cooper without us, I believe the group would have continued as planned and we would have done our best album and show ever.

Meanwhile, I could see our influence everywhere. The glam rock tide of the '70s probably owed something to us. Besides Kiss, bands like the New York Dolls, Mötley Crüe, Twisted Sister, and a whole bunch of other stylized rockers teed off on our harlot couture. When the Sex Pistols turned punk around in 1976, they were free in giving us credit. We thought the whole safety pins thing had come from Glen.

Alice Cooper had finally struggled to the top of the glittery rock pile and it was time to negotiate a new recording contract. This is when bands finally make any money. Dropping out at this point would make zero sense.

That contract was negotiated for Alice Cooper, but we were floored to find out that we weren't included.

After ten long, hard years, it appeared that Alice Cooper had ceased to be ours. Everything that we had created for that name had slipped through our fingers. It was a dark time for me. I felt my career had been swept under the carpet. One day I was a rock star. The next day I was uninvited. Boom. Dealt out. Gone.

19.

THE COLD ROOM

I NEVER STOP THINKING ABOUT GLEN. We loved him even as he broke our hearts. He was a great travel buddy. It was like having this surreal comic on board. His bits weren't forced. Those eccentric, whacked-out lines just calmly rolled out of him all night long.

But the day came when the greatness of his character was smothered by his drug needs. Nothing is as ugly as addiction. Before you know it, pleasure gives way to need and then need gives way to desperation. It's a pool of lies, and it doesn't give a shit about how good a person you are. It lures you in, it enslaves you, and it rarely stops until you're dead and everyone at your funeral walks out carrying a heavy burden of guilt that they weren't able to help.

I remember the first time we had pot, back in the earliest days of the band. An older tough guy—I had no idea where he came from—shared a joint with Tatum, Glen, and me in his car while we were parked in front of John Speer's parents' house.

Glen liked pot a *lot*, and it became one of his favorite things to be sneaky about behind the gymnasium. When he scored, it brought a taboo excitement to our rehearsals. It made us feel like real social outcasts.

As the drug culture progressed, the tokens of appreciation escalated, especially in Hollywood, where pot was merely an hors d'oeuvre to enhance pills—or something else. Not partaking in the dope made your visitors paranoid that you might be a narc, so you went along. We were good at pocketing stuff on the sly. Glen took all the stuff he could get to save for future dry spells. As our popularity went skyward, though, those dry spells became history.

The difficulty of dealing with the dark side of Glen was magnified by the company he kept. Living in the same house, you weren't going to say anything to Glen if he brought home some burnt-out couple with a kid who seemed to have no plans to leave. You just hoped someone would take care of it.

About six months after we left the Galesi Estate, the place burned down. Since Glen's new place was only a mile away, he drove over to watch the Galesi burn. "That old joint was a tinderbox anyway," he said, shrugging. Just our luck, though. Because Glen was spotted near the scene, some people started blaming the band for the fire. People naturally believed that the hedonistic rock band had torched it during some Satanic ceremony, but that wasn't so. We were well out of there by then.

(There were also some suggestions that "Italian lightning" was the cause, but I wouldn't put faith in that. The wiring in the house was frayed and pitiful. More than once, Cindy had been woken by a smoking fuse box and had to call the fire department.)

Glen knew that Michael, Neal, and I were writing a new album in the same neighborhood, but we didn't talk about it much. Meanwhile, he continued to struggle. He'd shape up and then go back down. Then he'd shape up again. I guess it depended on the temptations of availability versus the need to get it back together. You were never sure which Glen would show up.

I occasionally invited Glen to bring his guitar over to my house so we could jam in my basement music room, known as Claustrophobic Studios. We jammed for hours. Susan would sing hilarious songs she wrote on the spot, like "I Want a Genius," which was about dopey things some guy did; the choruses were her wish that she had a genius.

The years rolled on and beat the hell out of Glen. As his funds were depleted, his party crowds dwindled. The vultures who ransacked his house for anything valuable disappeared.

I would hear stories of Glen jamming with the Dead Boys at CBGB and bashing foreheads with Truman Capote at some Manhattan party. Then I heard that he lived in an apartment in New York City with hookers. It was hard to know what to believe. In the late 1980s, the city was being ground down by an epidemic of hard drugs, and a lot of lives got tossed in the trash.

Once in a blue moon, Glen would show up at our door alone. He'd ask to borrow money in the form of a joke ("I'll mow your lawn for two hundred dollars"). I'd hand him some money, and he'd leave and return in about an hour. He'd use our bathroom, then come out and lie down on the couch for a long while with his arm over his eyes. He'd get up and we'd have a heart-to-heart. In a while, he would leave and "hoof it" back toward the dark chambers of his house.

His folks were deeply concerned. They sent me money and a bus ticket for Glen to go back to Phoenix. I rounded him up and dropped him off at the bus station only to find out that he had walked back home via the funky neighborhood where his drug connection ruled.

The second time, I physically escorted him onto the bus. Glen told me that he owed me and to go to his house to get his vintage Fender Harvard amplifier. He said he wanted me to have it. I told him that we were even and to get healthy.

Phoenix wasn't the remedy. He disappeared. The only news that came in was pretty sketchy.

In 1983 or so, he got better and formed a band called Virgin. His sister, Janice, saw him again in '88. He was living at a friend's house, and they spent the afternoon swimming in the pool. But by '89 he'd slid deeper down than ever.

Then a guy named John Stevenson from Iowa came into the picture. Michael Bruce was working with John's brother, and Stevenson told Michael he wanted to meet Glen. Michael put the word out and tracked Glen down to a dive motel.

Glen's roommate was a rodeo cowboy, a bull rider. When John and Michael arrived, Glen and the bull rider were obviously strung out. It was New Year's Eve 1989, and the two talked Glen into going to his parents' house to watch the Iowa-Ohio football game on television, even though Glen didn't want his parents to see him in the shape he was in. Glen's dad watched the game with them, and his mom sat with them a while. It gave them a chance to get to know John. They hit it off well.

The afternoon was so nice that Glen took John aside and told him he was the first person he'd brought to the folks' house who they liked. John wanted to help Glen. He offered him a plane ticket and a place to stay in Iowa—far away from temptations. John was hopeful, but he flew back to Iowa thinking that was the end of it.

A week later, Glen called him in Iowa and said yes, he'd do it.

Clarion is surrounded by cornfields as far as the eye can see. This is the rich bottomland of America, where corn thrives by the hard work of honest people. They start their mornings with the hog report on the radio. Glen joked that the town was so small that every person had his own cop. "And ain't that nice," he'd say.

Glen continued drinking to various degrees, but he was now on the methadone program. He still fell into ditches, so to speak, but not that deep, black abyss.

One day a local woman named Lorrie Miller stopped by the town's convenience store, as she had a hundred times before. She had no idea who the longhaired guy was buying a beer and a slice of pizza. When he saw her, he turned on the charm.

Nothing goes unnoticed in a town that size, and the two quickly became the big item. Lorrie showed Glen around. They met Maria Holly, Buddy's widow. Glen and Lorrie did so many things together.

Glen fell in love with Lorrie and lived with her in a great old farmhouse in town. The future looked bright. He proposed, and Lorrie accepted. They were engaged and they set a date.

But their wedding day never came.

I find myself in Iowa at Lorrie's farmhouse.

The décor tells the story. Glass shelves with delicate old knickknacks. One shelf features Glen's model cars—just like the ones we built together in high school.

At the top of the stairs was Glen's special room. He called it the Cold Room because he kept the temperature in there low. Opening the door revealed the world of the great Glen Buxton: his guitar ready and waiting on a stand; an amp with cords and effects pedals; *TV Guides* stacked in chronological order around the floor; a couple of desks covered with gadgets and knives, bayonets, a German Luger, and piles of little stuff all begging to be inspected closer. He had pictures of Jeff Beck and Jimmy Page on a wall, along with a photo of the town's police department—the one he said was as big as the town. And most everything had a price tag on it.

There was no question that Glen had lived there, but I had arrived too late. He was gone. There in the fall of 1997, he lost his eleventh bout with pneumonia. Neal, Michael, Rockin' Reggie, and I had descended upon the isolated town for Glen's funeral, as had crowds of loving fans. The one motel in town was packed, so people pitched tents and shared RVs. They didn't mind. It was for Glen.

The Buxton family was there, Tom, Jerry, Ken, and Janice. Alice didn't make it. He released a statement to the press, though. I don't blame him for that. Your love for someone isn't measured by whether you can make his funeral.

Alice may not have wanted to turn it into a circus, which is what it was nearly turning into anyway. I told the fans there that it wasn't appropriate for me to sign autographs. The volume of requests won out, though. At first I felt like a chump, but then I thought about what Glen would have thought. Bingo! It broke the social rules! Sure, he would have approved heartily. And he would have loved the outpouring of appreciation from his fans. Neal, Michael, and I promised everyone that we would sign everything after the service.

It was October, and the air was both fall fresh and permeated with the scent of livestock and soil being turned. I walked around the sweet little town. Everyone there knew Glen and told me how much they'd liked him. It seemed the unlikeliest place in the world to embrace such a rebellious rock star, but then again, Glen had always favored down-to-earth people.

I thought back to the week or so before, when Glen called Cindy and me in Connecticut. He was just so *up* and talked for a long time. He told us he was engaged to Lorrie and was looking forward to marrying her in a matter of weeks. We'd been in touch. He'd call to ask to talk to our daughters Renee and Chelsea; he wanted to get to know them. He was trying to fill in the gaps in his life.

He was also tremendously excited about a reunion show he'd just done down in Texas. A guy named Jeff Jatras had made it happen. Michael, Neal, and Glen went, but I was weighed down with health issues and couldn't make it. Richie Scarlet, who played bass with Mountain at the time, filled in for me. They'd had a rousing time, and Glen told me that he had written some new songs. He wanted to do more gigs, but with me involved.

With a fervent sort of passion in his voice, he told Cindy that he'd finally gotten his life turned around. "I bet you didn't think I ever would," he said.

Cindy responded fervently: "I always knew you had it in you, G.B., but it was up to you to find that out. I knew you could do it. I'm proud of you."

We had no clue that he had an illness. Neal told us that Glen mentioned having chest pains during the Texas show. Neal told him to go to a doctor there, but Glen said he'd wait till he got home to Iowa. The pain he felt was incipient pneumonia, and on October 19, 1997—just a week after the show, and three weeks before his fiftieth birthday, and a few weeks before his wedding date—it brought an end to his wild life. Lorrie came home to find him lying on the bed. She called an ambulance, and he died at the Mason City hospital.

Now here I was in Clarion, still sick as a dog and on high doses of prednisone to get me by, meeting the folks who'd known Glen. Kids told me how cool Glen was, and how he'd taught them to play guitar.

The town florist recalled how Glen would buy flowers for Lorrie and stand there for hours writing out card after card because he couldn't quite find the right words to express how much she meant to him.

During Glen's funeral service, someone asked if I would like to get up and say a few words, but I was a mess—I can barely type about it now. I just couldn't. Reggie said he would do it—his faith had gotten him through his own dark days and he'd become a preacher.

They played "Stairway to Heaven," which I thought was a bit cliché, but Glen had liked Jimmy Page, so it worked fine. The pastor talked about how Glen always sat in the back of the church, saying things that made the congregation laugh. I could just picture it. I wanted to hear one more of Glen's zany shots. Just one more.

As Neal, Michael, Reggie, Ken, and I carried out his casket, Glen got his final ovation from his fans.

Somehow it seems fitting that the train runs by Glen's final resting place. At a later date—thanks to a Canadian fan, Paul Brenton, who collected donations from other Alice Cooper group fans—Glen's headstone would be their tribute. Shaped like a school desk, it has the musical notation of his iconic intro riff for "School's Out" and initials carved into it by his friends and bandmates.

He's finally found some quiet sleep.

20.

THERE'S NO BUSINESS LIKE NO BUSINESS

ALICE MIGHT HAVE HAD HIS fame without us, but he still went off the deep end. The true, gothic depths of his bad years managed to be kept secret for a long time. Really, only when he participated in a 2014 documentary, *Super Duper Alice Cooper*, did he finally let his hair down and tell the world he had actually gone to live in a strange world of hell.

It was songwriter Bernie Taupin who prodded Alice into talking openly about the cocaine addiction. Bernie, who had written all those great songs with Elton John, went to work with the newly solo Alice. Somewhere along the way they got into the Bolivian marching powder. Alice, who had generally abhorred drugs for so long, fell for cocaine completely. Living large in Malibu, he partied his way into the halls of doom.

Cindy and I were sure aware of it. Musician friends told us horror stories about what it now took to revive Alice enough to record or perform. A shady doctor appeared to have taken control of him, until Ezrin, whose father ran a hospital in Toronto, got the quack tossed out.

Cindy and I saw Alice's 1981 appearance on Tom Snyder's late-night talk show and we almost screamed when we saw this tarted-up, cadaverous shell of a guy. Only distantly in that glittering wreck could we see our old buddy, that ol' laugh riot Vince.

When he moved on to freebasing, it sucked out his life force. One day in the middle of all this, in the early '80s, Cindy and I met with him in a hotel room in New York. We sat on the bed and talked. He'd run out of excuses. Now he was trying to find the courage to say what was so screamingly obvious. He said to us that he had to quit this stuff or die.

"When I look in the mirror," he said, "I see blood dripping from my eyes."

As he spoke, a tooth fell out of his mouth. It lay on the bed between us. Cindy and I acted as if we hadn't seen it. But we shivered at the sight.

When we left, Cindy and I talked about it all the way home to Connecticut. We knew that if the group had stayed together, we'd have worked to get Alice back to health. But we also knew how impossible it can be to talk sense into an addict, especially an intelligent one.

From that day forward, he seemed to know he needed help. His wife, Sheryl Godard, a ballerina he'd met when she danced in his *Welcome to My Nightmare* show, helped him through it, then threatened to divorce him when he relapsed. Finally, in 1983, he got clean for keeps, and devoted himself to golf, fitness, religion, and family.

He now lives in a big sprawling house in Phoenix, where he and Sheryl raised three fine kids. I am so glad that my old Phoenix running buddy found a woman who lasted for life. You look at these two now and see them connected by a tremendous energy.

I always thought that Alice would come around. As bad as he looked in his emaciated years, I knew he would sober up. His true constitution, I thought, was the guy who ran alongside me in one-hundred-degree Phoenix heat. The guy who loved life and thought everything was pretty funny. And I am thankful he managed to dig his way back. I always thought his righteous character would do some soul searching and he would at least question what had really happened.

While Alice was off flirting with death, Cindy and I faced a different kind of uncertainty in the 1980s. People assume if you're a rock star once, you get a lifetime pass. With the guys in our band, people thought, Oh, *Billion Dollar Babies*, huh? Money to burn!

Not so.

The breakup—or shoving out, as I see it—was devastating. We all had health issues. Some royalty payments came in the mail, sure, but we had to find new careers. Cindy, who prospered as a fashion designer and owner of a boutique, still acknowledges that this was the hardest part of our lives.

But just as Alice and Sheryl started having kids, so did we. In 1982 and 1985, two daughters, Renee Ciara and Chelsea Monet, entered our lives and gave us more treasure than all the fame in the world could heap on our plates. When they got to be teenagers, naturally they thought the folks were uncool. But then they began to hear our music elsewhere, in London and Paris, and they came around.

It is amazing that our songs still get play after forty years. Alice's continual touring certainly helps move sales, but it's also a tribute to the longevity of the themes of our teen anthems. The audiences still leap to their feet when the songs get cranked up, and it sure warms you like a blowtorch to the heart.

The only proper direction for an artist is forward. Who needs venom? Neal and I teamed up with Joe Bouchard, the guitarist from Blue Oyster Cult, in a band called Bouchard, Dunaway, and Smith. We released *Back from Hell* and *BDS Live in Paris*. Then came the Dennis Dunaway Project, with Rick Tedesco, Ed Burns, Russ Wilson, and the expertise of our musical guru, Ian Hunter. In 2007 we released an album called *Bones from the Yard*. Then Russ and I played in the 5th Avenue Vampires with Richie Scarlet and Joe Von T. We released *Drawing Blood* in 2010.

These days I've been touring Europe and the States, and getting a hell of a lot of nice regard, with Blue Coupe, which I formed with Joe Bouchard and his brother Albert. We've released two albums, *Tornado on the Tracks* and *Million Miles More*. The fans still offer us a nice heat.

As for Neal, we always see him and Rose, who he's been with for about twenty years. We'll hit our favorite Mexican restaurant and be cackling and hooting and knocking each other around like we're our favorite piñatas.

In our first days of success, Neal was farsighted enough to buy a little land in Arizona. Years later he sold it at a profit, liked the profit, and kept making deals. He began doubling up on music and real estate. Now the "Rock N Realtor" in Connecticut, he's moved more houses than an earthquake.

Michael is harder to connect with. He has taken up a life of travel. For a while he was in Arizona, but now he's mostly in Mexico. Sometimes I can find him, but sometimes, when I need to tell him of some venture that concerns us all, finding him is impossible. Michael is one of the key people who went unmentioned in the *Super Duper Alice Cooper* film. I don't see how that happened but everyone knows he was a big part of the dream—and a big part of the songs!

And Michael keeps playing. In 2005 he put together a package called *The Second Coming of Michael Bruce—Alive & Re-Cooperated, Cooperated,* recorded by my dear talented friends from Iceland, Ingo and Silli Geirdal. The one sense of loss I have with Michael is that his travails took the wind out of his songwriting sails. He was once a songwriting machine. Who knows? Maybe he's got a chestful of knockout songs that require the attention of some lively musical mates. I do know that when we see him, it takes only a minute for us to begin looning about like a bunch of orangutans on laughing gas.

When Blue Coupe was working on *Million Miles More,* Alice stepped in and sang on the song "Hallow's Grave." He hit a homer on it. Anybody looking at me and Alice work would just see a couple of teenage troublemakers cutting up in the hall. For us, school's never out.

21.

THE HALL OF FAME

THE TELEPHONE IS RINGING...Oh, it's Shep sending an e-mail. Aloha, he says. He always uses that greeting because he lives in Hawaii. He wants to arrange a conference call. "We know we're nominated."

Nominated for what? Can he mean the Rock and Roll Hall of Fame?

When the call happens with Alice, Neal, Michael, and Shep, I am trying to think of the last time such a call happened. We sure sound like friends who have never had a gap in our conversations.

And we have been nominated for the Hall of Fame. It's true. In his casual, soothing tone of voice, Shep says to keep quiet about the whole thing for now. After a few questions and some laughs, everyone hangs up except Neal and me. We always like to compare notes after moments like this. We would like to have gotten Michael's thoughts, too, but he always hangs up too fast.

"It's about fucking time," Neal said. "We were eligible fourteen years ago!"

I admitted to being relieved and even surprised that they'd recognized Alice Cooper as a group.

"Yeah," Neal replied. "After everything that's gone down, I was prepared to see it go either way."

On September 7, 2010, the original Alice Cooper group and Bob

Ezrin were scheduled to record three songs in New York City. It was only coincidence that it was the fortieth anniversary of when we began work with Ezrin on *Love It to Death*.

My drive into New York from Connecticut took an hour, and I was in the grip of swirling thoughts the whole way. Once there, I found myself standing in front of the unassuming metal door of the Magic Shop studios. When the door opened, there stood a smiling Bob Ezrin.

"Hey, it's Dennis," he said with a big grin.

Bob is a refreshingly happy person. His hair was shorter and grayer, but he still had that same great, sparkling enthusiasm.

He asked if I needed any help unloading. I told him that I had two Fender Jazz Basses and Glen's old '56 tweed Fender Harvard amp. He came out to look at the amp, in the back of my car. "We've got to use it," he said.

The studio felt like an old-time movie theater. I heard drums and looked beyond the reflections in the big window and spotted Neal. His drums were all set up under some heavy blankets, as if he were working in an Arab tent.

Hey, Neal. Hey, Den. You made it!

Bob and one of the studio assistants came in carrying Glen's amp. They set it on top of a road case near a black Steinway piano. We decided to make Glen's amp into a shrine, so Bob sent his assistant out to buy a bottle of Seagram's 7 and a dozen red roses.

Bob watched as I lifted my mirrored bass out of its case. He asked if that was *the* bass. I said, "Yeah, it's the same one, the Billion Dollar Bass."

"I love that bass," he said.

As we dialed in the tones, I was impressed with the sound and asked him how to get such a big sound when I recorded.

"Easy!" Bob said. "Hire me!"

Michael Bruce arrived carrying his guitar. I went into the control room and patted him on the back. He put his case down, smiled, and said it had been a long journey. He meant the red-eye from Tucson, but of course he meant more than that.

The three of us began playing Neal's song. After more than three decades, we were working on a recording together. It felt like not a damned moment had passed since the last time. Our combined playing styles sounded as familiar as a blue sky.

When we stopped, the air was filled with sarcastic zingers. Again, it was as if we were picking up from yesterday's insultfest.

Alice would miss this moment. He was in London attending the *GQ* Men of the Year 2010 awards at the Royal Opera House.

Over lunch, we wondered if we were really going to get inducted into the Rock and Roll Hall of Fame. Refueled on food and friendship, we went back to the studio to tackle a song that I had written and recorded with the Dennis Dunaway Project and released on *Bones from the Yard*, called "Subway."

Alice loved this song. For years he'd been doing a show on satellite radio called *Nights with Alice Cooper*, and he'd played this song often. He'd also had me on the show. He and Bob wrote new lyrics and a melody to fit the theme of his album and renamed it "A Runaway Train."

Listening to our work was reassuring. It sounded like the original Alice Cooper group, even though it missed the fiery energy of our dear friend Glen. We couldn't have sounded any different if we'd tried, though. I was particularly happy with how enthusiastic Bob was about trying out everyone's ideas, even the spontaneous ones. It was like the glory days, a pure group effort. We were so psyched we could have knocked out a whole album in two weeks.

The session was in full swing when Alice arrived. He was exhausted from the flight from London, but he was beaming about all of us being together again. Photographer Bob Gruen walked in with a camera around his neck. Alice's tour manager, Toby Mamis, followed, along with Rob Roth, who was designing Alice's sets.

While Michael continued recording guitar parts, Alice and I got caught up on the wives and kids. We talked about Glen emptying his pockets at the Canadian border, and how he'd been like Harpo Marx because you never knew what he was going to pull out next.

As the sound rolled out of the speakers, we were in awe of Ezrin's studio tricks. Neal sat at the console and complimented Bob on the great drum sound. "It's live drums!" Bob replied, snarking about all the recordings now done with artificial drums. "When you hear real drums, you remember how great they sound."

At dinner break, Alice led the way down the sunny sidewalk to a favorite nearby restaurant. He was excited about our new songs. Shep showed up wearing a big smile. We all kept coming back to more Glen stories.

So long . . . See ya . . . Don't forget me, or nothin' . . .

As soon as the Rock and Roll Hall of Fame announced its nominations, my telephone was ringing, the mail was pouring in. I'm talkin' tsunami. The Hall of Fame staff called for display pieces, my official signature, and things like that. They had to prepare just in case we won. People called to wish me luck. It was overwhelming.

Our march toward glory took a notable turn when it was decided that the original group should perform at Alice's yearly Christmas Pudding show in Phoenix. It was to be a benefit for a church group that Alice and his wife, Sheryl, are involved in, the Solid Rock Foundation.

The original group had played the Pudding show before, but this was special. Our discussions about who should play Glen's guitar parts landed on Steve Hunter, who'd played on Alice's first *Welcome to My Nightmare* album. Steve had also played the lead guitar solo on "Generation Landslide," so he'd known Glen. Steve has a whip-snap sense of humor, which is why Glen took to him.

One day, we were in the rehearsal hall ripping through "Billion Dollar Babies." I sensed that Alice was having fun working with us. Then I saw that we were getting a frantic signal from Alice's right-hand man, Kyler Clark, to stop playing.

"You're inducted!" he yelled.

Neal yelled, "Are you fucking kidding me?" He stood up and bounced his drumsticks off his snare and they twirled through the air.

Alice laughed. "I told you guys that if you stuck with me, I'd have you wearing diamonds as big as scrub buckets."

Hugs, smiles, pats on the back.

Kyler said, "We have several phone interviews lined up, so follow me, gentlemen."

Michael arched an eye. "Oh, so *now* we're gentlemen?"

At the Christmas Pudding show, my parents were in the audience, along with a slew of other relatives. I worried that it would be way past Dad's bedtime; his health wasn't too good. But this would be only the second time my parents ever saw me play. The first time was in Tucson, in the late '70s, and they confessed that upon our first note, the crowd stood up on the folding chairs and they couldn't see a thing.

To our growing surprise, we learned that people were coming in from Canada, France, and Australia just to see the old gang together again.

Time to tune up. Alice was primping in the mirror while Michael, Steve, and I juggled things around to get our guitars into the cramped space. Neal twirled his sticks, signaling that he was ready to go. Alice's mom even came in and sat down.

As Michael and I warmed up with "No More Mr. Nice Guy," Alice joined in. Then his wife, Sheryl, and daughters Calico and Sonora chimed in with Steve's wife Karen Ann Hunter on some exciting harmonies. Kyler opened the door and said, "Showtime!"

"Let's go, boys," Alice said.

We heard Bob Ezrin's heartwarming announcement citing our induction, and the reaction of the eight-thousand-strong crowd felt like the best thing I'd ever heard in my life. Michael started the riff for "No More Mr. Nice Guy," the curtain opened, and Neal hit his first fill. And like a million times before, Neal and I looked at each other and locked in.

Alice's voice was strong. He had survived a dark era, and clean living suited him well. So here were five guys who had seen just about every possible thing a rock life brings, and yet here we were—in a different year, a different decade, even a different millennium—playing these songs with a sense of commitment that wouldn't die.

We played for an hour, and could have gone on for hours more.

The Hall of Fame event is held in the Waldorf-Astoria, a grand, gilded dowager of a palace in Midtown Manhattan. Kings, queens, moguls, and gangsters have stayed there. Walking down the central hallway, which rises over you like a cathedral, you half-expect someone famous to tumble out of the flower spray. All too much for rock-'n'-roll people.

I could just hear Glen looking around and cracking, "Hey. Ain't this the fuckin' nuts?"

We were going to get the recognition we didn't get when "Alice Cooper" got a star on Hollywood Boulevard and the band wasn't invited to the unveiling. Now we were going to get toasted by the best.

After a fun evening with friends eating chocolate in front of a fake fireplace in our elaborate suite at the Waldorf, and a good night's sleep, the morning of the big day arrived. Our itinerary requested that we arrive in the Grand Ballroom by 11:00 a.m. but we showed up an hour early. The giant room was lined with balconies way up to the ceiling. It was all lit.

Leon Russell sat down at the grand piano onstage. The commotion came to a standstill when he began singing one of the most moving songs I've ever heard, "A Song for You." The room was silent during the song, but then came the applause.

Wow! What an unexpectedly perfect way to start the day. And that was only the beginning. Tom Waits, Bruce Springsteen, Dr. John, and John Mayer ran through their songs. The crew set up all the Fender amps and Neal's kit, and we ran through our four tunes with kids from the Ronald McDonald House, who were to sing "School's Out" with

Alice and Rob Zombie. We ran through the set once and then got off-stage.

Bette Midler and Darlene Love ran through some songs, and then most everyone came onstage and sang "Da Doo Ron Ron" with Paul Shaffer and the CBS Orchestra, Elton John, and a ton of people. It sounded *amazing*.

That all happened before 11:30 a.m. Yes, a very special night lay ahead.

Electricity and fine fragrances filled the air as Cindy and I made our way into the crowded meet-and-greet. I wore a classic tuxedo with a black shirt and tie, but nobody was looking at me because Cindy had made herself a spectacular red dress with a generous smattering of sparkles attached. She highlighted her flowing blonde hair with brilliant Rock 'n' Roll Red Manic Panic hair color. Even more noticeable was the magical aura around her. She was loving every second of this.

I spotted Joe Greenberg and made my way over. His importance in the Alice Cooper success is shamefully underrated by history. Joe and Shep were a team to be reckoned with throughout our rise. But Joe would fall away from the management team with the same sort of sleight-of-hand disappearing act that the group had endured. He lives in LA now, where his talented son, Adam Hunter, is a stand-up comedian. You can be sure Adam gets great career advice.

An usherette escorted us to a large round table in front of the stage that was reserved for the band, our ladies, and Joe and Shep. These seats would have cost three thousand dollars each had we not been inducted. Neal fished through a large urn of ice on the table and found only bottles of wine. "Where's the fucking beer?" he barked. "This is supposed to be the Rock and Roll Hall Fame, and they don't have any beer?"

The word went down, and soon a special cooler of beer showed up. Ah, rock-'n'-roll days. Everyone laughed because he was right, and because it was perfect that Neal would have found something wrong right off the bat.

"I'm drinking Zero water," Alice said. "How rock-'n'-roll is that?"

Sheryl Cooper, and even Steve Hunter, were insiders, and deserving of this night. So were the roadies who had had to lug gear to kingdom come in the predawn hours, the seamstresses who had rushed to fix a broken zipper, the women who had held down the office and dealt with the sulfuric phone calls, the parents who had loved us despite it all, the lighting guys who had looked down on us, not to mention the longtime devoted fans who had gotten their sick little mitts on our records and played them while their parents yelled at them down the hall. This award represented every one of them, too.

Michael J. Fox was sitting near me at the next table. He caught my eye and said, "Hey, man, glad to meet you." When I told him I'd heard he was quite knowledgeable about Alice Cooper, he laughed and said, "You wanna know how into it I am? I know all the guitar parts on *Pretties for You*. That's why I'm here—to see you guys get inducted."

That floored me. I thought, Even *we* don't know those guitar parts.

At our table, Michael Bruce ordered another Jack and Coke. Cindy immediately took it away from him. Joe Greenberg looked at me, and we grinned. This was just like the Hollywood days: trying to sneak something past Cindy.

Glen's siblings, Janice and Ken, were at a table next to ours. They had expected to accept Glen's award on his behalf at the podium with the rest of us. That was fine with me, but the rules had been rigidly drawn before we set foot in that room.

"Chicken pot pies? Are you fucking kidding me?" There went Neal again. Everyone was laughing out loud, including people at nearby tables. Our daughters, who had seen their uncle in action many times before, rolled their eyes, but couldn't contain their laughter.

"Is this the Waldorf or a fucking Grange meeting in Ohio?" Michael barked, looking at the chicken pot pies. "Just like Grandma used to make!"

Alice poked his with a fork and said, "I hope this isn't our old chicken."

"I can see the headlines now," I said. "'Alice Throws Chicken Pot Pie into Crowd.'"

The awards speeches and performances were about to begin, so everyone returned to their seats and we were escorted backstage.

For my stage costume, Cindy had sewn small costume mirrors and trinkets from her Cooper days stockpile all over a 1930s tuxedo with tails and more down one leg of some black jeans. And I wore a handcrafted buckle with the *Billion Dollar Babies* logo etched into it that promoter Leas Campbell had made as gifts to each band member in 1973.

The feeling of walking to the stage with all eyes on us wasn't like trying on an old jacket, but it felt natural. We had done this a million times. And you look forward to this kind of attention the way you do sex.

They took us through a long kitchen, around to the far side of the stage, where we would wait by racks of dishes. I thought about swiping a Waldorf-Astoria fork in Glen's honor, but I didn't want it in my pocket while I was playing. So I resisted.

Michael walked up with another drink. "Cindy's not here, is she?" he said, smiling. "This one's for Glen."

I said, "Ask Alice about drinking and performing. He could tell you if he could remember it."

Alice asked, "How's your book coming, Den?"

"Good," I said. "Do you wanna be in it?"

Kyler said, "Let's go," and we went out into the Grand Ballroom, behind a curtain to a dimly lit ramp that went up to the stage. Darlene Love was at the podium giving an emotionally charged but most eloquent acceptance speech. Her bigger-than-life image was on a screen high up above her head. Darlene had been beaten down by the business but had risen up again, and she was genuinely deserving of and grateful for this long-overdue recognition. I wondered if Phil Spector, the producer who released her recordings under another artist's name, was watching from his prison cell. My personal feeling that I was finally getting some credit for all I had done seemed modest compared to what Darlene had been through.

The spotlights followed Love offstage to enormous applause, and Rob Zombie took the stage while the technicians swung into action switching all the equipment over. Originally the producers had wanted us to accept our awards before playing, but Alice insisted that it would be better if we played first. He was right.

"That's our cue," I said as the short film about the Alice Cooper group began. "Have fun, guys," I added. We went out to the stage. Four of us lined up in front of Neal's drum riser, with our backs to the audience. I looked up at the film and saw Glen playing his ass off.

That choked me up. I looked at Alice and said, "Can you believe it?"

"No," he said. "No, not at all."

Rob Zombie yelled, "And, finally, in the Rock and Roll Hall of Fame, Alice Cooper!" Neal clicked his sticks together for the countdown, and seven hundred watts of sheer power jarred the room.

I turned and immediately saw enough talented music idols and movie stars to intimidate anyone. And I saw Cindy and Sheryl and Rose and Joe and Shep. I looked up at the balconies but couldn't spot Renee and Chelsea, sensational looking as they were this night. But the music was our lady of the moment, although she didn't require so much attention that thoughts about our whole career weren't flooding through my head. And I couldn't help thinking about all the amazing bands that had been on that prestigious stage. Even Neal's hero Gene Krupa had probably played "Sing, Sing, Sing" on this stage with Benny Goodman and His Orchestra. It's impossible to imagine Krupa being any more dynamic than Neal was that night. His playing was every bit as explosive and as tight as ever.

We breezed through to "School's Out," at which point the kids came out in their Alice Cooper makeup. We started the song, and Alice announced Rob Zombie, who joined in singing lead. I moved over to share Michael's microphone so they would have the spotlight.

Finally, the big rave ended with me running through the kids' choir and soaking up the warm celebrity-charged applause. I laid my bass down on Neal's drum riser while Rob handed over Alice's award, and then we each stood ready and thankfully accepted our awards.

Alice's speech was perfect, even though his use of the word *we* seemed like a blanket term covering us *and* his current band, as if the two were one band. But I guess I prefer that to an awkward explanation. I am naturally sensitive to this subject, but, anyway, I liked his speech a lot, especially his citing our heroes the Yardbirds and the Who.

It was my turn. I thanked the rats in the snake's stomach for the ultimate sacrifice to art. I said that over the years some things change, and I removed my purple sunglasses, held them up, and then switched them for a pair of reading glasses. I thanked everyone I could think of, but I know I left some out. I thanked Glen Buxton and started to ask the audience to raise their glasses in tribute to him, but I got overwhelmed with emotion and the words just wouldn't come out.

Michael's speech was impromptu. He asked for prayers for the people in Japan who were then suffering the tragic impact of a tsunami. Michael is a caring person, and humbler than he used to be. I can only guess if he wonders about the rightness of doing that solo album. But young choices are the skeletons in everybody's closet. And I think, at that time, Humpty Dumpty had fallen off the wall and nobody could put him back together again.

When it was his turn, Neal told the story of how Cindy had found Joe and Shep for us, and then he saved the day by thanking all of our fans for being the real reason for the award. "This award," he said, "is because of you, about you, and for you."

Leaning down he boomed, "And now that Alice Cooper has collided with the Rock and Roll Hall of Fame, we thank you a fuckin' billion!"

The Grand Ballroom filled with warm applause from our industry peers. That's something we never imagined happening.

With Glen in our thoughts, emotions running high, and the proud feeling that after all we'd been through our dream had finally been recognized as a collective achievement, we began our triumphant walk off stage. We felt like gladiators marching from the Colosseum.

Only we went the wrong way. In rehearsals we were told to go stage left. Now we were being urgently pushed to go stage right. Like errant schoolboys we were turned around and marched *back* across the stage, grinning sheepishly. As we passed by the podium, I paused at the microphone and said, "Some things never change."

Then we went downstairs and raised hell into the night.

Dennis,

🏠 (well) dennis 👁 hope u
do good at all u do. W+ 🐔 we
get real good and people start 🎤 ing
4 us I'll always remember how u
said one ☀️-y day. "Hey why don't we
start a group and call it the 🥁 +s

      Good Luck.
          your frend
            Vince.

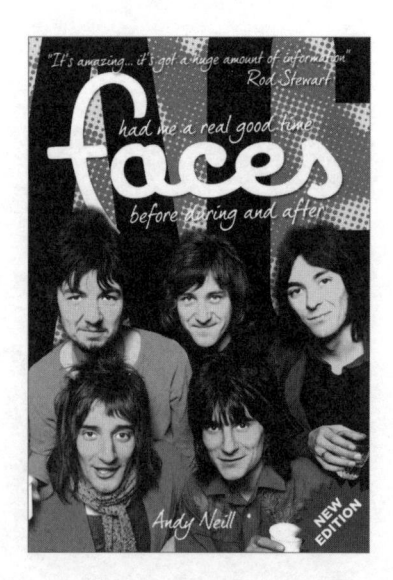

Had Me A Real Good Time
FACES
Before, During and After
Andy Neill

Forty-five years ago one of the world's best loved rock'n'roll bands, the Faces, formed from the ashes of the Small Faces and the Jeff Beck Group. Rod Stewart, Ron Wood, Ronnie Lane, Ian McLagan and Kenney Jones were in it for a laugh, and became the pleasure-seeking antidote to some of the more serious-minded groups of the early seventies. Their partying was legendary and their music was the ultimate in good time rock'n'roll.

Had Me A Real Good Time fully examines the roots, triumphs and tragedies behind a band as devoted to mayhem as they were to music. This is the real story of the Faces.

"It's amazing... it's got a huge amount of information" – Rod Stewart.

"Rich in detail and behind the scenes yarns." * * * * - MOJO

Available from all good bookshops
Or in case of difficulty www.omnibuspress.com

ISBN: 978.1.78323.619.0
Order No: OP56507